NOTES ON CONTRIBUTORS

Sarah Benton is a researcher, lecturer and editor.

Cynthia Cockburn is a researcher and writer based at City University, London, where she is a research professor in the Centre for Research in Gender, Ethnicity and Social Change.

Moniza Alvi's first volume of poems, *The Country at my Shoulder*, was published in 1993 by OUP. Her second, *A Bowl of Warm Air*, is due in 1996. She teaches in a comprehensive school in South London.

Michael Blumenthal is an American poet and novelist, currently living in Budapest. His collections of poetry include *Days We Would Rather Know* and *Against Romance*.

Elaine Feinstein is a poet and novelist. Her novels include *Dreamers* and *Lady Chatterley's Confession*, and her most recent volume of poems is *Selected Poems*.

Judy Gahagan's volume of short stories, *Did Gustav Mahler Ski?*, appeared in 1991. Her poetry and journalism has been widely published, and two pamphlets of poetry came out last year. She lives in London and Italy, where she works part-time for the Open University.

Carole Satyamurti teaches Psycho-social Studies at the University of East London and the Tavistock Clinic. She has published three volumes of poetry: *Broken Moon*, *Changing the Subject* and *Striking Distance*.

Steven Rose is Professor of Biology and Director, Brain and Behaviour Research Group at the Open University and is currently working on a book on biology and human freedom.

Jeffrey Weeks is Professor of Sociology at South Bank University, London. His most recent book is *Invented Moralities: Sexual Values in an Age of Uncertainty* (1995).

Andrew Samuels is a Jungian analyst

David Bell is Consultant Psychotherapist at the Tavistock Clinic.

Bill Schwarz teaches at Goldsmiths College, London.

Bill Bowring teaches civil liberties and human rights law at the University of East London, and is also a barrister. He is an executive committee member of the Bar Human Rights Committee, Treasurer of the International Association of Democratic Lawyers, and is International Secretary of the Haldane Society. He has published widely on human rights and related issues.

Kate Markus is a barrister practising public law, a former Chair of the Law Centres Federation. She worked for many years at the Brent Community Law Centre. She is Chair of the Public Law Project, and of the Haldane Society of Socialist Lawyers, and a Member of the Legal Aid Board.

Keir Starmer is a barrister practising public law and is editor of *Justice in Error* (1993). He is one of the authors of the *Democratic Audit*. He is Vice-Chair of the Haldane Society of Socialist Lawyers.

Ken Wiwa is a journalist and campaigner for the rights of the Ogoni people, and is son of the judicially murdered Nigerian and Ogoni human rights activist Ken Saro-Wiwa.

Kader Asmal is a Member of the South African Parliament, and is Minister for Water Affairs and Forestry in the South African Government of National Unity. While in exile he was Professor of Human Rights Law at Trinity College Dublin and on his return he was a member of the ANC's Constitutional Commission. He is now Professor of Human Rights Law at the University of Western Cape.

Michael Mansfield is a Queens Counsel, practising criminal law at Tooks Court Chambers, and well-known for his advocacy in terrorist trials and miscarriage appeals. He has written and broadcast widely on cases of miscarriage of justice, and is author of *Presumed Guilty: The British Legal System Exposed* (1994).

Jonathan Cooper is a research fellow at the Institute for Public Policy Research, and is also a barrister practising at Doughty Street Chambers, as well as working at the AIRE (Advice on Individual Rights in Europe) Centre.

Ethan Raup is a criminologist who was Research Director and Deputy Press Secretary for a US Senate campaign for Washington State. He was consultant to the Democratic Governors' Association. He is now on the policy staff of the Mayor of Seattle, Washington.

John Griffith is Emeritus Professor of Public Law at the London School of Economics, and is author of numerous works, including *The Politics of the Judiciary* (1991) and *Socialism in a Cold Climate* (1983)

Keith Ewing is Professor of Public Law at King's College, University of London, and is author of many works including *The Right to Strike* (1991), *A Bill of Rights for Britain?* (1990), and *Freedom Under Thatcher: Civil Liberties in Modern Britain* (1990)

Ruth Lister is Professor of Social Policy at Loughborough University. She is author of numerous works, including *The Exclusive Society, Citizenship and the Poor* (1990) and *Unemployment: Who Pays the Price* (1981). She is currently writing a book on feminist perspectives on citizenship.

Anna Coote is Assistant Director of the Institute for Public Policy Research, responsible for social policy. She is author of *The Family Way: a new approach to policy making* and editor of *The Welfare of Citizens: developing new social rights*.

SUPPORTING SUBSCRIBERS

CONTENTS

EDITORS
Stuart Hall
Doreen Massey
Michael Rustin

GUEST EDITORS
Bill Bowring with Kate Markus
and Keir Starmer for the
Haldane Society of Socialist
Lawyers

POETRY EDITOR
Carole Satyamurti

ART EDITORS
Jan Brown and Tim Davison

EDITORIAL OFFICE
Lawrence & Wishart
99a Wallis Road
London E9 5LN

MARKETING CONSULTANT
Mark Perryman

Sounding is published three
times a year, in autumn,
spring and summer by:
Soundings Ltd
c/o **Lawrence & Wishart**
99a Wallis Road
London E9 5LN

SUBSCRIPTIONS
1996 subscription rates are (for three issues):
UK: Institutions £70, Individuals £35
Rest of the world: Institutions £80, Individuals £45

BOOKS FOR REVIEW
Contact Soundings Books Editor,
c/o Lawrence & Wishart.

ISBN 0 85315 819 3

Text setting Art Services, Norwich
Cover photograph: Joanne O'Brien/Format

Printed in Great Britain by Cambridge University Press,
Cambridge

What is at Stake?

With his speech on stakeholding to a business audience in Singapore in January, Tony Blair took the plunge into risky political water. His earlier, somewhat ingenuous, attempts to formulate a political vision around the values of community did not have the potential for controversy and division which the 'stakeholding' speech immediately unleashed. These ideas of community mainly encoded a necessary antithesis to the ideology of harsh, possessive individualism, captured in Mrs Thatcher's infamous phrase, 'there is no such thing as society, only individuals, and families'. But this emphasis on the missing dimensions of the social had become a banal point of reference for every left-of-centre political voice, with no power to galvanise anything but a routine response. The moral superiority of the social is a litany which anti-Thatcherites mumble in their sleep, though without confidence that when the moment of decision comes, the voters will risk much for it. Even Mr Major, after his election as Tory leader, had tried to define himself to some degree against harsh individualism, and in favour of some idea of moral solidarity ('back to basics' being one comically doomed version, found dead on arrival by revelations of corruption, sleaze and sexual scandal among his colleagues). But that was even before his softer ideas were beaten out of him by the heavies of the right, who now hold the unfortunate man their prisoner.

Perhaps, who knows, it was decided in New Labour circles that it was not going to be enough for Tony Blair merely to be virtuous and engaging, but that Labour would need a mobilising idea too. Possibly it has been recognised that Labour must engage its own supporters in some more active way than hitherto, and that the pitch to uncommitted middle opinion is not, by itself, going to be enough to inform or motivate a radical government. It must have been realised that the language of moral renewal by itself was not going to generate enough political momentum.

Why then was the idea of stakeholding launched into the British political skies from Singapore? It is a curious place from which to initiate a new phase of British political debate. But the choice of location sought to inflect it, from the start, in a safe direction, as contextual insurance against the hazards of this line of thought - which were in fact revealed within hours of Blair's speech. (A speech in Singapore can now have the same instant political impact as one in Westminster, a fact of interest in itself.) Anyway, the setting emphasised that the idea of stakeholding signified, for Labour, a model of modern, dynamic, cohesive capitalism, the model of the 'Asian Tigers' of Singapore, Hong Kong, Taiwan, etc. It might help if the radical idea of a stakeholding society could be shown not to discomfit even an audience of business people of the most exemplary and competitive type. (Perhaps the New Labour style is to launch *all* its new intellectual initiatives to business audiences, preferably abroad, as a new kind of market testing?)

Over here, the message was given several conflicting interpretations, within hours. Heseltine sought, with glee, to embarrass New Labour by saying that these 'stakeholders' were merely the vested interests of corporatism reborn, or returned from their Old Labour cupboards - the Ghost of Solomon Binding.[1] Portillo said it was stealing a right-wing idea, the property-owning democracy, no less. New Labour, even Robin Cook at his least convincing, said in reply to Michael Heseltine, that this was nothing new, stakeholding implied no *new* commitments or policies. It merely rephrased the opportunities for citizens to participate in the labour market, obtain education and training, be a member of society, which Labour had been talking about all along. More a new slogan than anything else, Blair added. Embarrassingly, John Edmunds of the GMB and John Monks of the TUC popped up to say that actually trade unions *would* have something to do with it, and that legislation *would* be needed to strengthen workers' rights within companies. They were even working on it. What a prudent thing that this had been denied before John Edmunds had even said it! But the most important reaction was from the group of radical intellectuals who had developed the idea in the first place (Will Hutton, David Marquand), or who anyway thought it was relevant to a serious reforming project (Andrew Gamble and Gavin Kelly). They welcomed Blair's contribution. Will Hutton wrote: 'Yet stakeholding is a genuine departure; it attempts to offer a set of guiding principles that could organise a reformist political programme in five chief areas: the workplace, the welfare

---

1. Jack Jones and Hugh Scanlon made a 'solemn and binding' agreement with Harold Wilson, on the occasion of the climb-down from proposals for trade union reform in 1969, when Barbara Castle's *In Place of Strife* was withdrawn in face of trade union resistance. This was a low point of corporatism.

state, the firm and the City; the constitution, and economic policy more generally (*The Guardian*, January 17). He added, however, 'This is not socialism in the twentieth century.'

The reality is that stakeholding had become an important idea, developed by the most coherent and purposeful group of left-of-centre reformers now on the scene. Will Hutton, the most widely-read of these, developed the concept of stakeholding capitalism in *The State We're In*. This requires, he says, a significant change in the relationship between shareholders and other participants in the economy. It should reduce the present excessive rights and powers of shareholders, and enhance those of employees, managers, the professions, consumers, and the wider community. (In the public services, incidentally, both professionals and workers are stakeholders who have been pushed aside.) By announcing his commitment to the idea of stakeholding, Tony Blair has linked New Labour to a substantive radical debate.

'Singapore is a curious place from which to initiate a new phase of British political debate'

To place one's party within a political discourse which is already going strong, and has aroused much public interest (Hutton's book is a best-seller) is a different thing from staying within an ideological space (that of community and the social) which is either empty, or else is occupied mainly by interest-groups worried about the family. The main advocates of 'community' are, not surprisingly, the 'communitarian' movement, whose leading intellectual is the American Amitai Etzioni, and which is most vigorously promoted in Britain by Demos. This focus on the family, as articles in our first issue by Beatrix Campbell and Lynne Murray showed, can have worrying implications, especially for the role of women in the workforce. But it does not impact much on the economic area of debate which is likely to be central to the election. To that extent, New Labour's commitment to what it defined as enhanced 'community' was a 'safe' choice, whereas, wittingly or not, 'stakeholding' is a dangerous one. There is much that is worth saying about community, particularly about *specific* communities and ways of life - as Jeffrey Weeks's article on sexual communities explores in this issue. But Labour's evocation of a unified, consensual national community ('One Nation Socialism') has not been moving the party in the direction of a celebration of diversity and difference. On the contrary, there is a worry about who might turn out to be excluded from Labour's community, like Harold Wilson's earlier 'national interest', and how coercively this idea might be deployed against dissenters. We shall be returning to community, identity and difference in future issues.

The history of stakeholding

Debate about a society of stakeholders did not begin in the 1980s, with the reaction to Thatcherism and the need to imagine an alternative to its version of the market society. Stakeholders were formerly defined as those with 'a stake in the country', that is to say landed property, on which the right to vote once depended. Government was defined, in English liberal theory, as the minimum arrangement necessary to protect life, liberty and possessions. Locke argued that the protection of property was the main end of government, and although his argument allowed that 'property' included men's (*sic*) persons, and what they had made with their labour, the usual Tory and Whig interpretations were narrower than this. Property was measured in freeholds and in other claims on land. So the argument, by Levellers and Diggers in the seventeenth century, and Radicals like Tom Paine and William Cobbett in the eighteenth and nineteenth centuries, that political rights were due to *all* men (and with Mary Wollstonecraft to all men *and women*), in virtue not of property-ownership but of humanity, was an attack on the original idea of 'stakeholding'.

Here is what Cobbett had to say about this earlier conception, in an imaginary dialogue he wrote in 1832:

> **Cobbett** Have we not been governed entirely by men of rank and wealth?
> **Elector** Yes, we certainly have.
> **Cobbett** What *reason* have you to suppose, then, that the same sort of men are the only men capable of putting things to rights; and do you believe that any thousand men, caught by the legs, by straining a string across the road, could have managed their matters worse than to have made the existence of themselves and the government depend upon the imaginary value of little bits of thin paper?
> **Elector** Why, that is very true, to be sure; but if a man have not a great stake in the country, how are you to depend on his doing right?
> **Cobbett** As to *stake*, in answer to such an observation, old TIERNEY once remarked, that stakes of this sort generally belonged to the *public hedge*. But do you think that the Americans have got a good government; do you think

that their laws are wise and good; do you think that their affairs are managed by able men?

Elector Yes, I wish to God ours may be as well managed; for see how great and powerful that country has become; and see how happy the people are, under the sway of the Congress.

Cobbett Very well, then, that settles the point; for there is no pecuniary qualification whatever for a member of Congress: very poor men are very frequently chosen, and very rich men never. There have been seven PRESIDENTS: two of them have died insolvent, and were insolvent at the time when they were PRESIDENTS.

A *foolish* man may be in favour of men of rank and wealth before he hears this dialogue; but it is only a *roguish* one who can persevere in such a choice after he has heard it.

Democratic rights were accorded to all citizens in Britain during the following century or so. Though one notes that American democracy has gone downhill in this respect since Cobbett's day; it now largely excludes the poor in its less-than-fifty per cent voting turnout, and practically rules out anyone except the rich from running for major office. And in Britain we recently had in the Poll Tax a covert re-introduction of a property qualification for voting. During the twentieth century, these political rights led to substantial economic and social rights too, with full employment, universal income support, old age pensions, rights to housing, health and education. (Incidentally this was the heyday of Old Labour, as well as of Collectivist Liberalism and One Nation Conservatism). So now the people have to say once again, long after the achievement of universal political rights, and with the ebbing away of these and other social entitlements, *Well, where is our stake in the country now?* [2]

The connection between property and political rights was the original foundation of the debate about rights of citizenship and democracy in Britain. This link has been revived in Will Hutton's writing, in his insistence that 'stakeholding capitalism' depends on achieving a democratic, republican constitution. Only, he argues, if the authoritarian powers of the British state are cut down, its powers devolved, and citizens accorded enforceable rights, can a more inclusive political

---

2. At the time of writing, it was reported on the news that women on income support regularly do not eat in order to feed their children.

economy become a reality.

The explanatory links between the political and economic dimensions of stakeholding have not so far been set out convincingly. Both agendas - of economic and social inclusiveness, and of constitutional entitlement - are essential ones, but it is not exactly clear how and why one depends on the other. The American example suggests that a political practice which is more democratic than

'The class dimension of political discourse is only repressed at the cost of total political confusion'

the British one, in many respects including everyday habits of mind, can nevertheless coexist, and be substantially corrupted by, a ferocious preference for property rights over all other claims of well-being or justice. In so far as a democratisation of the constitution *would* change economic practice in

Britain, it is because it would probably lead to a new hegemony of social forces, and exclude our recent kind of minority dictatorship.

It is true that the devolution of powers to localities, regions and nations, the virtual enforcement, through a proportional electoral system, of cross-party cooperation, and the strengthening of citizens' individual entitlements (e.g. through the Social Chapter) *would* in Britain enforce more inclusive social policies. But to understand why this is so requires consideration not only of constitutional principles and mechanisms and their effects, but also of our underlying political culture. It is because those classes and blocs whose powers will be strengthened by constitutional reform would support more inclusive social strategies, that these strategies follow from these changes, not that a republican constitution generates these all by itself. It is the continuing legacy of paternalism among the upper and middle classes, and solidarism among the working class, in British society, that might ensure that a more democratic polity would also be a kinder and more egalitarian one. What continues to differentiate Europe from America, in respect of social inclusiveness, is not the superiority of its constitutional practices, but more solidaristic traditions and values, rooted in its class structures.

This does not make the importance of constitutional and political 'stakeholding' any less. But it does require recognising that they have economic and social effects mainly in virtue of the role of social classes and their relations of power. This discourse of classes, class fractions and their relations is one with which practically everyone - except Mrs Thatcher (who tells the Conservative Party that it neglects the middle class at its peril) - is now acutely uncomfortable. Yet arguments from the interests and outlooks of classes were quite conventional in nineteenth century bourgeois Britain, from all parts of the ideological spectrum. It permitted British liberals, for example, to identify their constitutional precedents and exemplars in Athenian democracy and republican Rome, and Matthew Arnold to argue in 1869 for the guiding role of enlightened state servants, in harmonising the interests of the Barbarians (the aristocracy), Philistines (the middle class) and the Populace (the rising working class), the 'three great classes of English society'. This dimension of political discourse is only repressed (as it has been) at the cost of total political confusion. (The Conservative Party may be having a nervous breakdown, but it is not usually confused about *this*.)

Moving the agenda on

There will be difficulties in moving the New Labour agenda forward on to the terrain of a stakeholder society. In some respects it was a surprising choice to give a label to this prospective programme, before there was anything ready to put in it. This is why there was such confusion and immediate backtracking in response to criticism. Nevertheless, the opportunity is important, and must be taken.

Part of New Labour's difficulty is that it has been trying to construct a political bloc which claims to *exclude* practically no social interest whatever. *De facto* the 'other' of 'New Labour' has for years been 'Old Labour'. So Labour has been running, ever since Neil Kinnock's election to the leadership, mainly against itself. Key speeches to party and trade union audiences have nearly always emphasised departures from traditional party thinking, and taken the form of public demonstrations (the most extreme case being Neil Kinnock's Conference attack on Militant) of how different New Labour was from what had gone before. The debate about 'stakeholding' is important for the party, since it makes it possible for once to re-include, because of both the radical pedigree and the ambiguities of this idea, virtually all of the left and centre in its interpretation and development. This is a major departure from recent Labour practice.

Contrast Labour's anxious political inclusiveness in recent years with the compulsive exclusions of the right. It has been anti-European (Mrs Thatcher's jibes at 'No-Nation Conservatives'), anti-working class (what is the meaning otherwise of speaking *for* the middle class?), anti-trade union, anti-asylum seeker, anti-illegal-immigrant, anti-scrounger, anti-single parent, etc. Their political programme constructs itself mainly by hostility to 'Others' of all sorts. So paranoid is this world-view becoming that it is hard to imagine what the Tories' *positive* community is, except as a bundle of phobias and hatreds directed outwards. Perhaps when the opinion polls show such a very low level of support, it becomes difficult to imagine one's own constituency in a convincing way, since it has in reality disintegrated, and is waiting to be ideologically re-formed as something else. The Conservative right's current paranoia thus represents the symptom of an acute anxiety-state.

But the idea of a political bloc with no outside at all has its own difficulties. Any criticism that is encountered is felt as an attack on the vital unity and wholeness of the bloc, and is therefore perceived to be a threat. This may be why so many key speeches are given before business audiences, and why policy pronouncements and commitments are so bland and ostentatiously inoffensive. If the bloc is *everyone*, then all conflict, except with actual Conservative spokespersons, must be avoided. (Tony Blair is even rather polite to most of them, except when defending Harriet Harman.)

But it is quite difficult to construct a political programme, with policy commitments, which does not imply gains and losses for specific fractions and interest groups in the population. The hesitations in setting out a tax policy make this particularly clear, since taxes must impact on changes of priority in every area of government. If there are to be no losers, then taxes can hardly be increased. (In fact the only new source of funding so far mentioned for Labour's spending programmes is a windfall profits tax. Not even the most crazed Euro-dependent farmer would expect such a windfall more than once in a Parliament.) But then how, once Gordon Brown's winning lottery ticket has been spent, is anyone to have more, even the most needy or deserving?

It is as if New Labour wants to give the impression that it will create a competitive but just society in which it can say, like the Dodo (no Old Labour man he) 'Everybody has won, and all shall have prizes'. The image of the 'stake' is here an interesting one; its dictionary meanings link it inseparably to wagers, gambling, games of chance.[3] Perhaps the image of the 'stake in the country', which developed as a political term of legitimation in the eighteenth century, in fact started its life around the gaming tables of the aristocracy. In a society obsessed

---

3   *Stake* (1540, of unknown origin). That which is placed at hazard; esp. a sum of money, etc., deposited or guaranteed, to be taken by the winner of a game, race, contest, etc.' *Shorter Oxford English Dictionary.*

with the National Lottery, when 80 per cent of the population spend money in the hope of winning prizes of more than £40 million, we must hope that 'a stake' comes to amount to more than a ticket in a game of chance. The exclusionary potential of this idea must also be recognised. The old idea, that without a 'stake in the country' one has no rights, could even come back again, and be used to push aside not those without property, but those who are out of the workforce, or who are otherwise said to 'shirk' on their obligations.

With society now constructed as a Great Lottery, it is a problem when some people have no tickets, nor much chance of acquiring any. Actually, the Lottery was invented at a moment when it was necessary symbolically to console those without other

> 'Wilson reduced the former 'other' of the privileged classes to a caricature of themselves'

more substantial stakes, by offering a magical prospect of plenitude; whilst also assuaging the guilt of the more comfortable classes with the knowledge that not they personally but their good causes benefitted from all this voluntary taxation.

Everyone is to win?

But the idea of a bloc without an outside, a politics without conflict, may not be easy to reconcile with the discourse of stakeholders. Enlarging the stake of some citizens, must mean reducing the stake of some others. Hutton is clear about this: whilst he recognises the necessary role of the financial sector in the British economy, his proposals would substantially reduce shareholder power vis-a-vis the managers of productive companies. This argument is to some degree a re-run, with a more purposeful intention, of the earlier debate about the managerial revolution and what it was supposed, wrongly it turned out, to have achieved. It also dimly evokes Keynes's 'euthanasia of the rentier', though the rentiers are still wide awake, and even Hutton is less radical than Keynes.

Harold Wilson, Labour's last election winner, adopted a different strategy from New Labour's today. He resolved the debate between the idea of a Labour Party depending largely on the loyalty of the manual working class, and the revisionist, Gaitskell-Crosland model of a classless party, in a brilliant ideological transformation. He reduced the former 'other' of the privileged classes to a caricature of themselves. The capitalists whom it was safe to oppose became marginal or even fabulous figures, such as speculators, 'Gnomes of Zurich', and the like, whilst the privileged, aristocratic governing class were pictured in sepia on the grouse-moors. This enabled him to hold on to his traditional Labour supporters, who still defined themselves by loose but still-visible class identifications and antagonisms, whilst gaining new support by disorganising and dividing the middle classes. Some fragments of the new middle class, especially those whose position depended on education, hard work, and merit, not on inherited wealth or social position, identified with his 'northern' hostility to and mockery of the old establishments. (Humour was a powerful weapon, since in jokes, as Freud pointed out, truths could be stated and sentiments expressed which would be unpalatable and therefore repressed in a naked form). Wilson thus gained both general electoral support - just enough - but more important, for a period of a couple of years before it was wholly squandered, the enthusiasm and commitment of a new social bloc committed to the 'modernisation' of British society. The structures of the conservative state and finance-driven capitalism, against which the stakeholder debate is now directed, were in fact those to which Wilson capitulated in 1966, and again later.

I t is not clear who are going to be the friends, enthusiasts and advocates of a programme whose guiding principle is, or was, to have no enemies. Wilson had a 'modernising intelligentsia' on his side, the ancestors, in their ideological range and commitments, of the 'pro-stakeholder coalition' today; and this was one important fraction that gave him a chance. The importance of the stakeholding initiative is that it potentially allies such an intelligentsia with a reforming government, and makes it possible to work out where the crucial lines of change (and inevitable division) have to come.

There is a temptation at this point to demand that the 'stakeholding' programme be immediately spelled out in terms of detailed policies, in the areas of corporate governance, welfare policy, the City, constitutional reform, and so on. The first to demand such specification were the Tories, who realise that virtually any new policy commitment will have its critics, and will allow the government to chip away at Labour's now formidable width of support, passive as much of it may be.

This problem arises partly because New Labour has been generally reticent in policy commitments, but more importantly because of the radical and therefore divisive potential of the stakeholder agenda. There are major losers from prospective reforms in the areas of the constitution, the rights of shareholders, the generation of employment (which must be paid for, in the first instance, by someone). Even if there can be hopes of some non-zero-sum gains from reforms, from higher rates of growth, reduced social costs, etc, these will be neither sufficient nor immediate. Indeed, since the Conservatives, through their inadvertent devaluation, seem at last to have achieved some national competitive advantage, there may be few or no short-term advantages from a Labour victory in terms of faster economic growth.

But if policy specification can be dangerous, how is this vital debate to be carried forward? Much more must be said if the whole initiative is not to collapse, in a retreat humiliatingly like one of Mr Major's numerous re-launches of himself. What is now needed is not public policy specification, but an initiative to set out the broader terms of the stakeholder argument, so that when specific policies *are* defined, or made public, they belong within some intelligible perspective.

In particular, the language of stakeholders might enable New Labour to identify more clearly for whom, and against whom, it is now speaking. An important point is raised by the demand that everyone should become a 'stakeholder'. (Whether or not this is the term one would ideally have chosen to define rights of citizenship and social membership is a secondary issue at this point.) This is that many citizens now are *not*, in effective senses of that term, stakeholders, and indeed that their stake, or secure position in society, is deteriorating, irrespective of aggregate national levels of prosperity. New Labour must be willing to speak to the condition of those who have poor or worsening prospects, and to identify them as citizens who are without, or who are at risk of losing, an effective stake. And on the other hand, it must be prepared to acknowledge that the system is unduly shaped in the interests of a minority, whose entitlements to profits, and whose right to move their capital wherever they wish, are excessive.

'the language of stakeholders might enable New Labour to identify more clearly for whom, and against whom, it is now speaking'

This minority is what is represented by the present Conservatives. New Labour has the opportunity, as Wilson did, to identify the exceptionally obtrusive and venal segments of this apparatus - the top-manager beneficiaries of privatisation of the utilities, for example, and the Tory nomenklatura who dominate most of the quangos - and to make them stand as the public symbols of this corrupt order. Just as Labour has always been attacked at its weakest points (the 'loony left' etc.), so the Conservatives are most vulnerable at theirs. There does need to be a sharper and more antagonistic tone to New Labour polemics, to give expression to discontent, and to transform into energy and hopefulness the depression and cynicism which has spread over this society. A renewed capacity to conduct an ideological argument of some kind is necessary if Labour is to mobilise its own potential support in a more committed way.

Meanwhile, it is important that policy documents and proposals should be written and debated. What is needed is to develop forums of debate which are parallel to and interact with the New Labour agenda. (*Soundings* intends to be one of these.) This can allow policy initiatives to be set out and support for them to be tested - greenhouses of healthy plants set growing which a Labour government, or government-in-waiting, can transplant and bed out in public when their time is ripe.

The reasons for reticence about forward commitments from Labour politicians need to be respected, but what should also be expected of them is involvement in and receptivity to wider debate. Tony Blair's method of conducting the argument over Clause IV and the party constitution, by meeting party members all over the country, was in this way exemplary, whatever one might think about the new constitution itself. Engagement with both the radical intellectual community, and with more representative groups of citizens and activists, is necessary if a radical government is to keep its bearings. (The last two Labour governments failed in this respect, and then died.) It is, paradoxically, by such a twin-track system, of a plethora of think-tanks, kite-flying, and active debate among radicals, then selectively absorbed by the politicians, that the right has sustained a rolling agenda of reform throughout its period of office. Though what is now most visible is the right's sectarianism and self-isolation, if one takes the last twenty years as a whole it has been formidably effective. The left has something to learn from this.

Tony Blair's 'stakeholder' speech makes possible, but does not ensure, a significant transition in the politics of New Labour. It allows the realities of large-scale social exclusion, of increasing inequality, and of irresponsible power, to be addressed again, but in a language not already deadened by past ideological assumptions. A political discourse which could give some coherence to a programme of reform was urgently needed, and this is a major step towards it. To this extent, Tony Blair chose well, and perhaps bravely. We intend to do what we can to ensure that something of value comes from it.

Knights against the nightmares

Sarah Benton

*Tony Blair is emerging as a chivalric hero, who will
rescue us from the demons of Thatcher's Britain. But
his politics of moral transcendence reflects the
dissolution of a more rooted politics, based in
people and their communities. Do we simply
succumb to the tenderness of his wooing, or can we
play a more active role in the battles?*

The political season began. Each conference was held, in the same sequence as
every year, following the same rotation of seaside towns. Each grouping had its
own agenda, compiled from the lists of concerns forwarded, by a more or less
tortuous process, from members to the central administration, who processed the
concerns and returned them, in a hygienically-sealed package, to the members.

This season, from mid-September to mid-October every year, opens the formal
political year and establishes the concerns, sometimes the nature, of that time.
What were the concerns for 1995-96? The TUC conference, Brighton, was about
a leak from Blair's office; it was about whether or not the TUC would dent Blair's
authority or reinforce it by its vote on the minimum wage - from which the
disagreeable element specifying the amount of the minimum wage had already been
removed. The Liberal conference, Glasgow, was about Blair's interview in *The
Times*, suggesting Liberals and Labour might make common cause on some issues;
it was about whether the Liberal members would undercut or augment Blair's
stature. The Labour Party conference, Brighton, was simply about Blair's authority
in the New Labour party. It was not about whether he would be good enough for

the party, but whether the party would be good enough for him. (It was. The party had displayed a 'new maturity' said Blair appreciatively, as it acted to expunge old infantilism.) The Conservative conference, Blackpool, was about whether that party could muster enough energy even to put up a challenge to Blair. 'If you count the number of times he is mentioned, then Blair is undoubtedly the star of this gathering', wrote David Hare from Blackpool.

What had happened to politics? The banners made it clear:

Blair sweeps Left aside

Blair faces revolt on minimum wage

Blair: I will fund Schools Revolution

Blair vows to cut class sizes

Tony Blair looks to have defused a row about the Minimum Wage

Those were the banner headlines of broadsheets and ITV on the weekend *before* the Labour conference. His coming triumph had been announced in advance. He had already been made into something more than an embattled politician.

At the conference itself there were no decisions about policies. There were only measures of Blair's authority. The old party had already disappeared and become a Jabberwocky with jaws that bite and claws that snatch; a rather tired and ridiculous old dragon but nonetheless worthy of the heroic endeavours of St George Blair. In this drama of rescuing the frail maiden Britain, he must be seen to be risking his political life, in a manly and chivalrous fashion. John Prescott must perforce be a brute beside whom Blair positively shimmers with knightly gentleness; eyes shining moistly above bared, fearsome teeth.

But if Prescott must be the dumb retainer, the old party the dragon, and Blair the gallant knight-hero, what is the new party - and who are we? And how come we have arrived at these new roles in the political drama? Must we either be rescued or slain, but never the heroes?

Politics of no place

Blair is who he is - or rather the Blair persona is what it is - as a result of the relation of several different forces. In the short term, the most important of these are: Blair himself; the Parliamentary Labour Party and the party in the country; the Conservative opposition in parliament and in the country; the pro-Blair media and the anti-Blair media; the current powers of the national state and of sub-national government, and the perception of those powers.

And, first, I want to look in more depth at these last, actual and apparent powers, to explore a bit further why the politics of socialism can no longer be based in a politics of space; it is the weakness of national and regional institutions that has created a context in which Blair's persona flourishes. And it is Blair's actual and perceived ability to work with these powers which will shape his future stature as a political leader. We, the watchers, supporters, critics, helped create his persona only at the beginning. It will be his response to random events and inexorable processes which will then shape the persona.

The imagery of chivalrous knights blossoms round Blair because his leadership suggests something mediaeval, something resonant of political authority before the era of the nation state and civic institutions.[1] He has come to leadership at a time when national institutions seem impotent within the global economy but before new forms, embedded in place, have developed. Transnational institutions have no popular authority; their potential is dissipated in apathy and cynicism. Community politics is a Pandora's Box, sealed in fear of what might be unleashed, and in elite indifference to the smallness of anything which is not global. Blair's style, of moral transcendence over politics, lifts him above the scorned 'pettiness' of party politics, but risks leaving him, and his supporters, with nothing pragmatic or corporeal.

Before the nation state, the power of rulers was the power to command fealty; the ruler's imperium measured the reach of that loyalty. Like Greek Gods, they could be despotic, capricious and get things wrong; but only through them could people approach the higher realm of life, touch what soars above the mundane and dispel some of the terror that lies in mystery. Only such figures had the temerity to take on that world which existed beyond the mundane community, whether that 'outside' was war, pestilence, or a crusade to retake Jerusalem. But such quasi-

---

1. Recourse to a stereotype of the mediaeval is common when describing persons who evoke powers outwith political institutions. For example, it was the most commonly used stereotype for the (very modern) fatwa against Salman Rushdie from the Ayatollah Khomeini; it is commonly used to characterise that very modern invention, the nineteenth century Saudi Royal Family presiding over the twentieth century powers provided by oil and weapons; it has been used by writer Colm Toibin of Mother Theresa's authority; and, discussing Royalty today, Tom Nairn has written of 'the mediaeval times which have not quite vanished either from the world or Great Britain'. It is not so much a simile for the unreason that flourished before the Age of Reason as a more specific sense of how power operated before the Age of Democracy - and the modern writer's sense of how out of place such forms of power are when exercised today.

divine figures could be domesticated; he may be a rotten king, but he's our king, our access to greatness; we're for him, because he's for us. Not until the nation-state era did the people dare kill their kings.

W ith the nation state, popular nationalism and civic democracy are coterminous. Power is de-mystified; power expresses what people, not gods, do, and can be politicised. The communal self possesses itself and can make its own destiny (which is the idea that Tom Paine hurled against Burke's obeisance to authority.[2]) But when Blair evokes community it is not the Liberals' humdrum community of dog-shit and litter campaigns, or the Radical community demanding new instruments of self-government; it is a mystical (vacuous?) community of feeling with no grounding in place or institutions.

In the ideal of the nation state, the community of feeling - what binds people to each other - and the institutions of politics occupy the same place. This was formally established through the decades of struggle for universal franchise and political reform. Old Sarum (a place with a hill, a thornbush and no people, which had two MPs while populous Manchester had none) became, in the 1820s, the emblem of corruption and anachronism. A founding act of political reform in Britain was to bring political people and place into conformity by shaping constituency boundaries and representation to actual people. Continuous popular mobility has kept the Boundary Commission in continuous operation, but arguments about what constitutes a coherent community, not just numbers of people, have to shape its decisions. The impact in the British parliament of non-place communities, whether these are multi-national companies or animal welfare groups, has been evident in the arguments over the Nolan Committee report. Parliament did not debate whether or not such interest groups must be formally accommodated in a twenty-first century democracy; several MPs did declare that driving them out was the 'most important political reform of this century'.

Today, my neighbour and I may vote for different parties, but we believe that

---

2. 'Every age and generation must be as free to act for itself, *in all cases*, as the ages and generations which preceded it' wrote Paine in *The Rights of Man*, asserting the right of people to choose and cashier their own governors against Burke's claim that 'the people of England utterly disclaim such a right' - for ever. See Paine's *Rights of Man*, in *The Thomas Paine Reader*, Penguin 1982; and Burke's *Reflections on the Revolution in France* and *Thoughts on the Present Discontents*, Penguin 1982. For us, who have Freud's *Moses and Monotheism* to read, Burke and Paine's debate over the killing of the king and the permanence, or otherwise, of the civic settlement which follows that killing, is redolent of other meanings.

in choosing the composition of the council or parliament we are choosing a body that has the power to change our lives for better or worse. Even in the places, which is most places, where there is little feeling of neighbourliness, the fact of the common council which treats us as a common body makes us into a community of sorts. (And all communities are only ever 'of sorts'.) Further, if we want to change the amenities or composition of our community we have to look to each other for support, and we have to look to the political institutions which govern that place to make the change. What those institutions are depends on the current level of 'subsidiarity'.

Those politico-communities are part of who we are; they fix our place, literally, in the world; and it is through those institutions of place-based community that we have our civic rights and our civic being. Our civic being is embodied in the institutions of place. The right to vote depends not on class, race or sex, but on having an address.

'The fact of the common council which treats us as a common body makes us into a community of sorts'

When communities of people (or interest) and of place do not coincide, existing democratic institutions malfunction. At best, hitherto unheard voices are heard. At worst, the institutions become holed with secrecy, arcane practice and only money opens the gate into the corridors of power.

When communities of people and of place do coincide, they incorporate and represent each other, and both are repositories of political power. This is one link in the chain of belonging - communal self-possession - political power. How vibrant political institutions are depends on how organically they are part of this chain. Today's mobile 'communities', the modern 'diasporas' from Asia and Africa, are feasible communities in that they share a common language, memory, identity and kinship links.[3] But they lack political power as a community because they literally have no common ground. Mobility is an unevenly distributed good - mothers,

---

3. In the multi-ethnic 'community' in which I live, nearly all the shops have been started and are run by people of these diasporas - Nigerian, Ghanaian, Turkish, Greek, Bangladeshi, Pakistani, Indian, Ugandan and Kenyan Asian... Most of the Asian and Turkish shops are foodstores, take-away shops, and newsagents, the African ones are mostly cloth and clothing stores. The three new shops run by white English are an estate agent's, a bookmaker's and a 'Phone Shop'. This last offers cut-price fax and phone services, to meet 'the need of ethnic communities', as the proprietor put it, to keep in touch via a modern technology that is too expensive or complex to possess at home. He has, he claims, 200 customers a day, over 1000 a week.

children and the poor are particularly tied to place. Perhaps more importantly, being together in body has an incomparable power to generate communal ideas and feelings, a sine qua non of politics.[4] But even if a disembedded community does organise to realise political demands, it must still, at some point, make those demands of a political institution. And to organise to realise that demand, it must, at some point, organise as a place-based community.

At this moment, all effective political institutions still originate in and derive their legitimacy from communities of place. That may change - but it is hard to imagine that political desire and action will be generated and sustained if people do not meet, touch and talk in the same place. Without a starting point in physical actuality for communal self-possession, many of the links of community are non-corporeal, such as music, religion, story-telling. That this lack is the high price paid for freedom of movement is attested to by many.

Communal self-possession - sovereignty in another discourse, including Rousseau's - is the starting point, whether that community is a neighbourhood or a nation. The idea of the community possessing itself, coming into its own, is an integral part of all nationalist rhetoric. We will seize back ourselves from the oppressors and usurpers and be our own men! But this invites a digression about why the rhetoric of manliness assimilates the discourse of self-possession, and why non-territorial movements for communal self-possession don't get their hands on the political institutions. It is enough to say here that communal self-possession makes democracy possible, probably inevitable over time.

Wandering souls

The First International in 1864 heralded a century of megalomania; nothing less than the world triumph of socialism would do. Yet the rhetoric of internationalism underestimated the extent to which politics is dependent on the limits of place-based communities. And socialism has proved unable to transcend the loss of political power from locally based institutions. If the coincidence of community, place and political power slip, civic democracy as we have understood it, as the politics of communal self-possession, falters. It more than falters. It becomes

---

4. 'The time has come for a concerted effort to bring back a central meeting place to "trade" shares', said a letter in the *Financial Times*, responding to an article which had also attributed London's decline as a financial centre to the physical dispersal of financial services. *Financial Times* 2.11.95, 7.11.95.

impossible. In its place, we have political forms which are more or less disembodied. Divested of local government, of direct or elected representation at work or in social services, the link between place and political power is lost. We are at a loss. We want to belong, but to do more than belong. We want also to have effect. (Those who are already able simply to 'be', by virtue of some status of worth in the world, are *not* those involved primarily in the politics of identity.) It is out of that (relatively) secure being, sense of worth, that the proselytising spirit of politics comes. If our values have worth, we must propagate them! And others must accept these values, to affirm our worth.

That spirit is the lost soul of radical politics. For more than a decade socialist values were routinely derided by Thatcher; the people delivered four massive judgments against the left. The outcast soul of left politics seeks a home. What is to be done but attach it to one symbol, one leader; to become part of his imperium? The price of refusing our fealty is to become an exile from this new political arrangement. If we don't sign up with Blair's party, who are we, politically?

'The price of refusing our fealty is to become an exile from this new political arrangement'

What came first - the slippage of community/place/power? Have we all abandoned democratic politics to put ourselves in thrall to a Leader? Is the tottering of the political nation state the same as the death of citizenship? And is the death of the old mass party system the same as the death of politics?

The creation of the legend

As the story has unfolded since Blair became leader in the summer of 1994, it has quickly become a story of one man's mission to save the party... No, not the party, more the spirit of justice and decorum from whatever dank cave it was languishing in. Whatever Blair thinks (and what he thinks isn't really the point) the Labour Party is irredeemably flawed as an instrument for delivering justice. The old notion of the Party as an army is dead. (With credit cards and 0800 lines, 'supporters' can provide more money than members - though still not as much as trade unions corporately offer.) The value of the party becomes its power to attest to Blair's authority. 300,000 members, 350,000 members - why, isn't Blair a great man, look how he can pull them in, how far his imperium stretches!

At first sight, this substitution of Leader for party is merely the familiar demon, the media at work. All branches of the media shrink politics to a small national stage inhabited by a recognisable cast of people through whom the 'issues' are played. By dramatising and by evoking myths, political journalists transform what is otherwise, like war, dull, meaningless and full of unreconcilable conflict. Journalists learn this by trial, error and mutual influence. In political journalism

'The creation of the Tony Blair legend is a mutual affair'

the media is not the open, sprawling network of post-modernist legend. Nor does it manifest a further post-modernist conceit - that the communications which count are all electronic, ethereal, non-corporeal.

Coverage of politics comes from a cluster of editors and journalists, who all know each other, travel the same circuit and listen to the same speeches (or scan the print-outs from the speech-maker's office). They are on first name terms with the principal party personnel and manoeuvre anxiously to be invited to the most illustrious of the free-wine banquets laid on by the organisations with the most largesse and the best guest-lists. How could it be otherwise? The pressures and lures of peer group, status, competitiveness and familiarity shape journalists as much as other groups.

Blair's gift to the media was to be young, to be different, to be comfortable with television, and articulate. Of course they snapped up this gift. Who wouldn't, after an election sporting John Smith and John Major as its highlights? Television and direct debits make it possible to be a direct political leader. But the technology on its own is inert, and journalists can only work with material that exists. It was not the media that dispossessed the party, turning the party into a supine body, whose last twitchings were good sport but not serious contest. The media did not dissolve life outside Blair's court. And we should not underestimate the degree of energy that can exist in a passive body towards its sacred head.[5] The creation of the Tony Blair legend is a mutual affair. We know, from accounts like John Rentoul's excellent *Tony Blair*, that a radical shift in the relationship between leader and party was planned and worked for. It is also clear that neither Blair's style of leadership nor his relationship with the party fits a

---

5. 'Pseudo Republicans' deride popular royalism as passive and mindless, wrote Tom Nairn, but they fail to see that 'it has something highly positive about it - an apparently inexhaustible electric charge.' *The Enchanted Glass*, Hutchinson Radius, London 1988, p53.

classic right-wing pattern. Thatcher's persona did. Like Hitler, in J.P. Stern's analysis, Thatcher's chief claim to unique leadership was 'to introduce a conception of personal authenticity into the public sphere and proclaim it as the chief value and sanction of politics'.[6] She attested to her authenticity - corner-shop, Alderman father, grammar school, Methodism, we all know the story - in countless speeches. The counter-signs - the elocution lessons, the going over to the Church of England, the choice of private education for her children, the county clothes style - were enrolled as the natural progress of someone with that background and its authentic ambition to get on.

'Blair is a soulless carpet-bagger to his enemies, a wandering knight to his admirers'

The fact that Major emerged as The Leader of his party at the 1995 conference was hardly more surprising than Blair's triumph. He too had done the work before the event. But in his speech he, for the first time, made much of his true Conservative origin, citing his childhood in a poor but hard-working, risk-taking family. In this he was echoing the Thatcher claim to authenticity. This speech was acclaimed as his best, most Leaderly speech ever.

Despite two biographies in a year[7], Tony Blair has not emerged as a man with an original kernel to which he must stay true and which attests to his integrity. This is his freedom and his fatal flaw. Blair's origin is mobile (through his father - illegitimate and fostered - he has biological grandparents who were, like Major's parents, music hall artistes); and this makes Tony Blair a soulless carpet-bagger to his enemies, or a wandering knight to his admirers. Origins are being dug up for him - the influence of Christian socialists when he was at Oxford, for instance. And no doubt these myths will grow, thus augmenting his authority (authority being, as Hannah Arendt argued, both etymologically and essentially a process of augmenting an origin).[8] Like Great Leaders, he does demand that we trust him, that we make sacrifices - of principle, of history, of what is *sacred* - for him; but, unlike Great Leaders, he does not treat the party as an embodiment of the elect. He is not in love with it. It is not a relationship of intimacy or passion, as it was with Neil Kinnock or Michael Foot. He himself says: 'I was not born into

6. J.P. Stern, *Hitler: The Fuhrer and the People*, Fontana, London 1984, p24.
7. John Rentoul, *Tony Blair*, Little, Brown and Company, London 1995. Jon Sopel, *Tony Blair: The Moderniser*, Michael Joseph, London 1995.
8. Hannah Arendt, 'What is Authority?', in *Between Past and Future*, Penguin.

this party; I chose it'.

At the 1995 party conference Blair's task was to make himself belong to the party without losing his freedom from it. I asked delegates after Blair's speech what it meant they would now do. The answer was: go home and work harder for their new party. Anything else they might do - 'saving' a hospital, preserving a green space, creating a community group, acting on litter or urban decay, would be done through other, non-party agencies. Blair evoked community but proposed no communal powers. This is a can of worms that remains sealed. His speech skilfully offered the practical details the hard-noses of macro-economics wanted, but also put delegates in touch with those myths that make sense out of being human.

This was not a testament to his oratory as such. If Kinnock didn't have this effect this was not so much because his actual words were weaker; it was because we knew he was too grounded in his, and the party's, past. Listening to Kinnock, people feared for him. Blair's speech carried conviction because delegates had confidence he could deliver. Their confidence came from the fact that he had delivered already. And he had delivered already because they had already pledged him their support, most notably in changing (abandoning) Clause IV. That is, Blair's speech was a joint product, while Kinnock's were hacked painfully out of adversity to meet hostility.

Blair's is an essentially post-Thatcherite mission - he was not chosen to do battle with the dreadful old dragon. Rather he was rescuing something good, some authentically gentle spirit of Britain, from the mire and crudity of post-Thatcherite Conservative Britain. He offered us back the quality of compassion which she has so mercilessly derided. Indeed, the chivalric quality of Blair would not have emerged had he been party leader against Thatcher. There were very few heroic ways of opposing her, the most effective being the martyr's valediction from the mortally wounded Geoffrey Howe. Everybody else who tried seemed shrill, ineffectual, spiteful; her contempt was withering. Her hatred was her most powerful weapon. The only response to annihilatory hatred is ridicule, or flight. Opposing Thatcher, Blair would have remained hopelessly young and perky, dependent on the weight of the Labour Party to give him moral force. As he couldn't have depended on the Labour Party, his stature would have remained slight and boyish; a cheeky chappy, not St George. (For those who wondered at the time why the Labour leadership had gone to the imperviously self-possessed and middle-aged John Smith, that is a principal reason.)

The wooing of the people

There is something feminine about the gentle, compassionate spirit which Blair evoked at the conference. The dynamism comes from its marriage with male hardness. The gentle spirit can only be incarnated through the masculine art of politics as represented by Blair. This is the significance of the figure of the knight who clothes his manliness in gay apparel and sexual ambiguity. (Young Blair had 'a slightly mediaeval look about him, a sort of Three Musketeers thing', says the man who played bass guitar in their group Ugly Rumours.) The knight is decorous, courteous, beautifully arrayed; Chaucer's knight carried himself as 'meeke as is a mayde'. A knight worships and serves ladies but also devotedly loves other men. Perhaps, in this post-feminist age, this is the nearest to manliness that a Labour leader can approach. Other forms - Kinnock, Prescott - remind us of the crudity and violence that lurk in masculinity.

Blair's flirtation with a more feminine style is new - even Michael Foot, that most gentle of Labour leaders, habitually roared at Labour crowds. And it is a flirtation with a mass style; a reputation for 'hardness' in private is assiduously cultivated by his aides. It is part of the paradox of politics that Labour leaders, on the whole, address their conferences as though the mass is a feminine being in need of rescue and protection, while Conservative leaders on the whole speak like women inciting men to take up arms and behave like true men. At the Labour conference, it was the delegates who wept; at the Conservative conference it was the leader. Major was close to tears recalling the spirit of that 'proud, independent, stubborn old man that I loved' and moving on to name us, the people, as a nation of manly risk-takers. That's who we were under Thatcher - independent pirates and warriors, grown out of the need for a nanny or the need to care for others other than through the traditional male route of making money. Perhaps that is why 'the nation's favourite poem' is 'If', Kipling's hymn to the ideal of manliness. Perhaps that is part of the thrill of being a Conservative Home Counties lady representative; without shifting her bottom from the conference seat, she can fly off in her head to lay waste to marxists, miners, muggers, whoever is the enemy of the hour. Left-wing critics are right to detect a spirit of vindictive ferocity unleashed at Tory conferences. Both Thatcher and Major have talked of exterminating socialism. Labour leaders' rhetoric in comparison is positively pacific; not since the war have they sought to incite the people. That is why Conservative critics are right to detect in Labour leaders an imagining of the people as helpless.

A successful marriage of leader and people offers a joining of masculine and feminine to make a whole creature; but it dances on the edge of sexual ambiguity. Was the woman Thatcher really a man? Is the man Blair, like Reagan, really ruled by a strong wife, as military dictators Marcos and Noriega were really in thrall to evil women?

The porousness of this sexual division manifests how much an artifice the 'public/private' division is. In the cliché, private life is feminine; it is, in Aristotle's account, dedicated to the care and preservation of life; it is utterly undemocratic. Citizenship and equality belong to the public domain, which is man's domain. But political rhetoric and postures constantly swoop in and out of the 'private' domain, addressing us both as private persons who want to keep out of the political forum, and as privates on the domestic front of the war against disorder. Political rhetoric exploits our reality as domestic, public, private, family, individual, collective persons. The exploitation is partly opportunist. But it also marks the new political reality engendered by the welfare state - a new state, which both re-makes citizens as a protectorate, and charges them with the sleepless duty of guarding this founding order of civilised Britain.

The fluidity of mass politics is germinated by such ambiguity. It is customary to mourn the loss of party loyalty, but such fixed political belonging would mean we would have to inhabit one side of an absolute political divide. Since the re-creation of the British state as a welfare state, that would mean that Labour supporters would be forever consigned to enthusing about living in a protectorate, dispossessed (like women), and Conservatives would be forever asserting their manly self-possession, if only through association with the military and police. That absolute divide does not accord with reality; with the real unsettledness of ourselves. Popular politics has always been energised by an ambiguity of gender roles, which allows us to switch from self-possession to being protected and cared for, without having to switch party and become someone else.

It is not, however, possible to reclaim all of oneself without moving seats. Every shift in political hegemony is preceded by symbolic defections. Before they first won power, Reagan and Thatcher also both promised to restore to the people a vital quality (in their case, the spirit was of hard work, enterprise and love of freedom) of which they had been divested by the existing regime. The appeal is for apostates, but this must be presented as a *return* to one's true home to avoid the slur of treachery. At the heart of the appeal is the idea that their party (Reagan's,

Thatcher's, Blair's) is now the true custodian of the very values which once led people to vote for the other side. The good people have been betrayed by their leaders. Both Reagan and Thatcher explicitly pitched speeches at working-class Democrat/Labour supporters who had seen their ideals traduced by corrupt leaders. Blair called home the caring middle class and was rewarded by the defection of Alan Howarth, just as Thatcher got Reg Prentice et al, and Reagan got the 'Reagan Democrats'. Political renewal starts from restoration.

> 'When Thatcher offered to rescue the people, she had to inflate hugely the malign power of immigrants, trade unions, socialists'

There are vital differences however. When Thatcher offered to rescue people, like a Fairy Godmother to the people's Cinderella, she had to inflate hugely the malign power of immigrants, trade unions, socialists. A common-sense ability to assess risk, whether that's the likelihood of winning the national lottery or of being murdered in a dark street, is overwhelmed by these nightmare phantasmagorias of Conservative imagining. Why such Conservative nightmares should be so much more fertile than the left's, and so little restrained by reason, is a pressing and difficult question. Whatever the answer, one of Blair's chief roles is to dispel the unreason of the right. (As a delegate from St Albans at the Labour Party conference said, the chief effect of Blair on his canvassing was that Labour was no longer a 'nightmare' in voters' minds.) He must strive all the time to seem sincere, not to appear like the Rev. Francis Davey, the terrifyingly wicked vicar in *Jamaica Inn*. What he is helpless to control is that voice which says, prompted by myth, history, the unconscious: *of course* taxes will go up, bureaucracies will grow, else things will fall apart. The righteous will be rewarded, the poor must be avenged.

Whether Blair will ever name enemies is a serious question. Where are Labour supporters to direct their hatreds?

Global media and human-scale politics

The lack of hatred disturbs many Labour supporters. Blair seems to be saying Labour should learn to love its old enemy capitalism. Despite the tone of reason, he also suggests this embrace will transform the beast - look, privatised British Telecom is giving its goods to the needy, a princely act. Unreconstructed socialists fear they have been told to cover their fangs in case they frighten the media which created Tony Blair.

There is delusion here; it was political acts, like voting, joining, giving money, that gave Blair his authority. The media can't do that. They *can* however be blamed for not covering those forms of political life that exist outside Blair's court. Television changes the proportion of things, it changes size and distance. Without the enlargement of media coverage, dissent or experiment seems eccentric or nugatory or Luddite.

'Only if Labour could find an even Bigger Idea than Thatcher's could it defeat the old bat'

This is not to say that a part of the Labour Left isn't Luddite. It remains imprisoned in an obsession with party rules and winning positions. But the media's marginalisation of the left as a whole has also involved the inflation of this particular section of the left, out of all proportion. And at the same time, in areas where the left has its strongest voice, for example as the guardian of the welfare state, it has been unable to galvanize a coherent, national, movement of the poor. In campaigns for employment or equal health care or a decent environment, it is often superseded by local campaign groups and professional associations.

Short of uniform, national mass movements, we are left with forms of dissent that only acquire a larger import when there is a dramatic confrontation or a media celebrity involved - and often not even then. The present discontent with the human relation to the non-human world is massive and presages an epochal shift. For decades the prophets of this shift were dismissed as eccentric. Now, when their concerns have become general, the scale of political change needed is so gigantic that only the UN, or at least the EU, has the scope to achieve it; or it is left to individual fanatics to forego their cars or supermarket trips. There seems to be no scope for a nation state, or a national political party, to effect change. The sphere of politics either expands to the global or contracts to the ethics of the individual.

Two decades ago, the eccentrics and fanatics would have tried to get their concerns on to the Labour Party agenda. Who would bother now? Outside the conference centre in Brighton, on the day of Blair's speech, there was only one group chanting slogans. They were a group of Hindus protesting about the Pakistani exploitation of Kashmir. In previous years, there would have been a thicket of hands from a score or more of different campaign groups. That was the politics of yesteryear. The groups haven't gone away. They've gone away from the Labour Party conference. Perhaps it is right to assume that British culture is peculiarly resistant to ideas, fearful of passions, tolerant but dismissive of oddness.

And for these reasons, the odd ideas and passions of the dissidents must remain local peculiarities. In a pluralistic society, there can be no single commanding idea.

This is a post-Thatcherite reality, obscured during Thatcherism. The power of her persona was such that all signs and portents, all events, all developments, were attributed to a single phenomenon - Thatcherism. This in turn was reduced to a single Big Idea. And thus the left was set off on a wild goose chase for an alternative Big Idea. Only if it could find an even Bigger Idea than Thatcher's Big Idea could it defeat the old bat. There is no Big Idea. And in recognising that we can draw a close to the age of megalomania. There is no one Idea to be launched and followed, no single centre of power to be seized, no one commanding height to be scaled. The power of American TV culture to make someone into a 'global' star within a week of whatever event brought him or her to public attention perpetuates the megalomaniac illusion. That in itself should bring us down to earth. An American friend tells me that in the week in which British newspapers were dominated by the Battle of Clause IV, not a single American (fellow socialist) he talked to had any idea of what Clause IV was or why it mattered. The day after Blair's great speech, the verdict on OJ pushed Blair and the Labour Party off every UK tabloid front page, and to the side of every broadsheet. For global, read the reach of American satellite channels.

But because an event in Britain is not the main news on American/global TV does not mean it has no worth. In other words, we have to scale down our desires; or perhaps just fit them to the right size. We cannot destroy capitalism. We cannot *vote* Britain into being an egalitarian socialist republic. That doesn't mean that nothing else is worth doing. And despite Blair's global crusading tone, it was this recognition that something could be done short of total victory for socialism that first persuaded many people at a conference in 1994 that he was a man worth listening to. Whether or not his authority grows depends on what roles the rest of us can play.

Different Together

Women in Belfast

Photo Narrative by Cynthia Cockburn

Turf Lodge, the Shankill, Twinbrook, Ballybeen, Malone Road - say where you live in Belfast and it pins an identity tag on you: working-class, Catholic, nationalist-going-on-Republican. Or Protestant and poor, recently re-housed. Or aspiring integrationist middle-class.

To drive the knowledge home,
territory is colour-coded, on police
maps and in reality. Kerb stones
painted red, white and blue, the
stencilled hand of the Ulster
Volunteer Force tell you: this is
Protestant space. Gaelic, murals of
the Great Famine and lamp posts
ringed in green, white and gold
assert: the IRA rules here.

33

Belfast's walls are crusty with paint: graffiti shouting hurt and rage are painted once, painted out, painted in again. Housing areas are crusty with barbed wire, peace lines, crash barriers and fancy architected fences - erected to give security forces an illusion of control.

So called 'Peace line' separating the Loyalist area of the Shankill Road from the Republican Falls Road

RUC barracks in residential West Belfast

The ceasefires have given everyone a welcome breather, but watchfulness and territoriality are habits you don't break overnight. The soldiers are still there in barracks. Poverty and unemployment haven't gone anywhere either.

But Belfast is shaped by its contradictions. Tatty but sort of lovely. The ugliness of bricked-up windows and gaping roofs is redeemed by the smell of damp grass from the ring-around of green mountains. And the narrower its ghettoes the more alive their sense of community.

One thing: there are more active talented resourceful women-working-with-women in working-class Belfast than in most places in Britain. Advice, refuge, support for young mothers, a chance of training, these things have flowered all over the place. Such projects are under-resourced. But they persist because public facilities are scant, and women make good with their own energy.

At the core of this collective provision is an array of Women's Centres, most of them deep in either Catholic/Republican or Protestant/Loyalist terrain. Some are still in old housing stock where they began, some have rooms in community centres or even purpose-built space. They provide a friendly drop-in

Women Too, the Windsor Women's Centre, is one of (currently) seven women's centres in working class communities of Greater Belfast.

corner, a crèche, a locus for campaigning and courses in a range of things: personal development, carpentry, aqua-fit.

Centres have campaigned for playspace

Who takes liberties with Irish masculinity? Advertisement for toilet roll.

Belfast women's activism is a small but bold counter-current to the field of violence in which they live. The violence is official, military, political, criminal and often very very personal. Him indoors, local paramilitary commands and the authorities are not overjoyed by women's self-organising, but don't have the nerve to attack it openly.

An *if* and a *may-be*: if the ceasefires hold, can masculinity be decommissioned?

Taking the piss with a limp spring-roll: is the new generation of girls headed for more autonomy?

Low-paid male manual workers contemplate Louise Walsh's sculpture Monument to the Low-paid Women Workers.

First get-together of the North Belfast young women's network, which spans Catholic and Protestant areas

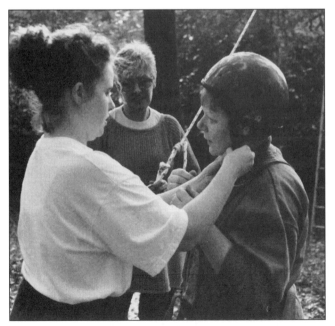

Learning trust through daring to climb: women from Poleglass estate

40

In Northern Ireland there is an extensive official and voluntary sector Community Relations industry that beavers away for Reconciliation. Its funding criteria seem to invite staged cross-community encounters, cultural exchanges and mutual confessions of prejudice. It is about a setting-aside of difference.

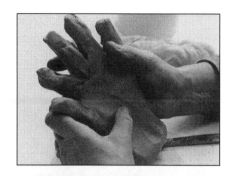

By contrast, the Women's Centres don't blame personal sectarianism for the war, so much as an oppressive state, unrepresentative politicians and inept policies. So they start somewhere else: invest in women and in community development. If you enable self-respect in brutally impoverished communities, they believe, respect for the Other will follow.

However you look at it, women's organising builds bridges. The community workers themselves manifest mixity: lesbian and heterosexual, university-educated and community-educated. Some coordinators of Catholic origin are working in Women's Centres on Protestant territory and vice versa. While the war was on this was often dangerous. But women were vigilant for each other.

*One of the first things women's centres
establish: a drop-in crèche.*

Several centres provide space and support for school-age girls

*Learning unaccustomed
manual trades*

Day-to-day working is consciously anti-sectarian, but being 'other' may mean being South Asian or Chinese, not only the one you call 'Prod' or 'Taig'. Activities often involve groups (of teenagers, say, or the Golden Girls) getting together with those from the other community, somewhere on neutral ground but without trumpeting it too much.

The Centres help each other. In 1989, when the Belfast City Council cancelled the funding of the Falls Women's Centre, impugning it as an IRA front, the Women's Centre of the deeply Loyalist Shankill led a protest against this finger-pointing and political vetting.

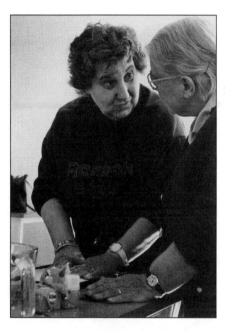

*This group of older women
call themselves The Golden Girls*

A different difference: not Protestant and Catholic, but Protestant and Muslim

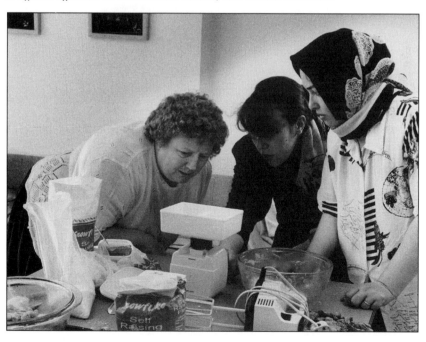

45

*Meeting of the Women's Support Network: how are working-class women
to get a voice in a new Northern Ireland?*

That was the moment the Centres set up a Women's Support
Network in which they now work together. They aim to see
women present in the processes that will shape the post-ceasefire
Northern Ireland and to get equity for women in the sharing of the
new funds promised by peace.

The Network is, they say, a *collective feminist* voice of women's
projects in working-class Belfast.

Individually women hold onto their political identities - some long
for a united Ireland, others feel deeply threatened by the idea. But
they have identified a commonality in being women, being
community based and being angry at injustice and inequality, that
allows them to affirm and even welcome this and other kinds of
difference.

This essay derives from a research project on gender and cross-communal relations in conflict zones, carried out by the author in the Centre for Research in Gender, Ethnicity and Social Change, City University, London. We hope this will be the first of a series of three such essays in Soundings, *subsequent issues representing women's projects in Bosnia and Israel. Thanks to the Lipman Trust and Womankind Worldwide for grants towards materials. And a resounding thank you to the women in Belfast whose skill and courage sustain the initiative described here.*

Five Poems

Returning to Russia

The winter here is very long, or hugely slow;
the broken pavements with their gristles of ice last
for a tonnage of unwanted future to be unloaded;

they say that at zero temperature the particles
are absolutely still, no force, no protest;
only the black trees pose, chaotic and hysterical

to mime the violence iced-in behind
the pale fuse of dusk; its light is the light
and lingering glance of long green eyes.

I've returned to this place like the seagull
returns, to where things lie spookily about,
returned from afternoons of racing-blue
and funny hats carousing in the new jokes
of the year, the tiny photogenic moments;
I've returned to the grey communal bread,
to a place inside myself I can't forget.

Muffled children poke the ice with sticks
incurious, in silence, not breaking it.
And another endless night lowers itself.

Judy Gahagan

Under the Brick

Concealed beneath a wasteland brick
a creased black and white photograph
of coupling - and we'd retrieve it
on those everlasting walks from school.
We'd turn it this way, that way, unsure
exactly how a couple fitted together,
put it back under the brick, but each day
find it again below the steel grey sky,
the London Country buses passing.
We'd pause, speechless, tilt our heads,
while their missing heads lived in
another world, outside the photograph.

At night I'd dream
and under the gritty newtown stars
the brick would hold down our secret,
would press on the headless bodies,
the limbs and their arrested activity,
the flesh more cracked and creased.

The lone couple, untouched by moonlight -
tiny creatures under a brick
in the middle of the wasteland.

Moniza Alvi

Spring Offensive

May's the month for optimistic acts:
seedlings - pansies, antirrhinums, salvias -
bedded in, gauche first-day-at-schoolers.
Your thumbs have blessed them, inner eye furnishing
dowdy beds with dazzling coverlets.

Through the lengthening dusk, snail battalions
creep on prehensile bellies from their dugouts.
They bivouac around your bright hopes,
slurp sapid juices, vandal lace-makers,
body-building on your would-be colours.

You stumble out at dawn and catch them at it,
scrawling silver sneers on wall and path,
and snatch them from their twigs, impervious to
endearing horns, their perfect picture-bookness.
You crush them, or worse; lay down poisonous snacks.

Yet, aren't their shells as lovely as petunias,
patterned like ceramic works of art
from a more coherent age? And might they not
defend with slow, tenacious argument
their offspring, soon to fizz and drown in salt?

Summer's on their side. Each night, new recruits
will graduate from dark academies.
You lie, plotting extravagant revenges.
Asleep, you dream a world where, very slowly,
children, friends, are running out of air.

Carole Satyamurti

Lazarus' Sister

On hot nights now, in the smell of trees and water,
you beg me to listen and your words enter my spirit.

Your descriptions unmake me, I am like wood
that thought has wormed, even the angels

that report our innermost wish must be kinder.
And yet, when your face is grey in the pillow, I wake you

gently, kissing your eyes, my need for you
stronger than the hope of love, I carry your body

where the hillside flickers: olive cypress ash.
But nothing brings relief. All our days

are numbered in a book. I try to imagine
a way our story can end without a magician.

Elaine Feinstein

Cambridge

Your neighbor has written a book.
Your neighbor's wife, too, has written a book
and your mailman and your landlord and your maid
and the young girl who bakes pies
at the Stop & Shop-- yes, she too
has written a book. Your best friend
is writing a book about the book
your first wife wrote, so you smile
and say "I'm so sorry,
I haven't read your new book"
to everyone you run into, just in case.

Once, you lived in a world of not many books
and were a happy bird: the earth
was a place of wide margins, little text.
Now, though, you're deep in the bookish dark
and ink runs through your heart like lead
with only the distant, the partial and the dead
to call you brother. You whirl at your will,
looking for air in this hard-bound,
hard-edged place of too much thinking.

O friends, I love you all,
but long for a little heart
among these hard-won pages.
Don't read my own book tonight:
just walk down to the river
where the moon's thin as a parenthesis
and even the ducks have abandoned the shore
for their bookish houses...
their relentless, cacophonous typewriters.

Michael Blumenthal

'The earth is
degenerating
in these latter days.
There are signs that the
world is speedily coming
to an end. Bribery and
corruption abound. The
children no longer obey
their parents. Every man
wants to write a book,
and it is evident that the
end of the world is
rapidly approaching.'

chiseled into an
Assyrian tablet,
cs. 2800 B.C.

The rise of neurogenetic determinism

Steven Rose

Neurogenetic determinism claims to explain everything - from violence in the streets to sexual orientation - in terms of properties of the brain or genes. These claims draw on the explosion of new genetic and neuroscientific techniques, but reflect a much older reductionist fallacy. This article analyses a sequence of falsely taken reductive steps and examines their consequences for both biological and social thinking.

We are now half way through what in the US has been called the Decade of the Brain. Europe, always slower to move on such matters, has just belatedly started its own such Decade. And we are even further into the massive international $3 billion-odd exercise known as the Human Genome Programme, the attempt to map, and subsequently to sequence, the entire DNA alphabet of the human chromosomes. (Identifying just what these DNA strands might do, what the genes might mean, is, as will become clear, a rather different matter, though often elided in popular consciousness.) For a neuroscientist like myself, it is an incredibly exciting time to be in the lab, at the computer or in the library. New results come flooding in at an almost impossible rate to digest. From the gene sequences of molecular biology to the windows onto the brain produced by the new imaging techniques, extraordinary pictures of complexity at all levels, from the chemical through the cellular to the systemic are emerging; of the brain as a dynamic entity, an ever-shifting sea of electrical and magnetic fluxes, of

'New results come flooding in at an almost impossible rate to digest'

chemical currents, of growing and retracting cellular connections, of coherent time-locked oscillations which some have even speculated form the basis of conscious experience. But data has far outstripped theory; rival schools, of connectionists (who claim that brain/mind properties can be simulated in the distributed architecture of parallel processing computers) and chaos theorists (who deny a permanent 'seat' to any mind/brain process) strive to make sense of an information overload that almost inhibits meaning.

Just as the Decade of the Brain has produced dramatic advances in information, so it has also generated ever more strident claims that neuroscience is about to 'solve' the brain and in doing so usher in a new era of what Delgado, an earlier enthusiast for brain surgery to cure violence, once called a 'psychocivilised society'. The emerging synthesis which I call neurogenetics offers the prospect of identifying, ascribing causal power to, and if appropriate modifying, genes affecting brain and behaviour. Neurogenetics claims to be able to answer the question of where, in a world full of individual pain and social disorder, we should look to explain and to change our condition. It is these claims, rather than the excitements of brain theory for its practitioners, which I wish to address here. If the reasons for our distress lie outside ourselves, it is for the social sciences to understand and for politics to try to resolve the problems. If however the causes of our pleasures and our pains, our virtues and our vices, lie predominantly within the biological realm, then it is to neurogenetics that we should look for explanation, and to pharmacology and molecular engineering that we should turn for solutions. Social and biological explanations are not necessarily incompatible, but at any time the emphasis given to each seems to depend less on the state of 'objective' scientific knowledge than on the sociopolitical zeitgeist. In the context of rising public concern about levels of violence, an ideology which stresses personal responsibility, and denies even the correlation between poverty and ill-health, is likely to reject the social in favour of the individual and his or her biological constitution.

Of course this is to simplify, to imply that the world is divided into mutually incommensurable realms of causation in which problems are *either* social *or* biological. This is not my intention; the phenomena of human existence and experience are always and inexorably simultaneously biological *and* social, and an adequate explanation must involve both. Even this may not be enough; both social and biological sciences deal with the world observed as object; personal experience is by definition subjective and any account which excludes this personal element from our attempts to understand the world falls into the reductive mechanical materialist trap against which both Marx and Engels inveighed. But such unity of subjective and objective may be even harder to achieve than that of the biological and social, and I cannot even begin to approach that issue here. (I tried to talk about it, however inadequately, in my recent book *The Making of Memory*.[1])

Let us then remain in the world of the objective. Clearly, for any serious scientist to deny the social in favour of the biological or vice versa would be unthinkable; we are all interactionists now. However, it is by their deeds that one must judge, and in any search for explanation and intervention it is necessary to seek the appropriate level which effectively determines outcomes. Whilst only the most extreme reductionist would suggest that we should seek the origins of the Bosnian war in deficiencies in serotonin reuptake mechanisms in Dr Karadzic's brain, and its cure by the mass prescription of Prozac, many of the arguments offered by neurogenetic determinists are not far removed from such extremes. Give the social its due, the claim runs, but in the last analysis the determinants are surely biological; and anyhow, we have some understanding and possibility of intervention into the biological, but rather little into the social.

This is not a new debate; it has recurred in each generation at least since Darwin's day, and most recently in the 1970s and 80s in the form of the polemical disputes over the explanatory powers of sociobiology.[2] What is new is the way in which the mystique of the new genetics is seen as strengthening the reductionist argument. At its simplest, neurogenetic determinism argues a directly causal relationship between gene and behaviour. A man is homosexual because he has a 'gay brain' itself the product of 'gay genes' and a woman is depressed because she

---

1. *The Making of Memory*, Bantam, London 1992.
2. See for example, E.O. Wilson, *Sociobiology: the New Synthesis,* Harvard University Press, Cambridge Mass.1975; S.P.R. Rose, R.C. Lewontin and L.J. Kamin, *Not in our Genes,* Penguin, Harmondsworth 1984; P. Kitcher, *Vaulting Ambition: Sociobiology and the Quest for Human Nature,* MIT Press, Cambridge, Mass. 1985.

has genes 'for' depression.[3] There is violence on the streets because people have 'violent' or 'criminal' genes;[4] people get drunk because they have genes 'for' alcoholism;[5] and there may be genes 'for' homelessness, according to the then Editor of the leading US journal *Science*. (The other day I even came across a claim that there might be genes for 'compulsive shopping'; there are clearly no limits to the power of the alphabet soup of DNA.) What isn't due to the genes may be left to biological insults occurring during pregnancy, birth defects or early childhood accident.

In a social and political environment conducive to such claims, and which has largely despaired of finding social solutions to social problems, these apparently scientific assertions become magnified by press and politicians, and researchers may argue that their more modest claims are traduced beyond their intentions. Such Pilatism, however, is hard to credit when so much effort is put by researchers themselves into what Nelkin has described as 'selling science'.[6] The press releases, put out by the researchers themselves, which surrounded the publication of leVay's and Hamer's books and papers (see footnote 3), claiming to have identified 'the' biological cause of male homosexuality, and raising a host of alarmist social and ethical speculations were couched in language which leaves little need for media magnification.

Reductionism

It is my argument that such naive neurogenetic determinism is based on a faulty reductive sequence by which complex social processes are regarded as 'caused' by, 'explained by' or 'nothing but' the workings out of biological programmes based in the brain or the genes. This reductive sequence runs through a number of steps which I shall outline later (see pp 65-9); the core issue, however, is reducibility, which, as Medawar once remarked, comes not as second but as first nature to natural scientists.

Thus when Popper, giving the first Medawar lecture to the Royal Society a few

3. See S. Levay, *The Sexual Brain* , MIT Press, Cambridge, Mass., 1993; D. Hamer, S. Hu, V.L. Magnuson, N. Hu and A.M.L. Pattatucci, *Science*, 261, 1993, pp 321-327; D.B. Cohen, *Out of the Blue: Depression and Human Nature*, Norton, New York, 1994.
4. A. Reiss and J. Roth, *Understanding and Preventing Violence*, National Academy Press, Washington DC 1993.
5. M. Galanter (ed) *Recent Developments in Alcoholism*, Plenum, New York 1994.
6. D. Nelkin, *Selling Science*, Freeman, New York 1997.

years back, offered eight terse reasons why biology was irreducible to physics (of which the fourth was that 'biochemistry cannot be reduced to chemistry'), he incurred the wrath of the distinguished assembly, moving the Nobel-Prize winning crystallographer Max Perutz into a vigorous response. His life's work, after all, had been to demonstrate the relevance of chemistry to biology, and a couple of weeks later he published a reply to Popper, basing his case on the way in which the molecular structure of haemoglobins varied amongst species depending on their environment. Contrast, for instance, the haemoglobin of a mammal which lives at relatively low altitudes, like a camel, with that of a related species, the llama, which lives at high altitude in the Andes, where the air is much thinner and the demands on the oxygen-carrying capacity of the blood therefore differ. The structures are subtly different, in each case better fitting the conditions which its owners inhabit. Is this not clear evidence that human physiology and biochemistry not merely depend upon, but are reducible to, the chemistry of their component molecules? Game set and match to Perutz?[7] I think not, but can not here argue that case in more depth. Suffice it to say that no amount of analysis, however detailed, of the molecular structure of haemoglobin can lead to an understanding of the function of that molecule as an oxygen carrier in a living animal, in other words its *meaning* for the system of which it is a part.

This is not of course at all to deny the power of reductionist analysis as part of our attempt to understand complex systems, nor does it reflect on reductionism as a methodology by which to experiment - there is essentially no other way to work. And it says nothing about abstract philosophical concerns with theory reduction. I am concerned here simply with the efforts to attribute causal explanation of complex social affairs through appeals to neurotransmitter metabolism, brain structures and genes. It is not necessary to enter into a full-blown defence of irreducibility to identify the flaws in the claims of neurogenetic determinism to explain complex social phenomena. Such phenomena are of their essence historically contingent and framed by meanings which the reductive process loses as surely as the information content of the page on which these words are printed is lost from a chemical study of the paper and ink which comprise it. And the issue at stake is not the formal philosophical one, but the question of the appropriate level of organisation of matter at which to seek causally effective

---

7. M. Perutz, *Trends Biochem. Sci.*,13, 1988.

determinants of the behaviour of individuals and societies.

The US Violence Initiative

Let me take a specific example of considerable current concern: the explanation and treatment of the wave of violence which seems to be spreading through the societies of the industrialised world. The debate about the causes of violence long predates the current furore; only the language in which it is cloaked changes. Two decades ago the focus was not genes but chromosomes, when it was claimed that there was a higher than expected prevalence of men carrying an extra Y chromosome amongst those incarcerated for violent crime. And at the turn of the twentieth century, for the followers of Lombroso, it was physiognomy rather than genes which predicted criminality. Before the time of modern science, it was simpler still; it was sufficient to invoke original sin, or predestination. Even if the extra Y has now gone the way of physiognomy and sin, predestination (albeit now spoken in a medicalised hush rather than a hell-fire rant) still lies at the heart of the argument.

Hitherto, in Britain at least, the focus of explanation has been on personal life history; the impoverished rearing practices of single mothers or the laxly disciplined schooling of the 1960s. But in the US even this explanation is being discarded in favour of a return to original biological sin; the fault, we are told, lies in our (or rather *their*) genes. The argument was put most clearly in 1992 by the then Director of the National Institutes for Mental Health, Frederick Goodwin, in his proposed Federal Violence Initiative. Noting that violence was concentrated in the US inner cities, and especially amongst blacks, who have, he argued, inherited a cocktail of genetic predispositions, to diabetes, to high blood pressure, and to violent crime, he argued for a research programme to identify some 100,000 inner-city children and to investigate the genetic or congenital factors which predispose them to such violent and antisocial behaviour. A few years previously, the psychologist Richard Herrnstein coauthored with James Q. Wilson *Crime and Human Nature* - in many ways the forerunner of Herrnstein's more recent coauthorship of *The Bell Curve* - which equally focused on the proposition that violent crime in the US is the prerogative of the poor and black and that its origins lie in 'failures' in their biological constitution.

Now there are many obvious objections to such a proposal. Some point to the fact that these discussions always seem to focus on working-class crime; no-one seems to study the heritability of the tendency to commit business fraud, or the biochemical correlates of wife-beating amongst middle-class men. Others worry about the complex and sometimes contradictory web of meanings involved in the very concept of violence. On the one hand an *identical* act - of a man picking up a gun and shooting another at close range - if sanctioned by the state in times of war becomes an act of heroism worthy of a medal, but if carried out in the midst of a drugs deal in a Manchester pub is a crime punishable by a long term of imprisonment. On the other hand, all sorts of *different* acts are lumped

'Predestination, through original biological sin still lies at the heart of the argument'

together: Cantona's attack on an abusive football fan, fights between demonstrators and police, the Russian bombing of Grozny, all merge, as if one word, violence, fits them all, and their underlying causes are all the same.

Goodwin's proposal led to charges of racism, and he has subsequently left the NIMH, but a modified version of his proposed Initiative, targeted on specific inner-city areas such as Chicago, is up and running, and estimated to cost some $400 million. A conference based on Goodwin's premises, blocked in the US, was held under the prestigious auspices of the CIBA Foundation in London in January of 1995, and the postponed conference in the US eventually got under way - in the face of pickets alleging racism - in September 1995. Not surprisingly, psychologists and psychiatrists, geneticists and molecular biologists have looked longingly at this particular pork barrel. In 1994 I was telephoned urgently by a well-known California-based therapist, just off to Washington to present a proposal to study biochemical and immunological 'markers' in 'violent, incarcerated criminals'. Would I collaborate with him, he asked, in analysing serotonin levels in fluids derived from spinal taps? Serotonin is a neurotransmitter whose metabolism is affected by a number of well-known drugs including, as it happens, the now notorious Prozac. To say nothing of the ethics of performing this type of operation on a - literally - captive population, the thought that such a study might provide a causal explanation for the endemic violence of US society is just the sort of simple-mindedness that the Violence Initiative fosters.

Amongst child psychologists the key word has become 'temperament'. This nebulous property is, they claim, to a significant degree heritable. Jerome Kagan suggests that some 10 per cent of the infants he studied show, from a very early age, a tendency to shyness which in later life expresses itself as aggression. To bolster this deterministic argument, he reports that he finds an analogous pattern of behaviour in kittens which grow into aggressive cats. Adrian Raine and his colleagues have studied a cohort of Danish males, now in their mid 20s, and shown that children born with birth complications, those who were products of an unwanted pregnancy and failed abortion, and those institutionalised during the first year of life, committed a disproportionate number of violent crimes (murder,

'Is there something unique about the genotype of the US population which dramatically predisposes it to violence?'

rape, armed robbery); they concluded that 'biological factors play some role in violent behaviour - and the role is not trivial.'[8] That children with such a desperate history become damaged and even criminal adults is an observation which would scarcely surprise even the most socially deterministic criminologist; the inclusion criteria for his sample are likely to cluster with many other impoverished aspects of the growing

child's life history. Most, however, would probably regard Raine's conclusion as a leap of faith justified only by a commitment to biologistic thinking.

No biologist could doubt the premise that individual differences in genes, and during development, help shape a person's actions and distinguish how one person behaves in a given context from how another behaves; nor that a study of the mechanisms involved in these developmental processes is of great scientific interest. But that is neither the reason why nor the way in which 'violence research' is currently being conducted. Rather, it is framed within a determinist paradigm which seeks the causes of social problems in individual biology, and it is fostered by a political philosophy - on both sides of the Atlantic - which rejoices in the privileges which come with inequalities in wealth and power and rejects steps to diminish them. The rate of violent crime and of incarceration is higher in the US than in any other industrial country. Can it really be the case that there is something unique about the genotype of the US population which so dramatically predisposes it to violence? Furthermore, rates of violence are not static; in both the US and the UK, violent crime has markedly increased in recent years - in the US the death rate amongst young males increased 154 per cent between 1985 and 1994. Such fluctuations between and within societies are quite incompatible with any genetic explanation.

---

8. A. Raine, P. Brennan and S. Mednick, mimeo paper at AAAS annual meeting, San Francisco, 1993.

The reductionist cascade

What this account demonstrates is the first two steps in a reductive cascade which characterises all such determinist thinking: *reification* and *arbitrary agglomeration*. In this section I will outline a series of reductionist assumptions which constitute the bases for determinist thinking. Alongside *reification* and *arbitrary agglomeration*, I will also describe: *improper quantification*, belief in *statistical normality*, *spurious localisation*, and *misplaced causality*.

Reification converts a dynamic process into a static phenomenon. Thus violence, rather than describing an action/activity between persons, or even a person and the natural world, becomes instead a 'character' - aggression - a thing which can be abstracted from the dynamically interactive system in which it appears and which can be studied in isolation. The same process occurs with 'intelligence', 'altruism', 'homosexuality', etc. Yet if the activity described by the term violence can only be expressed in an interaction between individuals, then to reify the process is to lose its meaning.

> 'Comparably crude generalisations in my study of memory in day-old chicks would be rejected out of hand'

Arbitrary agglomeration carries reification a step further, lumping together many different reified interactions as all exemplars of the one thing. Thus aggression becomes a portmanteau term within which all the many types of event and process catalogued above can be linked; all become manifestations of some unitary underlying property of the individuals, so that identical biological mechanisms are involved in, or even cause, each. Take, for example, the descriptions offered in a recent widely cited paper by Hans Brunner and his colleagues, associating a point mutation in the gene which codes for a particular brain enzyme concerned with neurotransmission with 'abnormal behaviour.'[9] The 'behavioural phenotype' in eight males in this family is described as including 'aggressive outbursts, arson, attempted rape and exhibitionism', activities carried out by subjects 'living in different parts of the country at different times' across three generations. Can such widely differing types of behaviour, described so baldly as to isolate them from social context, appropriately be subsumed under the single heading of aggression? It is unlikely that such an assertion, if made in the context of a study of non-human animal behaviour, would pass muster

---

9. H.J. Brunner, M. Nelen, X.O. Breakefield, H.H. Ropers, and B.A. van Oost, *Science*, 262, 1993.

- certainly if I made comparably crude generalisations on the basis of such sparse data in my study of memory in day-old chicks, the paper would rightly be rejected out of hand. Yet the claims the Brunner paper makes have become part of the arsenal of argument employed, for example, by the Federal Violence Initiative.

A third error in the use of this form of argumentation is *improper quantification*. Improper quantification argues that reified and agglomerated characters can be given numerical value. If a person is violent, or intelligent, one can ask how violent, how intelligent, by comparison with other people. IQ is one well-known example, but the quantification of aggression is also revealing, for it illustrates another feature of the reductionist cascade which leads to neurogenetic determinism, the use of an animal model. Place an unfamiliar mouse into a cage occupied by a rat, and often the rat will eventually kill the mouse. The time taken for the rat to perform this act is taken as a surrogate for the rat's aggression; some rats will kill quickly, others slowly or even not at all. The rat which kills in thirty seconds is on this scale twice as aggressive as the rat which takes a minute. Such a measure, dignified as *muricidal behaviour*, serves as a quantitative index for the study of aggression, ignoring the many other aspects of the rat-mouse interaction, for instance the dimensions, shape and degree of familiarity of the cage environment to the participants in the 'muricidal' interaction, whether there are opportunities for retreat or escape, and the prior history of interactions between the pair. And just as time to kill becomes a surrogate for a measure of aggression, so this behaviour in the rat is transmogrified into drive-by gangs shooting up a district in Los Angeles. Genes which affect the muricidal interaction are claimed to have their homologues in the human, and therefore to be explanatory factors here too.

Of course, in an entirely trivial sense this could be true. A genetic defect which leads to blindness in rats may have its homologue in humans, and blind humans are, one would assume, less likely to pick up a gun and fire than sighted ones. But this is not what the determinists mean when they make their causal claims for a specific genetic origin for violence.

Belief in *statistical normality* assumes that in any given population the distribution of such behavioural scores takes a Gaussian form, the bell-shaped curve. The best known example is IQ, the tests for which successive generations of psychometricians refined and remoulded until it was made to fit (almost) the approved statistical distribution - a manipulation exploited to the hilt in *The Bell Curve*.[10] But to assume that the entire population can be distributed along a single dimension to which a single numerical value can be ascribed is to confuse a statistical manipulation for a biological phenomenon. There is no biological necessity for such a unidimensional distribution (even for continuously varying genetic traits), nor for one in which the population shows such a convenient spread. (It is perfectly possible to set examinations in which virtually everyone scores 100 per cent; the British university penchant for 10 per cent firsts, 10 per cent thirds and 10 per cent fails, with everyone else comfortably in the middle, is a convention, not a law of nature.) Yet the power of this reified statistic should not be underestimated. It conveniently conflates two different concepts of 'normality', implying that to lie outside the permitted range around the norm is to be in some way abnormal, not merely statistically but in the sense which ascribes normative values. Thus homosexuality is abnormal in that only a small percentage of the population are gay or lesbian, and it has been, at least until recently, normatively unacceptable both legally and religiously. When Herrnstein and Murray called their book *The Bell Curve* they played precisely into these multiple meanings of reified normality.

Having reified processes into things and arbitrarily quantified them, the reified object ceases to be a property even of the individual, but instead becomes that of a part of the person - this is *spurious localisation*. Hence the penchant for speaking of, for example, schizophrenic brains, genes - or even urine - rather than of brains, genes or urine derived from a person diagnosed as suffering from schizophrenia. Of course, everyone ought to know (and does, at least on Sundays) that this is a shorthand, but the resonance of 'gay brains' or 'gay genes' does more than merely sell books for their scientific authors; it both reflects and endorses the modes of thought and explanation that constitute neurogenetic determinism, for it disarticulates the complex properties of individuals into isolated and localised lumps of biology, permitting neuroanatomical debates to range over whether gayness is embedded in one or other hypothalamic region or, alternatively, a differently shaped corpus callosum in the brain. Aggression is similarly 'located' in the limbic system, probably the amygdala. In the 1970s US psychosurgeons proposed to treat inner-city violence by amygdalectomising ghetto

10. R.J. Herrnstein, and C. Murray, *The Bell Curve:Intelligence and Class Structure in American Life*,The Free Press, 1994.

militants.[11] Things are a little more sophisticated today; a localisation in the brain can also take the form of some chemical imbalance, probably of neurotransmitters, so aggression is now 'caused' by a disorder of serotonin reuptake mechanisms, and drugs rather than the knife become the approved approach. Raine claims to be able to detect reductions in the neural activity of the frontal cortex in 'murderers' as opposed to 'normal' individuals by means of brain scans, and hence to be able to predict 'with 80% certainty' from this biological measure the likelihood of a person being a violent killer. It is not clear what such a measure might show in the brain of a Saddam Hussein, a Ratko Mladic or a Stormin' Norman. Presumably these would feature amongst Dr Raine's 'normals'.

It is at this point that neurogenetic determinism introduces its *misplaced sense of causality*. It is of course probable that during

'The cause of toothache is not too little aspirin in the brain'

aggressive encounters people show dramatic changes in, for instance, hormones, neurotransmitters and neuro-physiological responses, all of which can be affected by drug treatments. People whose life history includes many such encounters are likely to show lasting differences in a variety of brain and body markers. But to describe such changes as if they were the *causes* of particular behaviours is to mistake correlation or even consequence for cause. This issue has dogged interpretation of the biochemical and brain correlates of psychiatric disorders for decades, yet it still continues. When one has a cold, one's nose runs. But the nasal mucus is a consequence and not a cause of the infection. When one has a toothache it may be sensible to alleviate the pain by taking aspirin, but the cause of the toothache is not too little aspirin in the brain. Such fallacies are however an almost inevitable consequence of the processes of reification and agglomeration, for if there is one single thing called, for instance, alcoholism, then it becomes appropriate to seek a single causative agent; complexity is hard to deal with within the neurogenetic agenda.

Consequences of determinism

A number of single gene defects are known to lead to drastic dysfunctions of mind and brain. Huntington's disease, with its seemingly inevitable progress towards neurological collapse in middle age, is the classic example, but there are of course

---

11. V.H. Mark, and F.R. Ervin, *Violence and the Brain*, Harper and Row, London and New York, 1970.

many others; Lesch-Nyhan syndrome, Tay-Sachs disease; the list of rare but devastating conditions is long... But neurogenetics consistently overstates its case, moving seamlessly from single to many genes, from genes with predictable consequences in virtually all known environments to genes with small or highly variable effects, whose norm of reaction extends so far as to prevent any claims to predictability. In only a few per cent of all Alzheimers cases is there a clear genetic involvement; while evidence identifying gene markers for manic depression and schizophrenia have been advanced with extensive publicity, and then quietly withdrawn. At best, the hunt for the genes 'for' these conditions may be able to identify anomalous cases in which the genetic effect is to mimic a more widespread phenotypic condition (geneticists speak of phenocopies to emphasise the primacy of their genetic explanations in such cases; I have proposed the term 'genocopy' to help geneticists appreciate their more limited contribution). What both concepts emphasise is the extent to which multiple pathways may lead to a final common biochemical or behavioural endpoint. What both mask is the possibility that the endpoints may not be in every sense identical. Some diagnosed depressions are ameliorated by one type of drug, some by another, and these distinctions have even been made the basis of diagnosis, in which the pharmacological response rather than the clinical syndrome is made the basis for defining the disorder from which the individual suffers - once again insisting on the primacy of the biochemical over the behavioural, the biological over the social.

There are four main negative consequences of such determinism. The first is limited to the study of biology itself: the damage it does to conceptualising living processes. The primacy given to genetic causes fosters, even amongst researchers whose day-to-day practice ought to convince them otherwise, a linear view of living processes, in which the key to life itself lies in the one-dimensional string of nucleotide bases of DNA, the mythopoeic genome. Witness the metaphors with which molecular geneticists speak of the goals of the Human Genome Project - the 'Holy Grail', the 'Code of Codes', 'the Book of Life', 'genes for' particular conditions, as if the entire four dimensions of an organism - three of space and one of developmental and life history - can be read off from this linear code, like a telephone directory.

Few popular writers are more guilty of this than Richard Dawkins. From his first book *The Selfish Gene* to the most recent, *River out of Eden*, he has shown a rhetorical gift for making plausible the gene's eye view not merely of the individual but of the entire living world. Of course genes aren't selfish - this is a term which can only sensibly be applied to an organism, not a part thereof; but, whereas in my 1970s book *The Conscious Brain*, the elision in the title was a deliberate act of paradox, Dawkins seems really to believe that this is the way the world really is. Practising evolutionary and population geneticists and molecular biologists recognise that there are multiple mechanisms at play in the processes whereby species evolve or go extinct, and by which new species are formed. They include, of course, classical natural selection and possibly sexual selection, but they also may include genetic drift, molecular drive, founder effects and many others. But it remains the case that, for Dawkins as for Darwin, explaining how natural selection *per se* generates new species is a great deal harder than explaining how it succeeds in enabling already existing species to evolve so as to get better at doing their own specific things. Furthermore, the selective processes on which Darwinian evolution depends operate at many levels, that of the gene, the genome, the organism, even the population. For Dawkins only the gene, the primary DNA 'replicator', counts. It is a version of what in the 1930s was called 'bean bag genetics' in which each gene is seen as an individual discrete unit; the history of population genetics since then, in the hands of Sewall Wright, Dobzhansky and others, has been to transcend such simplicities, but the popularising schemata of Dawkins cannot deal with complexity. This is why he continually reduces organisms to genes and genes to text - to *information*. 'Life', he writes, ' is just bytes and bytes and bytes of digital information.'[12] He may think that he is nothing but a rather primitively designed PC, but I doubt that the rest of us see ourselves that way. 'Information' is not what life is about; it is about 'meaning', and the one is not even formally reducible to the other.

To clarify what I am getting at, consider the phenomenon that I study myself, memory. Memories are believed to be encoded in the brain in some manner based on the establishment of connections between nerve cells such as to create potential novel circuits - a little crude as a description but it will do for the present. Computer modellers from amongst the Artificial Intelligentsia have had a field day producing wiring diagrams of how such circuits could be created, and an entire theoretical universe has grown up over the past decade, called connectionism, which claims to be able to model memories this

---

12. R. Dawkins, *River out of Eden*, Weidenfeld and Nicolson, London 1995, p 19.

way. At a recent workshop on memory, an enthusiastic Oxford-based modeller claimed to be able to calculate that in primates a particular brain structure, the hippocampus, could encode precisely 36,000 memories. For him, a memory was synonymous with a particular bit of information. How many bits of information do I need to remember the peculiar sadness of the long September shadows, the colour of my son's hair, or even what I had for last night's dinner? These are simply not calculable in terms of information theory. Yet they are central to life - and I suspect they are for the Oxford populariser Dawkins as much as the Oxford connectionist. Neither they, nor my personal and intellectual engagement with them, are simply bytes and bytes and bytes.

What *do* genes do?

So what should one be talking about when one discusses genes? The shorthand phrase of a gene 'for' a condition is profoundly misleading - after all there aren't really even genes 'for' blue or brown eyes, let alone such complex and historically and socially shaped features of human existence as sexual desire or urban guerillas. The cellular developmental and enzymatic route which results in the manufacture of particular pigments involves many thousand genes; the route which leads to the behavioural manifestations we call desire clearly involves genes, but cannot sensibly be regarded as embodied in them. What there are, of course, are differences between genomes (that is, the entire ensemble of genes that any organism possesses). Thus in any particular genome, the absence of a particular gene may result in the emergence of differences in eye colour. The biologist looking at the effects of particular genetic mutations or deletions studies the functioning of the system in the absence or malfunction of a particular gene. Furthermore, the system is not a passive responder to absence or malfunction, but seeks, by means of developmental plasticity, to compensate for any deficit .

A considerable disservice was done to biology by the historical chance which meant that in the early years of this century two separate sub-disciplines emerged; genetics, which essentially asks questions about the origins of differences between organisms, and developmental biology, which asks questions about the processes which ensure similarity. The careless language of DNA and molecular genetics serves to widen this gap rather than help bridge it so as to open the route towards the synthetic biology that we so badly need. As is well known, chimpanzees and humans share upwards of 98 per cent of their DNA, yet no-one would confuse the two phenotypes. We have no idea at present about the developmental rules which lead in one case to the chimp, in the other to the human, but this, surely one of the great unsolved riddles of biology, seems a matter of indifference to most molecularly oriented geneticists.

The other consequences of determinism reach out beyond theory. If the homeless or depressed are so because of a flaw in their biology, their condition cannot be the fault of society, even if a humane society will attempt, pharmacologically or otherwise, to alleviate their distress. This victim-blaming in its turn generates a sort of fatalism amongst those it stigmatises: it is not our fault, the problem lies in our biology. Such fatalism can bring its own relief, for less stigma attaches to being the carrier or transmitter of deficient genes than to having been morally responsible. It is striking that in the US, leading gay activists have embraced the gay brains/gay genes explanation for their sexual orientation on the explicit grounds that they can no longer be held morally culpable for a 'natural' state, nor can they be seen as dangerously likely to infect others with their 'perverse' tastes.

The final consequence is the subversion of scarce resources. Funding for research and treatment becomes misfocused. The orientation of research funds in Russia towards the molecular biology and genetics of alcoholism is one good example; no rational attempt to explain the prevalence of vodka-sodden drunks on the streets of Moscow would seize on the peculiar genetics of the Russian population as its starting point. Similarly the Violence Initiative - directed towards seeking the origins of violence in American society in terms of the genotypes of blacks and poor inner city whites, problems of 'temperament' in toddlers and deficiencies in serotonin reuptake mechanisms in incarcerated criminals - is clearly going to keep a generation of psychologists, neuropharmacologists and behaviour geneticists in research funds for a good few years to come. One of the keys to success in science is to identify the appropriate level of analysis at which to seek the determinants of complex phenomena. Yet when the differentials between rich and poor are so great and widening, where the potential rewards of violence may be so great (and if large enough can even be socially sanctioned) - and especially where, as in the US, there are said to be more than 280 million handguns in private ownership, to look to biology to provide a determining explanation of what is going on is an expensive and foolish diversion.

Even in less dramatic instances, emphasis on genetic explanations and molecularly-oriented research prevents researchers from seeing and studying the obvious. The almost universal conviction amongst biological psychiatrists that schizophrenia is a genetic disorder means that they are unable to respond to the suggestive epidemiological evidence that the diagnosis of schizophrenia in the children of black-white relationships in Britain is severalfold higher than that of either of the parental populations.[13] No genetic model fits this finding as well as an explanation in terms of the racism of the society in which these children grow up. Yet it is well known that with a little ingenuity any phenotypic distribution can be explained genetically, granted appropriate assumptions about the incomplete or masked effects of genes, technically known as partial penetrance and incomplete dominance. It is not hard for a behavioural geneticist to offer as an alternative that the data could be accounted for by assortative mating - i.e. that you must be mad to begin with to have a relationship with someone of a different colour from yourself.

There is no doubt that the dramatic increases in neuroscientific knowledge are changing and enriching our understanding of brain and behaviour. There is equally no doubt that, wisely and appropriately employed, the new knowledge offers the potential to diminish the degree of human suffering, at least in relatively wealthy industrialised societies. But until the neurosciences and genetics can be broken out of their reductionist mould and relocated within a more integrated understanding of the relationships between the biological, personal and social, abandoning their unidirectional view of the causes of human action so as to recognise the appropriate, determining level of explanation for complex phenomena - that is until we can stop looking for the key under the lamppost because that is where the light is, even though a moment's thought will tell us we lost it a long way further up the road - their potential for good remains limited and for misapplication substantial and disturbing.

This text is a revised and expanded version of an article which originally appeared in Nature, *5 February 1995.*

---

13. G. Harrison, *Schiz. Bull.*, 16,1990, pp 663-671.

new left *review* 214

'The flagship of the Western intellectual left' *The Guardian*

160 PAGES EVERY TWO MONTHS

FINANCE AND EQUALITY – Robert Pollin
Charts a new stakeholder economics uniting efficiency and equality

THE CONSERVATIVES SELF-DESTRUCT – Andrew Gamble
The Thatcher/Major governments have undone formulas of Conservative rule stretching back to Queen Victoria

SYMPOSIUM ON *AGE OF EXTREMES*
Tom Nairn argues that Eric Hobsbawm is too pessimistic in his evaluation of late 20th century nationalism, **Göran Therborn** interrogates the account of modernity implicit in Hobsbawm's work and **Michael Mann** explores the century's social and generational shifts

THE RESISTIBLE RISE OF THE ITALIAN RIGHT – Lucio Magri
What can stop Berlusconi and the neo-Fascists from writing Italy's new constitution?

Benedict Anderson – *Blood and Belonging*

Régis Debray – DEATH AGONY OF THE SPECTACLE
Guy Debord's Situationist philosophy misses the banality and involvement of modern media

R. W. Davies – Stalin's Labour Camps: What the Archives Reveal;
Melissa Lane – Tom Paine and Civil Society; **John Grahl** – Agenda for a New Left

SPECIAL OFFER TO NEW SUBSCRIBERS
FREE BOOK AND FREE BACK ISSUE
New subscribers can claim a FREE BACK ISSUE – NLR 213 with **Peter Gowan** The Plundering of Eastern Europe, **Terry Eagleton** on Irish nationalisms, **Peter Townsend** New Labour's Error on Welfare, **Peter Dews** in defence of meaning, **Nadine Gordimer** on the legacy of apartheid provocation, **Ernest Mandel** on how he escaped from a Nazi jail, **Frances Fox Piven** Myths of Globalization, and **Fred Pfeil** on Guns, Guys and the US Government

FREE BOOK (please tick)	ANNUAL SUBSCRIPTION
☐ Christopher Hitchens **For the Sake of Argument**	**(six issues)**
or ☐ Perry Anderson **Zone of Engagement**	INDIVIDUALS:
or ☐ Perry Anderson **English Questions**	£22.50 (inland), £26/$47 (overseas)
or ☐ Slavoj Zizek **Mapping Ideology**	INSTITUTIONS:
or ☐ Jean-Paul Sartre **War Diaries**	£48 (inland), £51.50/$93 (overseas)
	SINGLE COPY: £4.50

✂

Name_____

Address_____

_____

_____Code _____

Cheques payable to *New Left Review* or

Credit card type: _____Expiry date_____

No: ☐☐☐☐☐☐☐☐☐☐☐☐☐☐☐☐

(Access, Visa, Mastercard, Eurocard, Amex accepted)

☎
CREDIT CARD HOTLINE
0181 685 0301
Fax: 0181 648 4873

Send to: New Left Review,
120-126 Lavender Avenue,
Mitcham, Surrey CR4 3HP

The idea of a sexual community

Jeffrey Weeks

Jeffrey Weeks explores the many - and complex - meanings of community.

Community, argued James Baldwin, 'simply means our endless connection with, and responsibility for, each other'.[1] And, as Raymond Williams once remarked, the term community is one of the few words which never has negative connotations, and is used pretty promiscuously in a host of political constructions across the political spectrum. It attempts both to express social realities and to offer an aspiration towards something better, more inclusive and tangible. In the form of contemporary communitarianism, the pursuit of community suggests a revulsion against the coldness and impersonality, the instrumentality and narrow self interest, of abstract individualism with its associated marketisation and commodification of human bonds. The idea of community, in contrast to social atomisation, suggests that men and women should be members and not strangers, should have ties and belongings that transcend the monad.

As such it has become a key idea in the debate on the post-modern world. Zygmunt Bauman has suggested that it has come to replace reason and universal truth in post-modern philosophy. There are no values or ethics that are not community based, it has been argued; for communities embody certain traditions

---

1. James Baldwin, *Evidence of Things Not Seen*, 1986.

- many of them, it has to be said, recently invented, but no less potent for that.

Communities are not fixed once and for all. They change as the arguments over time continue, and as other communities exercise their gravitational pull. But at the same time, the social relations of a community are repositories of meaning for its members, not sets of mechanical linkages between isolated individuals. A community offers a 'vocabulary of values' through which individuals construct their understanding of the social world, and of their sense of identity and belonging. Communities appear to offer embeddedness in a world which seems constantly on the verge of fragmentation.

A major problem, of course, is that a particular definition of community may undermine a wider sense of community embodied in the best of humanist traditions. The strongest sense of community is in fact likely to come from those groups who find the premises of their collective existence threatened, and who construct out of this a community of identity which provides a strong sense of resistance and empowerment. Seeming unable to control the social relations in which they find themselves, people shrink the world to the size of their communities, and act politically on that basis. The result, too often, is an obsessive particularism as a way of embracing or coping with contingency. And as critics of community have pointed out, social pluralism and the proliferation of associations do not necessarily mean variety for men and women personally: embeddedness means people can get stuck.

The challenge for modern advocates of community, therefore, is to imagine community without either neo-tribalism or self immolation. The key issue, I would argue, is not whether community, but what sort of community, and what sort of identity, are appropriate at any particular time. Michel Foucault distinguishes between three concepts of community: a *given community*, a *tacit community* and a *critical community*:

> a given community arises from an identification: 'I am an X'. Tacit community
> is the materially-rooted system of thought that makes X a possible object of
> identification; and critical community sees this system of thought as singular or
> contingent, finds something 'intolerable' about it, and starts to refuse to
> participate in it.[2]

---

2. Cited in J. Rajchman, *Truth and Eros: Foucault, Lacan and the Question of Ethics,*
   Routledge, London and New York 1991.

In the contemporary world, 'given' - or traditional - communities are losing their moral density as old values crumble and uncertainty rules. The latent sense of community that can be detected under the procedural republic of liberalism may provide the necessary support for a wider sense of solidarity, but in it lurks the danger that the communal values that are discernible will be conservative and exclusive - as indeed I believe Amitai Etzioni's communitarian advocacy of a strengthened spirit of neighbourhood and family must

'Community is one of the few words which never has negative connotations'

be. A critical community, on the other hand, results from a problematisation of a given or latent identity. It is open to new experiences and ways of being, which make new subjectivities possible. At its best, I shall argue, the idea of a sexual community as it is evoked in contemporary radical sexual political discourse embraces this notion of a critical community.

In this article I want to look at four key elements contained in the idea of a sexual community: community as a focus of identity; community as ethos or repository of values; community as social capital; and community as politics. I shall draw most of my examples from the best documented sexual community, the lesbian and gay community, with other examples as necessary. There are, of course, many problems with this choice. First of all, it presupposes a unity which is not necessarily there. The differences between gay men and lesbians are well rehearsed; there are many other differences: between rich and poor, white and black, North American and European, urban and rural, right and left, and so on. There is no reason to think that people who share one characteristic necessarily share others - but then, that is a feature of all communities. Secondly, it may understandably be argued that there are certain key elements of the lesbian and gay community that make it unique: stigma, prejudice, legal inequality, a history of oppression, and the like. But that, I would suggest, is what makes it a valuable path into understanding the nature of contemporary communities. The idea of a heterosexual community, much used recently in the literature of HIV and AIDS, is pretty much an oxymoron. Precisely because heterosexuality is hegemonic in our general culture, a general heterosexual community does not exist, though of course there are specific heterosexual communities (and as I have suggested, much of contemporary communitarianism assumes as a given that heterosexuality is the very definition of community).

In other words, it is because homosexuality is not the norm, is stigmatised, that a sense of community transcending specific differences, has emerged. It exists because participants in it feel it does and should exist. It is not geographically fixed. It is criss-crossed by many divisions. But a sort of diasporic consciousness does exist because people believe it exists. And this belief has material and cultural effects.

To put it another way: a web of narrative, a proliferation of stories, has developed in a particular set of historical circumstances, which gives meaning to the idea of a sexual community for many people. The effectiveness of sexual narratives or stories, as Ken Plummer has argued in his important book, *Telling Sexual Stories* (1995), depends on an ability to tell them, and an audience to listen to them. In recent years we have been witness to the emergence of large groups willing to tell their stories ('coming out'), and the construction of a mass audience for many hitherto implausible narratives, emanating from the private worlds of everyday life. And it is from the conflicts of everyday life that many of the greater conflicts of society are generated; and certainly the new narratives of sexual minorities have both subverted and challenged many of the narrative certainties of contemporary life. But there are other forces that are also shaking the foundations of legitimising value systems: the emergence of dissident sexual communities is only one index of the jumble of stories now bombarding us. In understanding the idea of community embodied in the new sexual cultures we can also begin to understand the complexities of communities in the post-modern world.

As a way into this question, let me now turn to the four elements of the idea of sexual community that I mentioned earlier.

Community as a focus of identity

It takes two people to make a lesbian, the American feminist Teresa de Lauretis has wittily remarked, and this underlines a profound truth. Sexual identities in the modern world, like other identities, can only ever be relational, shaped in a world of difference. But identities do not exist on an even plane. They are severely marked by a hierarchical ordering, in which lesbian and gay identities are subordinate.

The historical evidence is now massive that, despite the polymorphous nature of sexuality throughout history and across all cultures, the binary division in our culture, between the norm and the perverse, or in practice between hegemonic heterosexuality and dissident homosexuality, has a history, and a recent one at that. Despite the existence of distinct homosexual networks, meeting places, even nascent 'communities', for want of a better word, which are recorded in various European cities since late medieval times, it is only over the past century or so, coincident with the hardening of the binary divide, that distinctive homosexual 'forms of existence', with sexualised identities, communities and sexual political movements, have emerged. A sense of identity, shaped in a sense of community, and articulated through political movements, has been, I would argue, a dominant motif only since the late 1960s.

T he social movements concerned with sexuality that have emerged since the 1960s, the feminist and lesbian and gay movements especially, implicitly assume that it is through social involvement and collective action that individuality can be realised and identity affirmed. The new movements can be interpreted as a revolt against the forms of subjectification that the contemporary world has given rise to, a challenge to the technologies of power which define individuals in particular ways and pin them to particular subordinated identities and locations in society. They reveal the complexity of modern social relations, and the intractability of the contradictions and tensions these produce. They simultaneously offer alternative possibilities.

At the heart of the new movements is a rejection of imposed definitions, and a struggle for social space in which new identities can be forged. There is of course a historic irony in this process. The identities are being shaped on the very terrain that gave rise to domination in the first place. Racial and ethnic minorities historically challenged racist structures by affirming their racialised identities ('black is beautiful'). Feminism has historically affirmed the rights of women by asserting the positive qualities of femininity. Lesbians and gays reject the pathologising of homosexuality by 'reversing the discourse', and affirming pride in being homosexual. In the process, there is a search for a hidden history, a narrative structure which seems to express the truth of repressed or oppressed experience. But a better way of seeing what is happening is to understand it as a social positioning, where difference is asserted as a positive quality rather than an inevitable or naturalised divide.

Movements such as these are not simply expressing a pre-existing essence of social being. Identities and belongings are being constructed in the very process of organisation itself. They are effective in so far as they can speak a language which brings people into the activities, alignments and subjectivities being shaped; and the most effective language available is the language of community.

Like a movement, which both grows out of and creates a sense of wider identification, a community must be constantly re-imagined, sustained over time by common practices and symbolic re-enactments which reaffirm both identity and difference. A national community may be sustained by allegiance to the flag, national days, the ritual of elections or monarchy, by victories in war, war memorials and military pride, or by the less harmful ephemeral hysteria of athletic competitions or the soccer World Cup. A black community may re-enact its difference through defence of its territory against racist attacks or the symbolic presence of the police. It may also re-enact and celebrate it in carnival, the inversion of the daily humdrum existence where reality is turned upside down, the streets become the property of the oppressed, and the repressed experiences of the community can return, triumphantly, for the day. In the same way, sexual identity and community are expressed through annual events such as Lesbian and Gay Pride; or the losses of the AIDS community can be mourned and the lives of the dead celebrated through candlelit vigils and the sewing of memorial quilts. Without such re-imaginings a community will die, as difference is obliterated or becomes meaningless before the onrush of history.

Community stands here for some notion of solidarity, a solidarity which empowers and enables, and makes individual and social action possible. Sexual dissidence is ultimately dependent upon the growth of that sense of common purpose and solidarity represented by the term community. The appeal to the authenticity of one's sexual experience that has been the symbolic token of many of the pioneers of radical sexual change becomes culturally meaningful only in so far as it speaks to, and evokes an echo in, the experience of others in a latent community that is on its way to becoming a critical community. With the development of a sexual movement with a sense of its own history and social role, the idea of community becomes a critical norm through which alternatives are opened up.

Community as ethos and repository of values

Mark Blasius, in his recent book, *Gay and Lesbian Politics*, has argued that the lesbian and gay struggle has produced a sense of community and identity which provides the context for moral agency, and hence for the emergence of a lesbian and gay ethos enacted in everyday life. The lesbian and gay ethos, Blasius suggests, can be understood 'both as coming out and as integrating one's homoerotic relationships within all of one's social relationships'. In practice, though inevitably a prolonged and often anguished practice, that means a challenge to compulsory heterosexuality and the construction of an erotica 'that decenters genital sexuality and de-essentializes gender'. That in turn, Blasius argues, is the grounding for lesbian and gay politics in its various forms. I shall take this text as an example of the arguments being made for the ethical values of sexual community.

Blasius's most important contribution lies in his exploration of the underlying system of values that he sees as existing in the lesbian and gay world. Two significant trends are described: the shift from 'sexuality' to 'the erotic', which in Blasius's argument implies the displacement of traditional hierarchical patterns of the sexual in favour of plural forms; and the emergence of a 'new ethic' which embraces the erotic and is built around not so much an orientation, preference or lifestyle as a sense of self-identified and collectively invented community. They are in a real sense simply two aspects of the same cultural shift: a move towards the evoking, or inventing, of new identities, belongings and forms of intimacy.

Blasius suggests that the gay and lesbian community offers a sense of belonging, an ethos based on erotic friendship 'characterised by reciprocal *independence*' .

> Erotic friendship is an ethico-erotic relationship productive of equality; the participants (whatever they name themselves - lovers, exlovers, fuckbuddies, partners, etc) are inventing themselves and become the conditions for such self-invention of each other.[3]

He concludes that, in doing this, lesbian and gays are pioneering an art of living through one's erotic relations, and thereby introducing something new onto the historical landscape.

I agree with that formulation: the dense interconnections, networks, relationships, experiments in living, new forms of loving and caring (above all in response to the HIV and AIDS epidemic), which have been the outstanding

---

3. Mark Blasius, *Gay and Lesbian Politics: Sexuality and the Emergence of a New Ethics*, Temple University Press, Philadelphia 1995, p219, p221.

achievements of lesbian and gay politics since the 1960s, provide the grounds on which new value systems are developing. But have we said everything when we have said that? The recognition that the basics of a new relational ethos do indeed exist does not in itself answer that fundamental question of 'how should we live'; on the contrary, it poses it in a new way, and this, I feel, is downplayed by Blasius.

We all know how difficult it is to live up to the standards we have communally set for ourselves. Erotic desire can undermine the firmest resolutions. Fear and jealousy and betrayal are not abolished because we disapprove of them. A commitment to safer sex has not stopped unsafe practices. Friendship can turn to hate, and love, like desire, can die. There is a danger that in celebrating the new ethos of lesbian and gay life we may aspire to a utopianism that frail, mere humans can scarcely live up to. So as well as celebrating eros and the possibilities of community, we need to begin to spell out what an art of life, an ethos based on reciprocal independence, means in practice. Are certain forms of behaviour better than others? Are some things right, others wrong, some things true and others false? These are hard questions, because they suggest prescriptive rather than freely chosen answers. The challenge facing us is to avoid prescription and proscription at the same time as we invent forms of conduct which maximise human autonomy and freedom of choice whilst affirming our need for one another, the importance of the human bond. Again, the much used notion of community is an attempt to encompass that objective.

Community as social capital

The sexual movements of recent years have both encouraged and built on a sense of community, a space where hitherto execrated sexual activity and identities have been affirmed and sustained. Such a validation of community has been at the centre of the response to HIV and AIDS by the group most affected in the West, gay men. It has made possible a social and cultural response whose aim is to promote survival, defeat stigma, encourage community and develop self-esteem, the *sine qua non*, in Simon Watney's formulation, of a regime of safer sex. At the same time, the absence of a sense of community around sexual issues amongst other groups affected by the epidemic has been a critical factor in limiting the development of a culture of safer sex and personal responsibility.

For historical reasons, the earliest collective response to the HIV/AIDS epidemic came from the gay community, first of all in the USA and subsequently throughout the West, and even in the developing world. In the absence until the mid 1980s of coherent governmental or international responses, activists schooled in the lesbian and gay community established the first and enduring organisational responses to the epidemic - organisations such as Gay Men's Health Crisis in the USA and the Terrence Higgins Trust in the UK. These organisations pioneered practices of safer sex, rooted in community experience; developed models of care and mutual support, such as 'buddying'; acted as advocates for people with HIV and AIDS; lobbied, successfully, for a more strategic governmental response; and to some extent became key partners, even agents, of government in responding to the crisis.

These new voluntary organisations embodied a key philosophy developed initially in the sexual communities from which they sprang: that of collective activity and of collective self help (ironically, though from a different starting point, echoing the philosophical attitude of New Right critics of welfare). As one member of Body Positive, a support group for people living with HIV and AIDS, has commented, 'Self help is about taking control of your own life in your own hands and solving your own problems through helping others in the same situation'.[4] The emphasis on self help in relation to the new epidemic was at first a matter of *faute de mieux* rather than principle, a community response to the absence of government response in a climate of prejudice and fear. This grass roots mobilisation proved, however, immensely influential in the ideologies of the many other community based HIV and AIDS organisations that subsequently sprang up (my own research has shown that by the early 1990s well over 500 HIV and AIDS voluntary agencies existed in the UK, embracing all the major categories at risk). It represents, in the phrase used by Wann, a significant accumulation of social capital by the communities most at risk from the epidemic.[5]

Wann's argument is that a variety of social skills exist in the various communities that now make up an ever more complex and pluralistic culture, and that these are being deployed in a variety of community based activities. These provide a major resource in the sub-political spheres of social life that are ignored

---

4. P. McCory, 'On Self Help', *Body Positive*, no 181, 1995. This section on the HIV/AIDS voluntary sector is based on research from an ESRC-funded project, 'The Voluntary Sector Response to HIV/AIDS', which I co-directed with Peter Aggleton. The quotations are from interviews conducted with members of voluntary agencies.
5. M. Wann, *Building Social Capital: Self Help in the 21st Century Welfare State*, Institute of Public Policy Research, London 1995.

by the last ditch defenders of traditional statism but are being exploited by the market individualism of the New Right (as can be seen in the ways in which the purchaser/provider split in social welfare provision in part depends on the existence of voluntary activity whilst refusing to accept the radical challenge frequently offered by community action). Community based activities represent an attempt to gain control of the conditions of one's life, as again can be seen in the activities of the HIV/AIDS organisations.

In the early days of the epidemic, community based activities were rooted in a growing awareness of personal threat. As a respondent put it, 'We were all in it together...we were desperately in need of support with friends dying...and so we worked together.' Subsequently, the emphasis became more explicitly political, in the notion of self empowerment; this underlay not only the gay based AIDS organisations but also those that developed amongst women, black people and other threatened minorities. Hence such comments as: 'I think that is very bad for people's immune system, to be kind of dependent', 'it's more important to help people understand how to go about doing things rather than just taking over and doing things for them'. Of course, in practice, it became very difficult to maintain this commitment: self help groupings became service delivery organisations; professionalism replaced voluntary action; statutory funding tied agencies to formal procedures and stricter notions of accountability. Many voluntary agencies have become not-for-profit bodies closely linked to statutory requirements, and ties with the originating communities have often become strained, if they have not been severed. But the essential point remains: the developments occurred in the first place because of the social capital accumulated by hitherto marginalised communities.

Community as politics

For the movements concerned with sexuality what matters more than a single set of goals or a defined programme is the symbolic focus of the activities of the movements themselves, their struggle to gain control over the conditions of life. They cannot therefore be judged solely in terms of their political effectivity in attaining this or that legislative shift, important as this often is. Their ultimate importance lies in their cultural and informal impact on the lives of the individuals who align with them, and are addressed by them as active subjects.

The term 'movement' conveys some of this sense of informality but perhaps carries too strong a suggetion of a cohesiveness in organisation which is only spasmodically present. As Alberto Melucci has argued, social movements are normally '"invisible" networks of small groups submerged in everyday life'.[6] They tend to be concerned with individual needs, collective identity, and a part-time 'membership', and constitute laboratories in which new experiences are invented, and tested, in which reality is re-described, and individuals can develop alternative experiences of time, space and personal relationships. They attempt to shape a new 'grammar' of everyday life rather than political programmes.

One of their key functions is to translate actions into symbolic challenges that upset the dominant cultural codes, and reveal their irrationality, partiality and illegitimacy as products of power and domination. So they have a dual role: to reveal the macro and micro forms of domination that constitute modern life; and to demonstrate the possibilities of alternative forms of life that are not simply pre-figurative of some imagined future, but are actually being constructed in the here and now.

So the practical activities of such movements characteristically subvert conventional views of political activities. Consciousness raising, networking, carnival, festivals, candle lit processions both affirm a sense of collective being and challenge conventional patterns of life, transmitting to the system a picture of its own contradictions. They illustrate both the complexity of power relations, and the possibility of subverting them.

'What matters is the symbolic focus of the activities of the movements themselves'

In this way, despite their informality and *ad hoc* nature, these movements can in particular circumstances become active participants in the domain of politics. They regularly make demands on the conventional structure of politics, often couched in uncompromising terms. They also lean towards a politics of direct action, avoiding in most cases the forms of representative democracy. Contemporary social movements are frequently unstable in both their composition and strategic thrust, and there can be no *a priori* guarantee of their progressive nature. During the 1980s, as many feminists have ruefully noted, the women's movement was strongly divided over its attitudes to pornography, with a number of anti-porn feminists making common cause with far right moralists and

6. Alberto Melucci, *Nomads of the Present: Social Movements and Individual Needs in Contemporary Society*, Radius, London 1989, p6.

social authoritarians. Interestingly, and ironically, some of the neo-fundamentalist movements of recent years are themselves, in the delay in the triumph of their universalist hopes, explicitly redefining themselves as social movements with the same claim to social space, and to difference, as other, overtly progressive groups. The Christian Coalition in the USA, for instance, has achieved remarkable success in influencing the right wing of the Republican Party by playing down their Christian fundamentalism and stressing their more acceptable defence of traditional family values.

Politically, radical sexual communities and their associated movements point in two different directions at once - or at least embrace two distinct political moments: what I call the 'moment of transgression', and the 'moment of citizenship'.[7] The 'moment of transgression' is the moment of challenge to the traditional or received order of sexual life: the assertion of different identities, different life-styles, and the building of oppositional communities. In its recent form it has given rise to 'queer politics', which has sought to break with what has been perceived as the caution of contemporary gay politics with its integrationist approaches. The 'moment of citizenship' is precisely this movement towards inclusion, towards redefining the polity to incorporate fully those who have felt excluded. Its characteristic emphasis has been on the claiming of civil rights, formal equality - and most recently, in continental Europe at least, on the demand for 'partnership rights' for same sex couples. On the surface at least they seem radically different strategies, and find expression in different organisational forms: for example, in the UK, in the differences between the confrontationalist politics of Outrage! and the lobbying approach of Stonewall.

There are, however, closer similarities than there might appear between the two strategies. As Elizabeth Wilson has written:

> we transgress in order to insist that we are there, that we exist, and to place a distance between ourselves and the dominant culture. But we have to go further - we have to have an idea of how things could be different, otherwise transgression ends in mere posturing.[8]

---

7. See Jeffrey Weeks, *Invented Moralities: Sexual Values in an Age of Uncertainty*, Polity, Cambridge 1995, pp 108-23.
8. Elizabeth Wilson, 'Is transgression transgressive', in Joseph Bristow and Angelia Wilson (eds), *Activating Theory: Lesbian, Gay, Bisexual Politics*, Lawrence and Wishart, London 1993, p11.

The claim for citizenship is one possible way in which 'things could be different'. The notion of citizenship has been historically coloured by its familial and exclusively heterosexual connotations: the citizenship models embodied in the post-war welfare state were explicitly built around the nuclear family and a traditional division of labour between men and women. To claim full citizenship for dissident sexual minorities is to argue for the transformation of the concept. This is what I take Ken Plummer to have in mind when he proposes a new notion of citizenship, what he terms intimate citizenship. Intimate citizenship, he suggests, is concerned with those matters that relate to our most intimate desires, pleasures and ways of being in the world. Some of these relate back to more traditional ideas of citizenship.

'The notion of citizenship has been historically coloured by its familial and exclusively heterosexual connotations'

But intimate citizenship is much more concerned with 'new stories': questions relating to control of our bodies, feelings, and relationships; questions of access to representations and spaces; and the problems and possibilities of choice. In other words, issues that have been previously deemed to be outside the concept of social citizenship, because they were part of the private world, are now becoming part of public debate - precisely because it is only through public change that the protection of private space can be guaranteed. The achievement of intimate citizenship, in turn, however, is predicated on the existence of the shared identities, values, social capital and political belongings that we know by the term 'community'.

Conclusion: Community as necessary fiction

I have argued elsewhere that the idea of a sexual identity is a fiction (because it is based on the cultural construction of plausible narratives to make sense of individual lives).[9] But it is a necessary fiction because it offers the possibility of social agency in a context where equal access to social goods is denied. In the same way, the idea of a sexual community may be a fiction, but it is a necessary fiction: an imagined community, an invented tradition which enables and empowers. It provides the context for the articulation of identity, the vocabulary of values through which ways of life can be developed, the accumulated skills by which new possibilities can be explored and hazards negotiated, and the context for

---

9. Jeffrey Weeks, *op. cit.*

the emergence of social movements and political campaigns which seek to challenge the existing order.

There are, of course, dangers. The new elective communities can be as exclusive and stifling as traditional ones. Social pluralism and a proliferation of communities do not necessarily guarantee variety or autonomy for all members. The co-existence of different communities depends upon a recognition that the condition of toleration of one's own way of life is a recognition of the validity of other ways of life. That, in turn, requires that communities guarantee a freedom of exit and of voice for their members. The communities built around sexuality are no less likely than others to develop their own norms which may exclude as well as include.

But having said that, it should also be acknowledged that in the contemporary world, with its deep sense of uncertainty around values, the idea of a sexual community has developed because of a conviction that it is only through the enhancement of a collective identity that individual autonomy can be realised.

That is not all that could be said about the idea of community in general, or about sexual communities in particular. But it is enough, I hope, to illustrate my main point: in the contemporary world, the idea of a sexual community is both a necessary and an inevitable one. We cannot do without it.

In praise of gender confusion

Andrew Samuels

Not being certain of your gender is less of a problem than being too certain, argues Jungian analyst Andrew Samuels

Most people are wary now of anyone who seems too settled and sure in their gender identity and gender role. Think of the tycoon - so capable and dynamic, such a marvellous self-starter. Don't we know that, secretly, he is a sobbing little boy, dependent on others, maybe mainly female, for all his feelings of safeness and security? Or the Don Juan, talking incessantly of the women he has seduced, who turns out to have fantasies of being female himself and yearns to be seduced by another man. Or the woman who seems so fulfilled as a mother yet privately desires to express herself in ways other than maternity, to come into another kind of power, to protest at her cultural 'castration'.

So we have come to accept that behind excessive gender certainty lurk gender confusions like these. Yet many will probably consider that, as well as being suspicious of too much gender certainty, it is basically a good thing for everyone to be pretty certain about their gender, to know for sure that, in spite of all the problems with being a man or a woman, one is indeed a man or a woman.

As a therapist, I have come to see that quite another idea is needed to make sense of what people are experiencing in the muddled and mysterious world of late twentieth-century gender relations and gender politics.

Many of the people who come to see me for therapy are indeed manifestly and magnificently confused about their gender identity. Not only are they not at all sure how a man or woman is supposed to behave but they are not sure that, given what they know about their internal lives, a person who is truly a man or a woman could possibly feel or fantasize what it is that they themselves are feeling and fantasizing.

I noticed that, for these profound feelings of gender confusion to exist, there had to be an equally profound feeling of gender certainty in operation at some level. You cannot know the detail of your confusion without having an inkling about the certitude against which you are measuring your confusion. The client sobbing his little boy heart out knows very well that tycoons exist and evaluates himself negatively as a result. Indeed, we could even say: no gender certainty, no gender confusion!

What this means is that, to a very great degree, gender confusion is manufactured or constructed in people by the operations of gender certainty. If we agree that these certainties are part of socialisation, then it is hard to deny that the parallel confusions are equally artificial constructions and not deep personal wounds or failures.

Let me underscore the radical implications of what I am saying. We need to extend the by-now conventional insight that gender confusion lies behind gender certainty to see that *gender certainty lies behind gender confusion*. To the extent that gender confusion is usually taken as a mental health problem or a neurosis, we are making a colossal mistake here and even playing a most destructive con trick on those supposedly suffering from gender confusion. The problem is, in fact, gender certainty.

Let's look at how this works out specifically for men in Western countries today. The turgid idea that many men living in a feminism-affected culture feel confused about who they are *as men* takes on a rather different cast when looked at in the light of what I have been saying about gender confusion. Behind the apparent confusion and the pain that many men certainly feel lies the kind of unconscious gender certainty that we import from the culture by internalisation. From this angle, modern men are not at all confused - or, rather, feeling confused is simply not the main problem at depth. Their problem is being afflicted with a gender certainty that is no use to them, and maybe is actually harmful to their potential.

When men's movement leaders offer a certainty that seems to have been missing from the lives of men, they are unwittingly doing nothing more than bringing the unconscious gender certainty that was always there to the surface. As that certainty came from the culture in the first place, there's nothing radical or scene-shifting about it at all.

The really interesting question is what to do with the feelings of gender confusion from which everyone suffers these days. On a personal level, we need to measure the confusion against the certainty. If we do this, we may find we are not as badly confused as we thought we were. It is not necessary to be confused about being gender-confused. You can evaluate your confusion and decide what to do with it.

I think there *is* a lot we can do with gender confusion. I can see that it all becomes easier to do in words if you replace 'confusion' with something that sounds a lot more positive like 'fluidity', 'flexibility', or even (hateful word) by supporting 'androgyny'. But, although I realise it is a hard sell and won't win votes, I want to stick up for the word 'confusion' because it is an experience-near word, capturing what I do indeed often feel about my gender identity and what many clients I see in therapy feel about theirs.

'Gender is a story we tell about ourselves which is half private and half public'

So - what can be done with gender confusion? I think such confusion contributes something to social and political reform and change. Gender is a key element in modern politics because it sits halfway between the inner and the outer worlds. Gender is a story we tell about ourselves that is half private and half public. It is also something upon which most cultures have erected a welter of oppressive practices and regulations, mostly favouring men. Unfortunately, Tony Blair's new Labour Party may be turning back to a form of gender politics fuelled by the certitudinous 'family values' of the past.

But many men want to make a progressive contribution to gender politics and hence (as men) to the wider political scene. Perhaps they could do it in part on the basis of a frank reframing of how we evaluate the confusion-certainty spectrum in relation to being a man. It isn't necessary to refuse to be a man, or enter into spurious sociopolitical alliances with women that deny the existence of differing political agendas for the sexes. All that may be required in the first instance is a celebration of not knowing too well about who we are in terms of gender, not knowing too well what we are supposed to know very well indeed.

I can illustrate this from my workshops on male psychology. I ask people to do an exercise. I describe a rating scale running from zero to 10 that represents a continuum from 'old man' to 'new man'. Old man counts as zero; new man counts as 10. If the person is a man, he is asked to place himself on this scale; if a woman, she is asked to score the most significant man in her life, past or present.

Naively, I thought at first that this would be a straightforward business and we would just zip around the room with people saying 6, 1, 2, 8 and so on. But it never happens like that.

Many people insist on giving multiple answers. A man will say that he sees himself as a 2 *and* a 9. Sometimes this gets expressed more precisely: 'When I'm with a woman I'm more likely to be a 9, right at the new man end, but when I'm with men I find myself a 2 or a 3.'

Another man said: 'I would say I'm a 2. I consider myself traditional, but I'm trying to modify myself.' The number of participants of both sexes who mention words like *modify*, *change*, *improve*, is very high. Another man said: 'When I thought about it, I thought five. This isn't out of not wanting to choose, but out of confusion - the struggle, uncertainty and confusion of being a man.'

Many women mock the exercise but I've found what they say quite revealing. One woman said: 'I think my husband is a 2 but *he* thinks he's an 8.' Another woman said: 'I've been married for 33 years. My husband started as a 3 and after bringing up the children together, which was terribly important to him, I think he's become a ... 4!'

We need to access what is involved in gender confusion and gender certainty in a new language of fleshy images that speak more directly to people's experience. My eight-year-old son and seven-year-old daughter have been teaching me their theory of gender confusion and this has helped me to write about its positive aspects, and to distinguish what I am interested in (which is self-image at depth) from the more conventional, journalistic level at which men are simply regarded as mixed up because of what women have managed to achieve.

According to my children, there are four main categories which a person cannot escape: boy-boy, boy-girl, girl-girl and girl-boy. The categories are all considered absolutely equal and are very sophisticated in that anatomy is regarded as important but not decisive. (How hard to get that degree of realistic flexibility into academic discourse!) So my daughter can often refer to herself as a girl-girl while my son oscillates between being a boy-girl and a girl-boy. However, one day, my daughter may function as a boy-boy or as a girl-boy. Context is centrally important - it does depend on whom they are with. My children's system also helps us to get beyond a simplistic heterosexual-homosexual divide. As many adult boy-girls are heterosexual as are homosexual and the certitudes upon which homophobia rests are subverted in this way of speaking.

The point I am making is that the celebration of confusion embodied by these children may be a more effective, interesting and radical way to enter gender politics than either (a) the suspiciousness and judgmentalism of the therapist; or (b) the nostalgia-fuelled return to certainty we see in some aspects of the men's movement; or (c) the advocacy of an ersatz merger of men's sociopolitical interests with those of women. Gender confusion unsettles all the main alternatives on offer. Let's see how this works out in relation to men.

Nowadays, in the West, men are incessantly being seen as 'the problem'. This new stance reverses the trend of centuries in which women - the other sex, the second sex, the dark sex, the sex which is not one - have been the problem men set themselves to solve. Men are often depicted as sexually abusing, domestically violent, planet-despoiling creatures. There is little doubt that the point is a valid one. But, at the same time, a completely different set of images has arisen suggesting a breed of men who support the rights of women and children, and who are ecologically aware and non-violent.

So we are faced with a split in our collective image of men. Conventionally, psychotherapists tell us that such splits come about when something (such as gender confusion) causes unbearable anxiety. I think that immense collective cultural anxiety is actually being caused by the false certitude of masculinity itself - what I call 'the male deal'. It is the male deal which lies behind the deeply problematic gender certainty I mentioned earlier. And it is the male deal which grounds our culture's assumptions about religion, science - and politics.

In the male deal, the little boy, at around three or four years old or earlier, strikes a bargain with the social world in which he lives. If he will turn away from soft things, feminine things, maternal things, from the world of play wherein failure doesn't matter, then the world will reward his gender certainty by giving him all the goodies in its possession - all the women he can eat. In return for the gift of political power, he promises to be a good provider and to keep unruly and subversive women and children in their places. He also promises not to deviate from this function by loving other men too much (that is, becoming gay). Homophobia is really a political defence of the family of capitalism.

The question I want to pose is whether or not we can reframe the collective confusion about the male deal as an opportunity to rethink a number of things: the deal itself and its damaging as well as pleasurable effects on men; the nature of male authority and its roots in Western attitudes to work; the possibility of women and men facing the difficult economic times ahead as partners as well as adversaries.

Given that men control the sources of economic and political power, including the production of ideas and images of sexual difference, then, if men are on the move at some level, adding male political power to the ideals of male change could be decisive. In other words, we could be confronted with a social movement as significant as feminism but with the crucial difference that men are fortified with possession of all the resources from which women have been excluded.

Nothing is more suspect than the complaint, fuelled by 'victim envy', that society now favours women over men. Nevertheless, it would be wrong to end on the certitudinous note of male power. Taken as a whole, men certainly have power. But many black men, men who are physically challenged, men living in homelessness and poverty, young men dying in pointless wars or rotting in prison cells, and men whose countries have been invaded or occupied, might well dispute that they really do have power. Perhaps there's nothing other than gender confusion. Perhaps there isn't a monolith called 'men' after all. As a woman in one of the workshops said of her husband: 'Well, if you take 1-5 and put it on one side and if you take 6-10 and put it on the other side - *he's in the abyss.*'

Dennis Potter's *Singing Detective*

A Place in the Mind

David Bell

David Bell explores the interior
worlds of Dennis Potter

Dennis Potter's work has been increasingly in the public eye over the last ten years. He broke the mould of television drama, and achieved this, like any great artist, without intending to, but out of an inner compulsion. Because the television medium was the form in which he realised his dramatic intentions, his genius was not adequately recognised until recent times.

To my mind, he reached the peak of his talents in *The Singing Detective*, where he produced a narrative that broke down the barriers between inner and outer reality, not by obscuring the difference between them, but through a deep exploration of their relationship.[1]

It is in his exploration of the inner world and its relation to external reality that Potter brings concerns that are also central to psychoanalysis. Though, of course, all great artists deal with fundamental problems of our inner world, Potter, most especially in *The Singing Detective*, makes this concern quite explicit. The narrative structure is non-linear. It weaves back and forth between memory, fantasy

---

1. Page numbers in the text are from Dennis Potter, *The Singing Detective*, Faber, London 1986.

and reality. These narrative threads form an ever-increasing coherence as the drama develops over the six episodes. These formal characteristics of the drama constantly illuminate its content.

As elsewhere in Potter's work, there is a central concern with the struggle between creativity and destructiveness, with an unflinching capacity to lay bare for us the most unpleasant sides of human character and to show their sources. He describes an omnipotent character structure built up to deal with unbearable psychic pain, vulnerability and shame. However, this structure becomes detached from its origins and acquires an idealised life of its own within the personality. *The Singing Detective* was enormously popular because it addresses aspects of the human condition which are universal and which it is my aim in this paper to explore.

Because the narrative structure of *The Singing Detective* is non-linear and multi-layered, it is difficult to provide a synopsis of it without doing considerable disservice to the subtlety of the text. In fact, summarising the drama confronts one with the same difficulty as one encounters when attempting to summarise an analysis: everything is connected to everything else and the same story is told over and over again, yet every time in a slightly different way. The drama takes place over six episodes and the same elements are laid out in each episode. Disparate fragments become clearer as the narrative progresses and the relationship between them is revealed.

There are three threads to the narrative, each of which represents a different

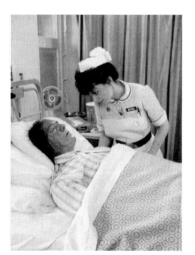

aspect of psychic reality: the current reality of the central character, his memories and, lastly, his imaginative or fantasy life.

Philip Marlow - not Raymond Chandler's detective hero, but a *writer* of detective stories - a man in mid-life, lies in a hospital bed, suffering a devastating exacerbation of the illness, psoriasis, which he has endured all his adult life. We learn that this is the worst crisis - his illness is at its peak. His whole body is covered in festering sores and the disease has so invaded his joints that he is almost completely paralysed and constantly in excruciating pain. The author makes it clear that his physical state may be taken as a metaphor for his inner world where he is facing a life crisis arising from his attempt to emerge from a paralysing inner imprisonment. The author refers, in the text, to the hospital ward as 'a place in the mind'.

The first narrative thread - his current reality - deals with his life on the hospital ward, his relationships with the ward staff, with other patients and, most especially, with his estranged wife, Nicola. The nurses and doctors appear mainly to be superior, arrogant, self-righteous and devoid of any human concern. They are irritated or embarrassed by any real show of distress. His relationship with Nicola is largely one of clever one-upmanship, which evades the longing for warmth which occasionally breaks through his shell. Despite himself, he develops a passionate attachment to the nurse Mills who looks after him.

To emphasise the concurrent realities, Potter uses the dramatic device of having a fellow patient, Reginald, reading Marlow's novel *The Singing Detective* to himself throughout the six episodes.

Marlow lies in his bed full of biting witty invective and relishing an apparent cynicism about life. During his stay, two patients in the next bed die, and are unceremoniously wheeled out of the ward. For much of the time, Marlow is apparently unmoved by the scenes of pathos, degradation and tragedy that surround him. This is, however, only apparent as his cynical comments almost always have a note of irony. He cries bitterly when Ali, a Pakistani heart patient in the next bed, of whom he had become fond, finally dies. When the pain or feelings of shame and vulnerability become too much for him, he takes refuge in his novel. He is re-writing it in his head.

The second narrative thread deals with a different reality: Marlow's childhood memories of critical events in his life which clearly have an important bearing on his current state. It is not clear at times what are to be taken as memories of actual events and what are fantastic distortions of these events, viewed from the perspective of his at times delirious state.

As a young boy, Marlow suffered a major psychological catastrophe which has had enduring effects on his personality. He remembers his parents as unhappily married, living in an empty world of bickering with the paternal grandparents. Young Philip's father appears mainly as a weak man, unable to save the family. Father's fine singing voice, much loved by all at the local club, evokes his son's adoration and admiration. However, his father's strength is more evident on the stage than it is in real life. Philip's mother is unfaithful to his father and he witnesses her lovemaking from up his tree in the woods. Her lover, Binney, is a musician from the band where mother plays and father sings. The boy is devastated by this betrayal and shows his disturbance at school by shitting on the teacher's desk. His tyrannical teacher is more than willing to accept that it was not her star pupil who committed this desecration and believes him when he pins it on the class fool, Mark Binney, the son of his mother's lover. We later learn that Mark ended up as a chronic psychiatric patient; he was the son of mother's lover.

P hilip's parents split up and his world is devastated when his mother moves him away from father and away from his rural life, to the big city. In anger, he confronts his mother, in front of some soldiers on a train, with his knowledge of her infidelity and later even more poignantly in a London underground station. It is, interestingly, at this point that Philip's mother notices the first signs of his illness (psoriasis). The first red patch has made its appearance.

In the sequencing of the narrative, this event is repetitively linked with gloomy and threatening images of trains, a terrifying scarecrow in a devastated landscape and Philip's mother calling after him. We later learn that these images refer to the central catastrophe - mother's suicide.

So, we are left in no doubt that at the core of Marlow's character is the problem of the terrible pain of unbearable persecuting guilt, which always threatens and from which he is always trying to escape. There appeared to have been no-one in his world to help him with this problem, least of all his loving but weak father.

The third thread from which the fabric of the narrative is woven is Marlow's imaginative and fantasy life. This falls into two distinct categories. Firstly, there are his imaginings, fantasies and deliria concerning his current reality. Here fantasy and reality are not distinct. For example, the viewer is led to believe that Nicola, his wife, is cynically betraying him with her lover Binney, both sexually and by stealing his work. It is only later that we learn that this is, in fact, a fantastic distortion of reality. Characters in his life on the ward exchange places with characters from his novel. In the second category, there is a quite different type of fantasy activity over which he exerts control (though, at the final crisis, as I will describe below, his control of the products of his imagination breaks down and he then feels controlled by them). It is more like the imaginative-creative work of the writer. From his hospital bed, Marlow is re-writing, in his head, his novel *The Singing Detective*. The story is a classic spy thriller. There are spies, prostitutes, a mysterious dead woman's body dragged out of a river (a

frequently repeated image). The eponymous hero is investigating the murder and gradually closing in on the traitor and cheap thug, Binney. The singing detective is glamorous, witty and sings in nightclubs. One always senses that he will get to the bottom of things and nail Binney.

Our hero is pursued by mysterious raincoated figures who spy on him and who, we are told in the text, work for an intelligence organisation. They aim to kill him so that the truth is not discovered. Marlow's identification with the glamorous singing detective - who unearths the evil - is never in doubt. The singing detective seems to combine some elements of his real father and also a wish fulfilling image of a strong father with whom he can identify and put his world to rights. We later see that he is also identified with the traitor and murderer - Binney. This, latter, identification is revealed through their use of the same words and in one scene they replace each other (this is a scene played first between Binney and a prostitute and subsequently between Marlow and the prostitute).

Actors play a multiplicity of roles spanning the different 'realities', a device which emphasises the interweaving of memory, fantasy and reality. Mother's lover (a childhood memory), Binney the spy (in the detective story) and Binney, his wife's lover in his fantasy-life, are all played by the same actor.

The songs have a different function from Potter's previous drama, *Pennies from*

Heaven, where the songs appeared to represent both a longing for a better world and the escape into a nostalgic sentimentality. Here they also represent artistic achievement - as Potter put it, 'the angel in us'.[2] They also bind the narrative together, often spanning the different realities. A character from memory strikes up a song, which is then taken up in the detective fantasy or in Marlow's imaginings concerning life on the ward.

An interior journey

The detective story convention, as Potter commented himself elsewhere, allows the plot to develop like a jigsaw. We, the audience, are in the position of putting together the clues from the first fragmentary images until the picture begins to appear. Marlow has embarked, in this crisis of his illness, on a journey of self-discovery and as the story opens, he uses a well known metaphor for this journey into his own unconscious.

We see Binney go down the steps into a sleazy nightclub and hear a voice-over: 'And so the man went down the hole like Alice. But there were no bunny rabbits down there. It wasn't that sort of hole. It was a rat hole.' We are later advised that the one thing you don't do down a rat hole is 'underestimate the rats in residence'...'they gnaw at your soft underbelly and do a lot of damage to your nerves'. I take this to refer to the gnawing pains of guilt.

It is a journey to confront great cruelty, persecution and a shattered internal world in which there are powerful destructive forces. There are frequent allusions to Nazi-like figures. At the centre of this world, there is the image of the woman's body pulled out of the river, representing the dead body of his mother after her suicide. The body, at one point, has Sonia's (the prostitute) face, at another, the face of Nicola, his wife. Although these images are all related, they occupy different realities and Marlow's increasing capacity to differentiate fantasy from reality is symbolised within the drama by his greater physical mobility.

A particular sequence is repeated as the narrative progresses: Philip, the boy up a tree, observing the couple in intercourse; the breakdown of the family; Philip's revelation to his mother on the train and subsequently on the underground platform; and his mother's suicide. In linking the watching of the adulterous couple, the family's breakdown, Philip's accusation

---

2. *Potter on Potter,* G. Fuller (ed), Faber, London 1993, p86.

against his mother, and her suicide, the author shows a profound insight into the depths of the inner world. From a psychoanalytic point of view, the child, excluded from the parental bed, harbours phantasies (sometimes conscious, but often deeply unconscious) of spying and attempting to control the parental lovemaking.

Awareness of exclusion, with all the attendant feelings of separateness, frustration and jealousy, often leads to frightening murderous impulses directed towards one or both parents. In such situations the child derives much support from seeing his parents well and healthy and *not* controlled by him. However, when events (in this case the mother's betrayal of father and her subsequent suicide) give external support to these unconscious wishes and fears, a psychic catastrophe results. Omnipotent destructiveness is confirmed and the capacity to differentiate inner and outer reality is compromised.

When Philip witnesses his mother's intercourse with her lover, it is a double betrayal. It is the betrayal of father by mother but it is also linked in young Philip's mind to the ordinary oedipal betrayal - the child excluded from the parental lovemaking. Young Philip projects onto the sexual couple all his feelings of hate, disgust, violence and murderousness, and announces from up in his tree that when he grows up, he will be a detective. This detective fantasy satisfies two wishes - on the one hand, the detective is someone who makes a career out of spying and therefore, in unconscious fantasy, of controlling the corrupt sexual couple. It also satisfies the longing for a strong father who can expose the corruption and restore order in the family, put the world to rights. The singing detective character satisfies both aspects. He seems totally in charge of the corrupt world around him - his eyes are everywhere; but he also represents justice, truth and morality. The murderer of the woman will be found. The capacity to sing captures the admired characteristic of the actual father now linked in the fantasy to the all-powerful detective.

When the young boy's omnipotence is confirmed, and, with it, omnipotent guilt for the destruction of his family, his faith in a good world is destroyed. The horror of this is represented in the drama by scenes of a devastated landscape, with only a scarecrow to be seen, glimpsed from a train window. The scarecrow is later given the form of Hitler, that icon of destruction, gesturing and mouthing words in a manner both obscene and grotesque. In another much later sequence, the scarecrow has the face of the sadistic school teacher who cruelly punished young Mark Binney for Philip's crime.

Philip's feelings of guilt seem to have origins from earlier in his life, even before his mother's suicide. Amidst a scene of bickering and terrible unhappiness at home, the young Philip thinks:

'My fault. Me. It's me. Me. It's all my doing. Me. It's me. My fault. Mine...'
He hurriedly mutters a prayer:
'Our father which art in heaven, Hallow'd be thy name....'

And the text continues, 'The boy's gabbled voice is quickly faded over by the face of the distressed man he is to become, in the hospital ward' (p70).

Potter describes Marlow's dilemma with great insight. He has built up a system of defences which does protect him from the unbearable mental pain. Yet his inability to confront his own inner world has acted like a crippling illness. It is as if he is frozen in time - in that instant of his observation of mother's lovemaking and of her later suicide. He has reached a crisis and the text makes it clear that it is a final crisis. A new treatment will have to be used. Concretely, a new experimental drug, symbolically a new way of looking at things.

Until this point, Marlow has taken refuge in a cynical world well described in the text. It is a world populated by figures who mock vulnerability. These figures are idealised and his perception of the world (as seen, for example, in his attitude to his wife) is fundamentally distorted. He is full of witty invective which is both cynical and bitter. His clever banter is really serving to keep him going and to evade the full impact of the feelings of despair and humiliation that are never far away. Potter records Marlow's desperate bravado: Watching his cigarette smoke, he says:

'Ali see the way it coils and drifts (nasty cackle), just like every human hope.'
'I used to want the good opinion of honourable men and the ungrudging love of beautiful women.'
He laughs ... then realises he meant it (pp12-13).

Or, elsewhere in the text, excitedly caught up in his cynicism, he turns to Ali, the

Pakistani cardiac patient in the next bed, who has been told that he mustn't get out of bed or strain himself in any way:

> 'What's the point' [in life]? 'What are we waiting for? Why endure one more moment than you have to? Go on! Get out of bed, Ali. Go on, jump up and down! And then hold a pillow over my face! Come on.'

The text continues:

> 'He stops abruptly, like one suddenly recognising the true extremity of his feelings, and the depths of his bitterness and despair' (p14).

L
ike the hero of his story, Marlow expects corruption everywhere... and finds it everywhere. His mental paralysis derives from his inability to distinguish internal figures from external reality. He sees the world through only one lens - helpless and contemptible victims are at the mercy of cruel tyrannical figures. The only way to survive is to play the game, to be on the side of the winners and evade any feelings of ordinary human dependence and vulnerability. The hatred and mockery of human helplessness that underlies this way of thinking about the world is, of course, underwritten by the cruel irony of his physical state. His condition is almost a paradigm of infantile helplessness - he cannot move nor wash nor manage his own toilet and, despite himself, is falling in love with the nurse who attends to him. She carries out maternal functions and becomes, therefore, in Marlow's mind, his own beloved mother. He says, 'I seem to have regressed into the helpless and pathetic condition of total dependency, of the kind normally associated with infancy' (p27).

M
arlow, however, finds strength and is helped to uncover his inner world by a 'clever psychotherapist', though Marlow maintains at first that this is not a therapeutic endeavour, but a game of cat and mouse, winner and loser. Like so many patients he claims at first no real interest in his therapy - he says this is 'kidnapping - I'm here under protest'. This is quite thin, however, and he also shows real insight into his desperate need to understand himself.

On being offered tranquillisers and antidepressants, he replies: 'I'm not taking those things. I've got work to do. Got a lot of thinking to do. If I don't think, I'll never get out of here.' His refusal of antidepressants and tranquillisers is also a refusal of their psychic equivalents - namely, his use of his artistic talents to create and live in antidepressive fantasies which evade his inner world, rather than confront it. This is not something he can manage alone. He says, in a state of rising panic:

> 'I can *not* stand it really truly can not stand this any more. I can't get on top of it or - or - see clear or think straight or tell what is from what isn't and if I don't tell someone, if I don't admit it - I'll never get out of it, never beat it off, never never never.' [3]

So, what is it Marlow has to 'think' or 'admit'?

He tells himself via his story that it is the murderer he is looking for, but he can't decide who it is. He says, brooding (trying to think who will be the culprit), 'It's always the least likely character who turns out to be the killer... well it can't be me. That's for sure. It can't be me. I didn't do it'.[4]

Dr Gibbon, the psychotherapist, has a very shrewd and different idea. Gibbon has read Marlow's story:

> 'I know all the clues are supposed to point in the direction of the
> murderer...But what if they also reveal the *victim* a little more clearly?'

He is suggesting a different reading. The pursuit of the murderer of the dead woman in the detective story represents Marlow's pursuit of the murderer of his mother which, deep in his unconscious, he believes to be himself. However, Gibbon suggests something quite different - namely, that Marlow is the *victim* of a catastrophe. Internal figures won't let him see this and torture him with his guilt. He cannot bear the humiliation, as he sees it, of the recognition of his need for help.

Melanie Klein described how all of us, in phantasy, destroy our loved objects, partly out of ruthless wishes to possess them and control them and partly out of hatred of our very need and dependence on them. She would have agreed with Marlow, 'We all have blood on our teeth.' [5]

---

3. Marlow is saying here that he fears not being able to distinguish inner from outer reality.
4. Freud commented in his paper *Negation* (Standard Edition 19, 1925) that repressed unconscious material often makes its first appearance in consciousness through appearing as its negation. As a patient of mine put it in his first association to a dream in which he killed a man in authority, 'Well, one thing's for sure, it wasn't my father.'
5. Melanie Klein, 'A contribution to the psychogenesis of manic depressive states', in *The Work of Melanie Klein, Vol. 1, Love Guilt and Reparation*, Hogarth, London 1975.

However, the hatred and attack on the loved object are denied. Instead, the world is split into idealised loved objects and frustrating objects which are hated. The attacked internal objects become dangerous persecutors and are projected outwards. Thus is created an amoral world where only survival matters and guilt is denied.

Klein showed how a critical phase of development ensues, termed the depressive position. In this there is a realisation that the hated attacked objects are the same objects as those we love and, if there is sufficient capacity to bear the pain and guilt arising from realisation of damage done, there is movement into a different world which is integrated and which has a moral dimension. This move towards the depressive position entails a fundamental shift in orientation to reality.

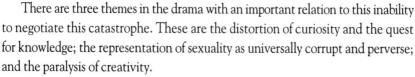

As integration occurs, projections are withdrawn and thus arises a capacity to differentiate inner and outer worlds. The wish to restore the damage done to the loved object forms an important basis for artistic creativity, in Klein's view. This is central to my reading of Potter's narrative.

Marlow's difficulty, then, centres on his inability to bear the persecutory pain of the 'depressive position'. Instead he has taken refuge (a 'psychic retreat'[6]) in stories and fantasies, and built up a character structure which, though freezing him developmentally, has also kept him alive.

There are three themes in the drama with an important relation to this inability to negotiate this catastrophe. These are the distortion of curiosity and the quest for knowledge; the representation of sexuality as universally corrupt and perverse; and the paralysis of creativity.

The development of knowledge about the self and the world is rooted in our earliest observation of family relationships. Thus in a certain sense we are all detectives in our pursuit of intimate knowledge; but, in Marlow's case, this 'detective function' has been deformed, linked as it is not to discovery and understanding, but to the control and exposure of betrayals in a cynical world

---

6. John Steiner, *Psychic Retreats*, Routledge, London 1993.

devoid of ordinary human values.

This world view stems ultimately from the belief that the parental sexual relationship *is* a betrayal. Here is the second theme, the representation of sexuality, which in this play is replete with hatred and sadism. Potter deals explicitly with this issue. The representation of a sexual couple and an observer is a motif which goes through a radical transformation as Marlow encounters his crisis. The central and repeated representation of the sexual act occurs when we see Philip up his tree, looking down on his mother's lovemaking.

In the first representation of this episode, Philip, up his tree, is clearly curious about nature, and this curiosity appears as mainly based on his love of the natural world. We see him take a ladybird and replace it tenderly on its branch. However, after catching sight of his mother and her lover walking through the grass, there is a sudden transformation in atmosphere, as the motive force for curiosity about nature and the world changes in an instant from love to hatred and the determination to control. He squashes the ladybird beneath his finger and says:

> 'I can't abide things that creep and crawl and - They got to be got rid of an, um? I can't abide dirt. It'd get everybloodywhere, doun it?'

Down below, two human creatures, mother and her lover, are, so to speak, creeping and crawling through the undergrowth. As Philip observes the rhythmic movements of the couple's lovemaking, the scene is interspersed with the now grown-up Philip lying in his hospital bed watching 'just as the boy watched' a man receiving cardiac massage - the same rhythmic movements. The representation of the sexual act is suffused with violence, horror and disgust. Later in the text, Potter shows that lies about sex and mental illness are closely related.

> Nicola has come to see him on the ward. He is clearly improving.
> He tells Nicola he is going mad.
> Marlow: (with precision), 'I mean going off my head. Round the bend. Bonkers. Losing my marbles. Cuckoo...'
> Nicola: (Uneasy) 'Do you want to talk about it? Or?'
> Marlow: 'Sex!'
> Nicola: 'What?'
> Marlow: 'That's what it's all about. Sex. Sex and lies' (p197).

Dr Gibbon clearly sees the importance of this and, in his first meeting, drew Marlow's attention to his description of the sexual act in his novel. 'Mouth sucking wet and slack at mouth, tongue chaffing against tongue, limb thrusting on limb, skin rubbing on skin. Faces contort and stretch in helpless leer, organs spurt sticky betrayals. This is the sweaty farce out of which we are brought into being.'

A s the narrative progresses, Marlow's picture of sexual intimacy changes. It acquires a warmer, more human quality, as Marlow develops a capacity to bear sexual longing and tenderness. At first however this breakthrough of warmth and longing for Nicola is quickly covered over, and Marlow returns to his psychic refuge where sex again assumes the form of a pornographic scene.

Right at the end of the drama, Marlow leaves the ward arm-in-arm with Nicola, leaning on her. Reginald, the observer of this happy couple, views them in a benign way. He reads the last line of the novel:

> 'And-her-soft-red-lips-clam-clamp-clamped-themselves on his.'
> He closes the book and says, warmly, 'Lucky Devil' (p248).

Their sexual closeness is now viewed benignly, admiringly.

Hanna Segal, Klein's best-known interpreter, has linked the capacity to bear the pain of guilt to the capacity for creative work.[7] She describes how works of art derive their aesthetic depth from the artist's capacity to face the pain of the guilt derived from the damage done to loved internal objects, and to overcome this. The work of art itself is an act of reparation. We, the audience, are gripped by works which we identify with - both with the artist's confrontation with the pain of their shattered internal world and also with their ability, through intense psychic work, to overcome it and depict it in a work of art.

Marlow had been dissatisfied by his novel, written many years earlier - it is even referred to in the text as a piece of pulp fiction. In his hospital bed he is reworking his piece of 'pulp fiction' and turning it into an artistic achievement.

I suggest that the narrative is also the story of its own making. In the first edition, Marlow had been using his imaginative fantasies to escape from his internal situation. However, in his life crisis, he is rewriting his life as well as his novel, now *not* to evade his internal world, but as part of his confrontation with it.

---

7. Hanna Segal, 'A psychoanalytical approach to aesthetics', [1952] reprinted in *The Work of Hanna Segal*, Free Association Books, London 1986.

I would now like to examine in a little more detail the character structure that has provided Marlow with his defensive retreat. It is a cold world full of cynicism, and is well depicted in the detective story. The figures in the underworld of spies, prostitutes and traitors have no morality, no concern for the suffering around them, nor for the activities in which they are directly implicated. Theirs is the law of the jungle - kill or be killed. Binney, the spy, represents this attitude. He trades secrets with whoever offers him the most, including doing deals with the Nazis. Marlow wants Binney to be the murderer - desperately - but, at numerous points in the text, it is clear that he identifies himself with Binney. In a confusion of fantasy and story, he becomes Binney, uses the same words and sleeps with the same prostitute. Marlow's principal identification is with the singing detective who confronts Binney with his utter lack of concern, his ruthlessness and his emptiness.

Referring to the world in which he is trapped, he says: 'One thing about this place - it strips away all the unimportant stuff - like skin, like work, love, loyalty, like passion and belief.'

As Marlow says: 'I can think the thinking, I can sing the singing. But you won't catch me feeling the feeling. No Sir.' In this refuge, Marlow feels protected from the pain of what Melanie Klein called the depressive position; yet through identification with the cold heartless figures, he perpetuates the sources of his own unbearable guilt and shame. Patients described by the analyst Herbert Rosenfeld dreamed of or made frequent references to mafia-like figures.[8] These figures often made their appearance just when the patient was allowing the analyst to have a warmer contact with him. Just at this point, the patient becomes terrified of some dreaded attack - as if he had betrayed some secret.

As the drama reaches its climax in the final episode, Marlow's condition has been improving though, typically, he is at first reluctant to admit that the treatment is working. His increasing physical mobility is accompanied by (and is a metaphor for) the *psychic* mobility that comes from the capacity to differentiate internal and external reality. He manages to sustain warm feelings towards Nicola without quickly perverting them. Previously, any warmth was quickly followed by a retreat into his refuge from which he poured scorn and hatred on her. There is now real doubt as to whether she is really corrupt and betraying him. In the final crisis the

---

8. Herbert Rosenfeld, 'A clinical approach to the psychoanalytic theory of the life instincts: an investigation into the aggressive aspects of narcissism', *International Journal of Psychoanalysis*, 52, 1971.

fleeting images cohere and Marlow is faced with the full recognition of his mother's suicide. He confronts his memory of seeing her in her coffin and manages to sustain the psychic pain which this image brings. In the last episode, we find Marlow emerging from his crippled state as he faces the full force of his guilt: not only his unconscious guilt for his mother's suicide, but also the reality-based guilt for his betrayal of his classmate and for his exposure to humiliation.

Marlow finds support in a renewed link with his father. We see Philip and his father walking home through the fateful woods in a memory of his return home after his mother's suicide. The father, in a moment of agony and inner strength, screams out his pain and then turns to his son and says, 'Philip, I love you'. Philip is, however, unable to accept his father's love. He is suddenly terror-struck and tells his father to be quiet as someone might hear. He points to the scarecrow. This is now in the 'observer position', observing the tenderness between father and son, and is felt to hate and attack them. The scarecrow now occupies the position once occupied by Philip who observed a different couple with terrifying consequences. It stands for a terrifying image of human destructiveness. It has no feeling, and annihilates at will. This moment presages the onset of unbearable persecution by feelings of guilt for the death of his mother.

As the camera, Marlow's eye from his hospital bed, approaches the image of the scarecrow in the wintry gloom, we hear Nicola's changing, crazed, little girl-like voice: 'Ding Dong Bell, Pussy's in the well'. We see a nude portrait in Binney's house, smeared with blood - 'Who pushed her in? Who pushed her in?'

Marlow's capacity to face fully these internal horrors and understand their nature enables him to regain inner strength and mobility. As we come out of Marlow's head, so to speak, and back to the ward, we find his condition greatly improved. As Marlow recognises his own real guilt at his involvement in the persecution of young Mark Binney, he is helped by the psychotherapist to bear this pain in one of the most poignant scenes of the whole drama. The psychotherapist bursts into song, showing how in Marlow's eyes he has become identified with the good and strong aspects of his father. Following this confrontation with his pain, we see Marlow on the ward. He is trying to walk.

'Look at me! Look at me! I did it! I walked! I can walk! Look. Look at me.'
Nicola: 'For heaven's sake - supposing you fall over - Philip. Hold on to me, you're not ready for this!'

Marlow: 'Hold on to *you?*'
She looks at him wryly, well understanding the other resonances
of the question.
Nicola: 'There aren't too many others around any more Philip.'
They seemed to study each other, his face was still wet.
Marlow: 'Be-bob-a-loo-hop.'
Nicola: 'Yes, but isn't it time you climbed down out of your tree?'
(p 242-243)

Slightly later, Marlow says in a delighted tone, 'Nicola isn't in the river'. This is a
reference to a dead body found in a river in the detective story. It is the body of a
prostitute, but it also clearly represents the dead body of his mother. He now seems
delighted that Nicola is not his mother and that she is alive. Shortly after this, two
mysterious men appear, wearing trench coats and trilby hats. They are referred to
anonymously as First Mysterious Man and Second Mysterious Man.

First Mysterious Man: 'Where are you going?'
Marlow: 'Home.'
Second Mysterious Man: 'But that's off the page ennit?'
The First Mysterious Man uses the flat of his hand on Marlow's chest, pushing
him back.
First Mysterious Man: 'You're going nowhere Sunshine. Not until we
settle this.'
Marlow looks around for help and can see none. He moistens his lips.
Marlow: 'Settle what?'
First Mysterious Man: 'Who we are. What we are.'[9]
Second Mysterious Man: 'That's right. That's absolutely right.'
Suddenly, they grab hard at Marlow's arm. He cries out.

These mysterious raincoated figures bear a close resemblance to the internal mafia
described by Rosenfeld. They make their appearance in the drama just at the point
when Marlow is making real progress and turning towards good figures (his
psychotherapist, his wife) for help. For Rosenfeld's psychotic patients these figures

9. This, incidentally, would appear to echo Segal's idea that the naming of parts of the
self, that is, giving them a real identity and owning them, is an important aspect of the
depressive position.

appeared often in the form of hallucinations. For Marlow they are fantasies, which do, however, have real effects, distorting and crippling his thinking.

Marlow is an author as well as being a patient and his novel is his attempt to visualise this internal situation, in order to deal with and overcome it. Yet this is not entirely true, for in the last episode the boundary between Marlow's fictitious creations and reality completely breaks down - a policeman appears and tells him Nicola has killed Binney and has committed suicide by jumping out of a car. This had been an episode in Marlow's fantasy, but it has (apparently) become reality. The anonymous men have walked off the page and into the ward to torture him.

But there remains the final denouement. The singing detective, Marlow's creation, comes crashing on to the ward, gun blazing. There is a violent shoot out. Everyone around Marlow - we may see these figures as representing parts of himself - is killed; Marlow watches horrified. He says that it is murder: his alter ego replies, 'I'd call it pruning'. The first mysterious man gets a bullet but, as the gun blasts, we see it is Marlow who has been killed by his alter ego, who announces

'I suppose you could say we'd been partners, him and me. Like Laurel and Hardy or Fortnum and Mason. But, hell, this was one sick fellow, from way back when. And I reckon I'm man enough to tie my own shoe laces now' (p 247).

We return to reality, normality, the calm of the ward with patients and nurses. Marlow leaves the ward, wearing his detective trilby jauntily, arm in arm with Nicola.

Marlow has faced heroically his devastating internal situation, but the ending of the narrative is ambiguous. There has been a catastrophic breakdown of the boundary between fantasy and reality. Binney and the anonymous men earlier seemed to have come to life showing their independence of the author by the realisation that they were being written. It is as if the author's creations have now been endowed with the omnipotence of the author and come off the page into the ward. Suddenly, Marlow is the victim of his own creations. I did find myself wondering whether this represented the author's recognition that the very act of writing a novel, controlling and manipulating characters in fantasy, can fuel a writer's own omnipotence. Part of the act of writing involves recognising this omnipotence, struggling with it rather than being overtaken by it. Marlow doesn't quite achieve this recogition, but Potter certainly does.

In a television interview some years ago Potter discussed the structure of *The Singing Detective*:

> by being able to use, say, the musical convention and the detective story
> convention and the 'autobiographical' in quotes, convention, and making them
> co-exist at the same time so that the past and the present weren't in strict
> sequence because they aren't - they are in one sense, obviously in the calendar
> sense, but they're not in your head in that sequence and neither are they in
> terms of the way you discover things about yourself, where an event of 20 years
> ago can become more, it can follow yesterday instead of precede it... out of this
> morass, if you like, of evidence, the clues and searchings and strivings, which is
> the metaphor for the way we live, we can start to put up the structure called
> self. In that structure we can walk out of that structure and say at least now we
> know better who we are.

I would like to thank Elizabeth Spillius for the help she has given me with an earlier version of this article.

Felipe's feast

Bill Schwarz

A review of Felipe Fernández-Armesto's Millennium
(Bantam Press, London, 1995)

When it comes to matters of history I find it hard to rid myself of a deep recidivism. Historians, by and large, seem to know more about the world than their intellectual peers. I'm aware that to say this displays an unbearable complacency, reveals a predilection for a positivism which finds few fans, and requires a defence of an academic division of labour which cannot be justified. I'm also aware that the great bulk of historical knowledge is locked up in a world of its own, and has a capacity to instil tedium which cannot be equalled. But every so often I come across a work of historical exploration and I wonder how any mortal, subject to the same dull turbulence of modern life as the rest of us, can possibly have written it. Reading Felipe Fernández-Armesto's *Millennium* produced in me this kind of wonder, an intellectual vertigo which exhilarates and forces one to reflect on one's own practice.

With a chutzpah and colossal confidence which makes Eric Hobsbawm or Perry Anderson seem parochial, Fernández-Armesto has set out to write the history of the world over the past thousand years. What is more, he has determined to construct this history not from the conventional purview of 'the West', but from its frontiers and margins. The resulting work rightly belongs to the blockbuster school of historiography: massive, epic, and slightly crazed. As we discover in the text, the book appears simultaneously 'in an unprecedented number of languages'. Anyone squeamish of history in seven-league boots had best steer clear.

But although in conception the book is a blockbuster, in method it is resolutely quiescent. He spurns all large, conventional abstractions preferring to construct a history which is 'convincingly imagined and vividly evoked'. This refusal to endorse any kind of 'mega-explanation', in a work like this, is pretty disabling: for it is precisely large historic transformations which form the substance of his story. There is of course an argument, though its founding principles remain mute.

In fact Fernández-Armesto retrieves what once was the staple of historical inquiry: the idea of a civilisation. He defines civilisation, principally, by its cultural forms, and by its proximity to a sea or ocean. Given the long duration of his historical object, the central theme of his narrative becomes the dynamic rise and fall of competing civilisations, or in his terms, the 'interaction' of civilisations. In a telling formulation he writes: 'If cultures and civilisations are the tectonic plates of world history, frontiers are the places where they scrape against each other and cause convulsive change'.

In this perspective the dominance of Europe or the West was both historically contingent, and relatively short-lived. It was 'later, feebler and briefer than is commonly supposed'. The expansion of Europe, he suggests, was launched not from the 'outpouring of pent-up dynamism' but from 'the insecure edges of a contracting civilisation'. He goes on: 'By looking at some of the shy and retiring empires, which generally forego their proper place, we shall be better able to see the late middle ages and the early modern period for what they really were: eras in which a number of expanding civilisations in different parts of the world clashed as their dynamics drove them into collision. The traditional picture, of a largely passive extra-European world, which

> 'A colossal confidence which makes Eric Hobsbawm or Perry Anderson seem parochial'

awaited, in retreat or decline, in stagnancy or arrested development, the imprint of an uniquely vital force from Europe, will have to be discarded, in favour of a more fluid image of the past'. Given this dynamism of the early modern non-European world, and the current decline of the contemporary Atlantic civilisation, he is quite right to centre what the orthodox historiography has striven to displace. And in so doing, he has forcefully shifted the terrain of debate.

But there are problems as well. Most of this is asserted rather than argued. His narrative does little to confirm or deny these hypotheses. There is some ambiguity about his conception of early modern Europe, which veers between seeing it as contracting and expanding. And he allows himself to say some daft things about the decline of civilisations occurring because of a determination of their peoples to talk themselves down. (The half dozen pages on the decline of Britain, fascinatingly juxtaposed to a discussion of the fate of Argentina in the twentieth century, revolve around an analysis of the cartoons of Max Beerbohm which adorn the author's drawing-room.)

In reacting against teleological history apportioning an inevitability to the rise of the West, he goes for a radical contingency, in which chance and perception determine historic outcomes. It follows that the substance of his narrative has little to say, in terms of recognisable social explanations, and a lot to evoke. But actually, as he happily concedes, what he chooses to evoke as representative of each historical moment in each civilisation is more or less arbitrary: for crucially, there is precious little for him to say.

And'this underlies the oddity of the book. It is a world-history composed of a mosaic of literary vignettes. (The chapter on China in the early centuries of the millennium begins: 'The farewell dinner was a protracted affair. Final leave was not taken till dawn, at the foot of a new pontoon bridge, a few miles north-west of Shanyin, on 4 July 1170...') Some of these are wonderfully funny and illuminating, evidence of a keen historical eye; others work less well, suggesting a hurried self-indulgence. But either way, in terms of the larger architecture of the narrative, it doesn't seem much to matter. For history, here, is made up of wondrous episodes whose meaning lies only in the fact that they happened.

But actually, for all his formidable learning, he has little time for what - today - is taken as conventional history. His is both more old-fashioned, looking back to earlier literary models, and more avant-garde, attempting not only to aestheticise historical explanation but to defamiliarise at the same time. He loves the wry iconoclasm which follows. The entire book is based on a literary conceit. He imagines himself to be a galactic museum-keeper from the future, charged with curating 'the millennium'. The opening sentence of the Preface reads: 'I have a vision of some galactic museum of the distant future, in which Diet-Coke cans will share with coats of chain-mail a single small vitrine marked "Planet Earth, 1000-2000, Christian Era"'.

Not far away, I imagine, resonates the influence of Borges. Most of all, Borges' vivid depiction of the Chinese encyclopedia, ordering the world on principles which to the Western eye look wilfully surreal, could be taken as the guiding principle, and human affirmation, of what this book is about.

Much fun can follow from this, as well as genuine insight. Thus, for example, 'the sudden rise and demise of the Third Reich and Soviet Empire' in eastern Europe is linked to a longer history of 'volatile hegemonies' in the region, comprising Mongol rule in the thirteenth century, Polish-Lithuanian dominance in the fourteenth century, and so on. This compression of historical time can prove startling. And maybe, just as we might usefully think of decentring 'the West' in terms of space, we should follow Fernández-Armesto and be more assiduous in decentring our own known generations, and the civilisation they represent, in terms of time. The moral or human force of this is strong.

But there is a more disturbing dimension to this too. For in a curious twist of fate, this determination to adopt the persona of the curator of the future, to rise above the petty squabbles of our own times, can also be evidence of a more familiar, more antiquarian disposition. With a glass of decent port to hand, it can echo precisely the ethos of the patrician academic, insisting on the moral superiority of adopting the longer view while the conflagration flares outside.

In a moment of revealing self-irony (or I imagine it is ironic), the second paragraph of Fernández-Armesto's history of the millennium dilates on the contrasting manners required of an Oxford, compared to a Cambridge, college. This same sensibility deemed it appropriate to open the Prologue with reminiscences of Prunier's restaurant, 'in the elegant London street that joins Piccadilly to St James's Palace'. In fact, images of food and restaurants run through the entire book. This is too studied to be mere chance. The metaphors are revealing. The historical vignettes which make up the overall narrative are like little, exquisite *hors d'oeuvres* which can be sampled at random. In a larger sense history becomes a matter of taste. The author describes his own obsession with history in such terms: 'Responding to the visible, palpable survivals from the past which still surround us releases - for those with appropriate sensibilities - delicious secretions of intellectual pleasure'. Here we have world-history in the epicurean mode.

Law and Justice

Introduction

Bill Bowring, Kate Markus
and Keir Starmer

We are said to live in a society governed by the rule of law: that is a society in which dealings between citizens and the state, and among citizens themselves, are governed by law rather than arbitrary power. It can come as no surprise, then, that law plays a fundamental role in shaping the society that we live in and in regulating it. Unsurprisingly, the form and operation of law, although often disguised and presented in neutral terms, tends to reflect the existing economic and political relations of capitalist society in the late twentieth century. The rule of law, often, is not an accurate description of a state of affairs, but a slogan - or an outright deception. Many undemocratic and highly oppressive societies have written constitutions based, allegedly, on the rule of law. In such societies the theoretical existence of the rule of law is promoted as a cover for practices involving major breaches of human rights. The rule of law is thus a concept which can conceal real relations of power. And, although the extent to which justice may be perverted varies widely in different societies, it is clear that it is a concept that needs analysis. This raises fundamental questions for everyone engaged in the legal process, and everyone affected by it.

The Haldane Society of Socialist Lawyers has worked for half a century to uncover the role of law in society, and to engage in the struggles that the exercise of law invariably throws up. For example, consistent with the society's long tradition of work with the trade unions, it joined with the miners in their fight for justice during the 1984-5 strike, and more recently has been involved in campaigning on issues such as the erosion of local democracy, criminal justice in Northern Ireland, the poll tax and world human rights. As the year 2000 fast approaches, there is a pressing need for the society to continue with this work. Such a definition of justice, self-evidently, includes the notion of social justice. And the changes of the last two decades in Britain have perhaps impacted more profoundly in this field than in any other. The Commission on Social Justice recently reported that nearly two-thirds of people live in households where income is less than the average, and one in three children now grows up in poverty; more than one million people are long-term unemployed, and earnings inequality is greater than at any time since 1886; and racially motivated violence is estimated to have risen faster than almost all other forms of crime over the last decade.

However, socialist lawyers have another role. In addition to the daily task of tackling existing injustices (in and out of court), there is the longer term strategic task of arguing for the law and legal institutions which will reflect the kind of society we aspire to. During 1995 the society launched a campaign designed to take such discussion into the next century: *Justice 2000*. This is intended to provide a focus for this longer term task by enabling progressive lawyers not only to draw together past experiences, but also to propose an alternative legal framework befitting a society committed to democracy and the eradication of poverty, inequality and exploitation. There follows some of the themes the society identified.

After the Brixton disorders in 1981, Lord Scarman conducted an inquiry and made recommendations for the involvement of local people in inner cities in community policing, the planning of local services, education and employment. Though the implementation of these recommendations, largely through the development of the Urban Programme, may have had its roots more in a fear of further riots than a genuine belief in democracy, there is no doubt that the consequences did bring democratic benefits. Community bodies, including Community Relations Councils, Law Centres and advice agencies, flourished.

As government policy changed in the latter half of the 1980s, most of those organisations suffered loss of funds or attacks on their independence. At the same time, sweeping new police powers have been introduced and the last remnants of human resistance are under attack. With the removal of the right to silence, innocent people are more likely to be convicted. And alongside the legal changes, there has been an assault on many of the social rights of the poor. The government now even attempts to erase people's sense of identity by making entitlement to the 'job seekers allowance' dependent upon set values for acceptable personal appearance. Those who don't fit the mould are simply scrapped. Single mothers are demonised and may soon lose many of their rights to housing; juvenile offenders are incarcerated with no regard for their futures.

The government is no longer concerned about the social unrest that might follow from its drastic measures, for it believes it already has in place the machinery for quashing it. Parallels can be drawn with other countries that also pretend to democracy. In 1901 a well known US lawyer, Lyman Abbott, said to the New York Legal Aid Society dinner: 'If ever a time shall come when in this city only the rich man can enjoy law as a doubtful luxury, when the poor who need it most cannot have it, when only a golden key will unlock the door to the courtroom, the seeds of revolution will be sown, the firebrand of revolution will be lighted and put into the hands of men, and they will almost be justified in the revolution which will follow.' No such fears motivate the governments of Britain or the USA in the 1990s.

Social unrest often follows from the limitations of our democracy. There is a range of possible responses to this by the state through the legal system. In the past, the government operated on the basis that protest had, to a certain extent, to be accommodated, in order to legitimise the state and to create stability. But the state's approach to achieving stability has changed in the last fifteen years and its attacks on democratic structures have become harsher. Like many anti-democratic societies around the world, it has removed a range of democratic and social rights and replaced them with repression of expression and protest.

In many ways the emergence of the anti-roads movement reflects a complete loss of confidence by local people in existing procedures. Public inquiries into road schemes tend to exclude any real participation by the people most likely to be affected by the building of a new road or motorway by denying them information, proper representation and resources. In reality, the positioning of a motorway is far more likely to be affected by the requirements of large corporations, whose interests are communicated to government officials by highly paid consultancy firms, than by the needs and wishes of local people. Put in this context, protest, far from undermining democracy, is an essential feature of it.

'For trade unions legitimised coercion rather than democracy rules'

Grave issues of principle have also arisen in Northern Ireland. Since 1968, when the Nationalists in Northern Ireland took to the streets to protest against discrimination in housing, employment and voting rights, the British government has invoked the law ostensibly to suppress terrorism, but in ways which have put the rule of law itself into question. When one measure failed, another was introduced: first internment without trial, then the removal of the right to jury trial, and finally the removal of the right to silence. So fundamental are these human rights breaches that Britain has frequently been found to be in breach of the European Convention on Human Rights. As is so often the case, the first victim of emergency legislation is the law. As the Irish conservative Edmund Burke said: 'People crushed by law have no hope but from power. If laws are their enemies, they will be enemies to the law; and those who have much to hope and nothing to lose will always be dangerous, more or less.'

Organised labour has also been the subject of a massive wave of regressive legislation, with the sole aim of weakening the influence of collective labour rights. In the name of democracy, seven statutes have been imposed on trade unions denying them their autonomy and weakening their collective strength. The threat of sequestration now hangs over every trade union, and the criminal law over individual members. Legitimised coercion rather than democracy now rules.

The legal system, which is orientated almost exclusively to individual rights, has erected huge obstacles, whether legal, procedural, financial or cultural, to the effective expression of collective concerns. Collective action by the working class has thereby been largely suppressed, often in the name of the defence of democratic rights. It is precisely because these forms of action are so potent that they are so strongly resisted, and for that reason it is vital that they are defended. Collective actions in the courts should, in the Haldane Society's view, be developed both to help protect the rights of workers, and with a view to developing a more open and fair system of justice in the future.

No system of justice can work fairly unless all of the players and the administrative machinery are sensitive to fundamental human rights. It is necessary to examine the whole of the structure of the courts, and of the appointments and role of the judiciary, to ensure that equal justice is achieved. If a more just system were to be implemented, the legal profession itself would have responsibilities in protecting a new system of justice.

It is from these perspectives that the Haldane Society, through Bill Bowring, Kate Markus, and Keir Starmer, has accepted the invitation of the editors of *Soundings* to produce this special thematic section of the journal. We have brought together a wide range of contributors: practising and academic lawyers, social policy theorists and researchers, and a former political exile who is now engaged in constructing a new legal order.

We start this special issue with an extraordinarily poignant voice: that of Ken Wiwa, whose father was judicially murdered in Nigeria. Here was law in the form of a blatant sham, but one which, with a few honourable exceptions, was ignored by the rest of the world until too late. The Abacha regime in Nigeria cares nothing for human rights or even the procedural niceties.

The new South Africa is different. Ken Wiwa's voice is followed, appropriately, by an address by Professor Kader Asmal, for many years an exile, but now a Minister in South Africa's Government of National Unity. His text, first delivered as a speech at Liberty's Human Rights Convention, in London in June 1995, opens up a perspective diametrically opposed to that offered to the people of Nigeria. The ANC's struggle can only be vindicated, he says, by a permanent structure of fundamental rights.

Of course, the United Kingdom is no stranger to the gulf between law and justice, and Mike Mansfield QC, well-known for his tireless advocacy in terrorist cases and miscarriage appeals, and author of a fine recent book on injustice in Britain, addresses the issues raised by the Colin Stagg case. Jonathan Cooper looks at the 'MOD Four' case, and the fact that grave violations of human rights cannot be remedied in English courts. He argues that the system for upholding democracy in the United Kingdom is heavily flawed. But the European Convention on Human Rights has its own limitations, and will not necessarily remedy the position of minorities in Britain.

There is another - perhaps the paradigmatic - liberal democracy, with its own problematic relation to questions of law and justice, not least in relation to the 'death row' phenomenon. Michael Howard has recently been casting envious eyes at the 'three strikes and you're out' laws and boot camps now being introduced in the United States of America. Ethan Raup presents a graphic account of the politics and strategy of the US 'reforms', and will provide an invaluable resource to those seeking to oppose the Tory politics of knee-jerk populism.

All of this poses the question of whether legal reform is possible or feasible; and, if so, what should be the measure of present failure and future improvement. Professor John Griffith, who has been the best-informed and most compelling critic of the undemocratic and often reactionary nature of the judiciary, says that the influence of the senior judiciary has increased and ought to be diminished. He fears a new wave of 'judicial supremacism', in which judges are beginning to contemplate, in suitable cases, the overturning of the work of the democratically elected legislature. Indeed, this already happens when European Community law is concerned. Incorporation of a Bill of Rights or of the European Convention could simply give more power to non-elected judges. Griffith therefore calls for a Constitutional Court; but one appointed not simply from the judiciary, but from a range of persons able to deal with the mix of legal, political and social problems with which they will be presented.

Social and economic rights have traditionally been neglected, on the grounds that they are not justifiable, and would be too expensive and impractical to implement. In our view, this is a reflection of a society's priorities. One area in which the British government has been found particularly wanting is that of trade union rights. Professor Keith Ewing examines the Wilson case (where a trade unionist refused to sign a 'personal contract'), and draws from the experience of the International Labour Organisation to show that if there is a change of government, social and economic rights, particularly union rights, must be given far more prominence.

Professor Ruth Lister has for some time been at the forefront of research into social policy. She reflects on her experience as a member of Labour's *Commission on Social Justice*, and on her disappointment that the debate on the Commission's Report seems to have 'disappeared behind closed doors'. She fears that the New Labour leadership, for all their enthusiastic welcome for the Commission's Report, will simply 'cherry pick' those elements which chime most closely with the New Labour agenda. And Anna Coote of IPPR confronts a number of the issues surrounding social and economic rights, especially the arguments made in order to marginalise their importance.

To what extent can, or should, critique of the law and legal system and condemnation of injustice be informed by theory? In the final article in this special issue, Bill Bowring looks at the often unspoken liberal underpinnings of even the most radical legal discourse, and at the efforts of the Critical Legal Studies movement to provide an alternative. Post-modern theory has, in recent years, begun to exert something of an hegemonic influence in critical legal circles, but he casts doubt upon the remedies proposed by post-modernists. He also looks at the alternatives offered by Habermas's recent inquiries into law, and the critical realist movement.

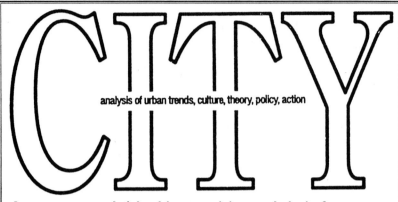

CITY

analysis of urban trends, culture, theory, policy, action

**A new quarterly* looking at cities and their futures...
with views from academics, architects, artists,
cartoonists, community activists, journalists,
photographers, planners, even property developers...**

Each issue is published in book form with a broad theme.

The theme for the introductory issue (192 pages) is:
"IT ALL COMES TOGETHER IN LOS ANGELES?"
Is L.A. *the* post-modern city or image of the future?

What about Tokyo, Hong Kong, Jakarta, Shanghai, Moscow, Milan,
Sarajevo or London, Manchester and Bristol? <u>And what can we do?</u>
We look at this range of experience and consider some answers.

Contributors include: Steve Bell, Peter Buchanan, Peter Hall, David
Harvey, Will Hutton, Alain Lipietz, Doreen Massey, Enzo Mingione,
Suzanne Moore, Alison Ravetz, Brian Robson, Peter Sellars, Deyan
Sudjic.

* Incorporating 'Regenerating Cities'

SUBSCRIPTIONS

☐ Individual £30   ☐ Institutional £75

For overseas subscribers add £5.00

Name _____

Address _____

_____

_____ Post Code _____

Please make cheques payable to 'City' and send to:
CITY, 5 Dryden Street, Covent Garden, London WC2E 9NB.

The murder of Ken Saro-Wiwa

Ken Wiwa

At midnight of a mild November night in Auckland, New Zealand, I retired to my hotel room. I felt a strange sense of calm, resignation even. I was unaware that a half way around the world, my father had just been executed. Despite feeling weary but relaxed, I could not sleep. A few hours later, when I heard movements and low voices outside my bedroom, I sensed that something was up.

The previous week had been fraught with tension following the announcement that a tribunal had just sentenced my father and eight other Ogonis to death. Since there was no right of appeal against the verdict, I had embarked on a punishing round of interviews in the world's media to try to raise awareness of their plight and thus get the world to intervene to save them.

As luck would have it the biennial Commonwealth Heads of Government Meeting (CHGM), was due to convene in Auckland the following week. So with the help of the Body Shop who had led the campaign on behalf of the Ogoni people in the UK since 1993, I flew across the world.

In Auckland, I had no real idea of what I was going to do, but it seemed an ideal opportunity to get the Commonwealth to plead with the Nigerian authorities for clemency for the Ogoni nine. At the airport I met my friend Richard Boele, an Australian of Dutch origin who had worked on the Ogoni issue for the Unrepresented Nations and People's Organisation at the Hague.

Earlier in the year Richard had bravely posed as a tourist in Nigeria to compile an excellent report on the human rights abuses of Ogonis by Nigerian soldiers in the area. Together with a team of volunteers, an organic plan for the CHGM evolved, which co-ordinated press briefings and interviews with trying to get lobbying opportunities with the various government delegations in Auckland on the back of the publicity.

Our efforts turned out much better than we had anticipated; at the beginning of CHGM, French testing of nuclear weapons and Britain's support for Chirac over the issue threatened to dominate the conference. But by the end of the CHGM, Nigeria was the talk of not just Auckland but the world. Of course we cannot claim the credit since in carrying out the executions at such a sensitive time, the Nigerian regime were defying world opinion.

However, whatever triumphs we felt we had achieved in Auckland in the early days of CHGM, a sense of foreboding soon descended on me. When the Nigerian delegation arrived in Auckland, I met a friend of my father's on the delegation who looked me squarely in the eye and urged me to be strong over the next few days. That day news filtered through that executioners had arrived at my father's cell only to be turned away because all the necessary paper work had not been completed for the prisoners to be released into the custody of the hangmen.

In desperation we tried to contact more government delegations to impress upon them the need to move fast. That afternoon, I met Prime Minister Chretien of Canada and informed him of developments. He assured me that they were doing everything possible. I felt slightly cheered by his words; the Canadians had been unstinting in their support throughout our crisis. But joy soon turned to anguish when I noticed for the first time that Nigerian security agents were present at a press conference I gave following my meeting with Prime Minister Chretien.

Later that evening, having felt we had done everything we could, I met the rest of my team to have dinner. Though I felt tired, dinner went down well and there was much joking and laughing at our table.

I took the news of my father's death stoically and cast my mind back to a letter my father had once written from his detention cell. 'My son', he wrote, 'prepare for the worst, neither death nor imprisonment scares me'. I remember receiving the letter and barely dwelling on the implications of those words.

In the months following that letter, I had reorganised myself to campaign to save my father's life. The nuts and bolts of living became secondary to the campaign - first to highlight my father's plight, then to articulate what the Ogoni struggle meant.

In that campaign I was bolstered by the fact that the Ogonis had a strong case and by a sense that my father, like many crusaders before him, might have to spend some time in jail. That would be the worst. It was all part of the game called human rights struggle. Not once, despite my father's brave words, did I prepare myself for the very worst.

Earlier this year my father had smuggled another note from his jail cell and in it he wrote 'the environment is man's first right'. He had written them on hearing that he had been awarded the 1995 Goldman Environmental Award for Africa for his contribution to grassroots activism. For my father and the Ogoni people the award was further justification, and some comfort in our struggle to safeguard our rights from the predatory forces of a giant multinational company and a brutal military regime.

When, on 26 July 1993, in an address to the Third General Assembly of the Unrepresented Nations and Peoples Organisation (UNPO) at the Hague, my father had accused Shell Oil company of 'waging an ecological war against the Ogoni', he was speaking from a position of some optimism. Barely six months earlier on 4 January, 300,000 of the half million Ogoni had come out in support of the ideals of the Movement for the Survival of the Ogoni People (MOSOP), now led by my father.

MOSOP had been formed in 1990 to challenge the situation whereby a community which had contributed to the exchequer an estimated $30 billion in oil revenue found itself without basic amenities, and living in a wretched environment being daily assaulted by oil exploration.

But my father's sense of euphoria was short-lived because both the Nigerian authorities and Shell were already planning to neutralise the growing campaign of the Ogoni people. Leaked documents of meetings between Shell officials in February 1993 advised that 'international networking... is at work and gives rise to the possibility that internationally organised protest could develop' and went on to suggest that 'movements of key players, what they say and to whom is more effectively monitored'.

And there it was that by some crazy coincidence my father was arrested in July of that year and charged with sedition over some political crime during the ill-fated elections of that year. He faced the death penalty until a change of government probably spared his life. But his experiences in detention, rather than deterring him, merely stiffened his resolve. Bolstered by the support he had received from the international community during his detention, he became more outspoken and bolder. It was this misconception that the international community would come to his aid which led to his demise.

When General Abacha seized power at the end of 1993, the change in government signalled a renewed and more sinister crusade against all libertarian and opposition groups in Nigeria. But General Abacha was a friend of my father. Despite the signals that Abacha was more ruthless than any other dictator in Nigerian history, my father felt he could push the Ogoni case bolstered by his international contacts and personal friendship with the new Head of State.

'The misconception that the international community would come to his aid led to his demise'

So six months later, when my father once again found himself in the framework of Nigerian justice, after four prominent and moderate Ogoni chiefs were murdered, he must have believed that it was yet another part of the process. At first my father was charged with inciting a crowd of Ogoni youths to murder the moderate Ogoni chiefs. The implication was that my father had been a radical, power-crazed despot who wanted the moderate leaders out of the way.

But the prosecution found it very difficult to fit my father with the crime; they were forced to accept reluctantly that he did not address any crowd on the day of the riot and was actually being led away by the security forces at the time of the riot which let to the deaths of the four chiefs.

Next the authorities fell upon the idea that my father's campaigning activities had let to a breakdown in law and order in Ogoni which ultimately resulted in the riot which led to the deaths of the Ogoni chiefs. From this wild extrapolation and deviation from the basic tenets of civilised law, they arrived at a verdict which my father and eight other Ogoni activists paid for with their lives.

The Nigerian authorities have tried to paint the tribunal which tried my father as a valid instrument within the legal system in Nigeria. However many independent observers at the tribunal, from within and without Nigeria, came away from the court room with the distinct impression that this was a politically motivated trial with very little basis in fact. The British lawyer Michael Birnbaum QC also found that the tribunal showed very little concern for internationally accepted standards of law. He compiled a thorough report for Article 19 based on his findings at the tribunal, having spent a week there as an observer.

After the executions, Nigeria was roundly condemned by leaders around the world for the 'judicial murder' of the nine Ogoni activists. Nigeria and Shell have caught the flak of international outrage and public opprobrium. Both organisations have subsequently launched damage limitation exercises aimed at supplying information to discredit my father.

The results have led to assaults on his character from some heavyweight commentators in the press here in the UK. We have also seen the bizarre notion of a government feeling the need to take out an advert abroad over a point of law in their country. To outsiders it smacks of weakness and desperation. The advertisement merely adds fuel to the fire. Whoever has been hired to do public relations for the Nigerian government is taking them for an expensive ride to ridicule.

Shell have also weighed in with their public relations machinery. Articles have suddenly appeared from people with very little knowledge of Ogoni praising Shell's efforts on behalf of the people. I have also seen and heard some Ogonis praising Shell's efforts on behalf of their people.

I cannot even pretend to be disappointed or surprised by this because I have observed over the last year that organisations like Shell and this Nigerian regime do not care about justice or concepts like fair play. They are only concerned with protecting their economic interests and their image. And in that goal innocent people are expendable. I know this from bitter experience.

If anybody wants to question this view, they should simply ask either organisation for their detailed and long-term plans for the Ogoni people and their environment. And should they provide these, I would be interested to see what mechanisms were proposed for independent and constant monitoring of such plans.

My father and eight Ogonis were judicially murdered. It is a phrase that trips off the tongue, but to be at the receiving end leaves one dumbfounded. Redress is arduous, and in the long run possibly futile. The murdered men are gone forever. However, if civilised behaviour is to be upheld as a desirable maxim, it is as well that governments, commercial organisations and individuals abide by and support rigorously the application of civilised legal standards across the world. Anything else can only lead us back to a darker age.

THE OGONI COMMUNITY ASSOCIATION

The Ogoni Community Association UK was set up in 1993 by the Ogoni people living in Britain as an affiliate to the Movement for the Survival of the Ogoni people. It aims to focus world attention on the plight of the Ogoni people by peaceful campaigning and to promote their emancipation through the Ogoni Bill of Rights, adopted by general acclaim of the Ogoni people on 26 August 1990 at Bori, Rivers State.

WHAT YOU CAN DO TO HELP

■ *REGISTER AS A SUPPORTER with the Ogoni Community Association or send a donation to the Association or the Ogoni Foundation. Address: 3-4 Albion Place, London W6 0LT. Tel: 0181 563 8614.*

■ *WRITE STATING YOUR CONCERNS about human rights and environmental abuses in Ogoni and Nigeria to the Nigerian High Commissioner at: The Nigerian High Commission, Nigeria House, 9 Northumberland Avenue, London WC2B 5NX.*

■ *DEMONSTRATE outside the Nigerian Commission in London. Demonstrators are there most evenings from around 5pm to 7pm. Registered supporters will be informed of organised demonstrations.*

■ *BOYCOTT SHELL: Demonstrate outside Shell petrol stations; sell (all but one) Shell investments you or your company may have; write and protest to John Jennings, Chairman of Shell at : Shell Transport and Trading Company Ltd, Shell Centre, London SE1 7NA.*

■ *GET MORE INFORMATION on environmental campaigns from Greenpeace (0171-354 5100) or Friends of the Earth (0171-490 1555). For human rights campaigns contact Amnesty International (0171-814 6200).*

THE OGONI FOUNDATION

Charity Registration Number: 1050502

The Ogoni Foundation aims to relieve poverty and sickness - in particular to provide aid to the needy in Nigeria or persons formerly resident there. It also aims to advance the education of people living in the UK and Nigeria in the Ogoni languages, traditions and cultures by providing a Saturday school. Finally, to help preserve the environment in Africa and the world through provision of educational information and projects, and by assisting local conservation projects.

Principles into Practice:

Bills of Rights at Work

Kader Asmal

Kader Asmal, formerly an exile and now a member of the South African government, discusses South Africa's proposed bill of rights, which will eventually become part of the nation's new constitution.

A constitution, and in particular a bill of rights, must reflect the soul of the nation. All bills of rights contain certain common elements, but no two are identical. The reason is simple: a bill of rights takes its character from the struggle through which it is won. The South African struggle has produced its own distinctive bill of rights which is a monument to years of opposition to tyranny. But it is more than a monument. It is the embodiment of our nation's needs and aspirations. It is the Jewel in the Crown of the new constitutional order under which South Africans live. My purpose is to describe briefly how it came about and to explain what, in practice, it means for the nation.

A few short years ago, South African socio-political life appeared to be irreparably damaged by years of one-party rule and prolonged executive lawlessness. Over the decades a systematic policy of racism caused massive suffering and death, uprooted millions, disrupted family life and forced thousands into exile. The courts had become effectively inaccessible to the majority and the legal system was largely discredited. The rule of law did not exist. South Africans were at war with one another. There seemed to be little hope for peace, let alone democracy.

Yet, the period from 1990 to the present produced a remarkable turn-about. The story has been well-chronicled, and I shall not attempt to repeat it. Suffice it to say that, against the tide of universal expectation, we became one nation under one flag, committed to open government and democratic process.

We now live under the sovereignty of an Interim Constitution which is widely praised as just and democratic, even if it is flawed and untidy in some respects. Though the nation faces residual tension, even conflict, there is no doubt that the overwhelming majority of South Africans enthusiastically support the new order.

The process is, of course, not over. Indeed, constitutional negotiators are hard at work preparing the draft of a final Constitution. And the durable culture that goes with successful democracy still seems a little way off, and requires articulation and nurturing. Yet the ground-work has been well done. Thirty-eight constitutional principles effectively serve as a broad set of instructions for the current drafters of the final Constitution. The entrenchment of these principles was the direct result of the negotiating process, where minority parties, for whatever reason, felt they needed to prevent a majority party from rewriting the constitution on its own terms.

The ANC had long advocated a system of constitutional supremacy with a justiciable bill of rights, as expressed in our 'Constitutional Guidelines' of 1988, which built in turn on the Freedom Charter of 1955. Other groups, led by liberal democrats, had also long fostered the constitutional entrenchment of human rights protection. It is ironic that the former National Party government, which had previously dismissed a bill of rights as unnecessary and undesirable, had become a trusting convert to the idea by 1990. Whatever the motives, and there were negative ones, this was one of the issues on which there was universal agreement, and the parties were at one that any constitutional settlement would have a bill of rights as one of its foundation stones.

These rights (which are contained in Chapter 3 of the Interim Constitution) are adjudicated on, in the final instance, by the Constitutional Court, an independent body of immense significance in the new order. The rights in Chapter 3 are for the most part stated simply and broadly. Limitation and suspension of the rights are subject to the most stringent conditions. The courts interpreting Chapter 3 are bound, and I quote, to 'promote the values which underlie an open and democratic society based on freedom and equality'; and the courts are further directed to refer to public international law and foreign caselaw where applicable.

Hence, although we have arrived at our own home-grown arrangements in our own way, they are in the best of company internationally. We have the constitutional basis for peace and progress. Though not yet there, we can at last aspire to Gandhi's description of democracy 'where the weakest should have the same opportunity as the strongest'. And, instead of seeing South Africa pilloried, and for good reason, at international forums on human rights, our country can be an enthusiastic and acceptable part of the celebration of human rights.

The intention of some of the parties at the negotiating table was that the rights in Chapter 3 would operate primarily in the vertical relationship between the state and the individual; that is against the state only, and not against corporate bodies and individuals. There is scope for horizontal application, that is where individuals or private bodies are concerned and not the state, since the interpretation clause of the chapter directs the courts to 'have due regard to the spirit, purpose and objects' of the chapter when 'interpreting any law and customary law' - which undoubtedly encourages a rights culture to permeate all areas of the law.

'The bill of rights was one of the issues on which there was universal agreement'

It was feared in some quarters, however, that the exclusively vertical application of the bill of rights would allow private institutions to discriminate on racial grounds. In effect, apartheid would be privatised, not eradicated. It must be noted that chapter 3 is a transitional bill of rights only, and the verticality/horizontality question will be high on the agenda of the drafters of the final bill. Even now, a creative interpretation by the Constitutional Court may well see horizontal application approved. An important factor to consider is that some of the large companies in South Africa wield immense economic power, and they should not be permitted to infringe the rights of individuals merely by virtue of their 'private status'.

Chapter 3 applies to all law in force, and the Constitutional Court has the power to declare null and void any legislation which infringes a right contained in the Charter. A limitation placed on any right may be justified, however, if it is reasonable and justifiable in an open and democratic society based on freedom and equality. The last-mentioned five words - based on freedom and equality - illustrate the efforts of two distinct human rights traditions in South Africa, libertarians and egalitarians. The former tradition values individual liberty most highly and the egalitarian tradition is more decisively equality-orientated. In terms of limitation and interpretation, freedom and equality are carefully given equal status. It is clear, however, from the tenor of the fundamental rights chapter, that equality is the central aim, equality which emphasises equal treatment in substance, and moves beyond mere formal equality, since corrective action is necessary to compensate for past deprivation and disadvantage. As Franklin D Roosevelt noted: 'True individual freedom cannot exist without economic security and independence.'

The equality clause guarantees not only equality before the law and equal protection of the law, but also contains anti-discrimination and affirmative action clauses. Restitution and redistribution of land are also included in the equality clause.

'Such quantum leaps have made it an exciting experience living and working in South Africa through the transition'

The right to life is stated in broad terms in the chapter and left for adjudication by the Constitutional Court. This immediately raised the question of capital punishment, and the death penalty was emphatically outlawed in 1995 by unanimous decision of that court in an incandescent finding which augurs well for future South African enlightenment. Another issue with regard to the right to life is abortion; and, although the question is subject to Parliamentary inquiry, the current conservative legislation has not been challenged in the courts as yet.

The bill of rights protects the classical civil and political rights. For the first time in South Africa there is a constitutional entrenchment of the right of all South Africans to cast their vote, and the right to campaign for a political party and to stand for political office. This illustrates the extent to which the country has, as it were, 'leap-frogged' - from one that forbade most people from voting and joining mainstream political movements, to one that entrenches their right to vote and to join whichever party they like. It is quantum leaps like this which have made it such an exciting experience living and working in South Africa through the transition.

A number of rights were included to ensure free and fair political activity during the elections, and these have much wider application than the election process in April 1994. This group of rights includes the right to freedom and security of the person, freedom of association and of movement. These rights would perhaps be taken for granted in many other countries, but under the apartheid regime freedom of movement was denied as a matter of policy by tyrannical measures such as pass laws, house arrest, detention - indeed, in the crudest form, the dispatch of dissidents by official death squads, as we are discovering daily in court disclosures.

Certain interests not universally thought of as rights have been elevated to rights status, such as the right to access to information and to administrative justice. Both were included to do away with the obsessive secrecy and executive autocracy of the previous government under which clandestine wars, political assassinations, bannings and detentions went unchecked. The administrative justice clause introduces a 'reasonableness' standard for administrative acts performed or decisions taken. In addition officials may be required to give written reasons for action taken, and are unable, generally, to hide behind the veil of official secrecy as in the past.

It was felt that the inclusion of certain socio-economic rights could not be postponed until a final bill of rights came into force. These are in the area of children's rights and rights to education, expressed in the most innovative manner. Children's rights, for instance, include the right to basic nutrition and basic health and social services. Accordingly the Department of Health has granted free health care for children under six and pregnant women. Already we are seeing fine principles put into practice.

The environmental right is formulated negatively, in that everyone is entitled to an environment which is not detrimental to his or her health or well-being. This must place an onus on the government to provide water and sanitation, housing and electricity, roads and parks, in fact everything which is conducive to health and well-being, particularly to formerly deprived communities. The Reconstruction and Development Programme is addressing these needs on a massive and imaginative scale, and is proving to be instrumental in changing the whole thrust of public financing and development, with major impact on the private sector.

It is more than likely that additional socio-economic rights will be included in the final bill of rights, expressing the rights in positive rather than negative terms and covering, for instance, a right to work, and environmental or third generation rights such as the right to conservation areas. The extension of socio-economic and environmental rights is not approved by all parties in negotiations. Some believe that the bill of rights should contain only those rights which can be enforced in every case, for fear of bringing the rights instrument into disrepute where budgetary restraints or lack of capacity or resources make performance impossible. This view is often held by libertarians, whereas egalitarians - and I am among them - would argue that these rights are not optional extras; that problems of affordability must be resolved; that such rights are vital in the great task of bringing about practical and not mere formal equality.

The right to property and the right freely to engage in economic activity were hotly debated in the negotiations, and opinions were divided mainly along libertarian and egalitarian lines. The egalitarians feared that these rights would allow those who had become rich during the apartheid years to secure these 'ill-gotten gains', thereby further entrenching economic disparity between rich and poor and threatening the fabric of society. The compromise reached gave both rights a place in the chapter, but each was qualified in some detail. The property right is qualified by a provision relating to expropriation to enable the government's land restitution and redistribution programme to return land to those forcibly evicted under the previous government, and to give the disadvantaged access to land for the first time. In the same way, the right relating to economic activity is qualified by a section which states in broad terms that the Reconstruction and Development Programme shall take preference. In the field of labour relations, the same give and take occurs, and the right of organised labour to strike is countered by a lock-out entitlement in favour of management. Various issues to do with labour promise to be among the more difficult facing South Africa in the immediate future.

To have any practical use, the rights in Chapter 3 must be exercised on the ground, and where they are infringed enforcement must be sought. As an example of principle into practice, one may consider human rights violations by the police. Formerly it was a pointless or even highly dangerous undertaking to make complaints against the police. Where investigations took place, the police generally investigated their own misconduct, and not surprisingly were frequently exonerated. The Minister of Safety and Security is to establish an independent complaints directorate (ICD) responsible for investigating complaints of police misconduct and abuse of power. Under this arrangement, members of the public can rely on an even-handed and thorough investigation of complaints. This is but one example of 'principle into practice'.

A very significant step forward with regard to rights enforcement is the extension of *locus standi*. Group actions, public interest actions and class actions are permitted when exercising rights contained in Chapter 3. Juristic persons can also use the rights contained in the Chapter. Since corporate bodies can clearly exercise rights in terms of Chapter 3, the question may be asked whether rights may be enforced against them.

W hatever advance it represents on past South African law and practice, the fundamental rights chapter represents a level of compromise reached after much dispute and vacillation between the major parties. It is to be welcomed as a bridgehead on which a fuller and more thoroughly debated and representative bill of rights can be built. The main concerns will be horizontality/verticality and, more importantly, which of the further second and third generation rights should be added, considering the linkage between enforceability and affordability.

I have no doubt that the foundation is there for a permanent structure of fundamental rights which will meet our needs, and help to confirm our country's new international role and place. It is a vindication of our struggle.

The struggle for liberation in South Africa has not been only a struggle for the vote. It has also been a struggle for freedom from hunger, poverty, landlessness, and homelessness. Our final Constitution must reflect the multi-dimensional and all-encompassing nature of the struggle for liberation. Our freedom is impoverished if our Constitution reflects only some of the rights and freedoms for which we have fought.

JUSTICE 2000

The Campaign of the Haldane Society of Socialist Lawyers

"If ever a time shall come when in this city only the rich can enjoy the law as a doubtful luxury, when the poor who need it most cannot have it, when only a golden key will unlock the door to the courtroom, the seeds of revolution will be sown, the firebrand of revolution will be lighted and put in the hands of men, and they will almost be justified in the revolution which will follow"

Lyman Abbott 1901

Lawyers need to strive to achieve their role in the transformation of society and the protection of justice. With this campaign, the Haldane Society aims to start a debate that will generate principles informing that struggle, both now and in a future democratic society here and internationally.

For futher details: HSSL 20/21 Tooks Court, London EC4A 0171 242 2897

Systemic Injustice

Michael Mansfield QC

*In spite of the spectacular series of overturned
convictions in the early 1990s, nothing has
fundamentally changed for wrongly convicted
defendants. In fact, the many changes introduced
by Michael Howard have loaded the machinery
even more heavily in favour of the prosecution.*

The enduring problem with the British system of Criminal Justice is a singular
lack of fundamental principles clearly stated, which at least set an agenda or target
or minimum standards. As we approach the millennium not only are we as far as
ever from even incorporating the European Convention of Human Rights into
domestic legislation, we also have one of the worst records on human rights
decisions in the Court of European Rights at Strasbourg. Worst still our attitude to
the court's decisions is one of arrogant disregard, dismissal and denigration. In the
Brogan case (detention) we derogated; the death on the rock decision was derided
and the government claimed it would ignore it; and recently the Gallagher decision
on exclusion orders was dismissed as a mere technicality.

All this must be set alongside the Home Secretary's blatant and equal disregard
for domestic legislation. There were, by the end of 1995, nine Judicial Review
decisions against the Home Secretary covering such issues as compensation for
the victims of crime, disclosure of information for prisoners serving life, wrongful
denial of parole, autonomy of local police authorities and the entry rights of the
Reverend Moon. The Learmont Report, delayed as it was until after keynote
speeches and suitable tub thumping at the Tory Party conference in the autumn,

was another indictment of this Home Secretary. Heads fell but not his, and despite cabinet rules about the responsibility of ministers for the activities of their departments, the Home Secretary has set one of the worst examples of adherence to the law.

I t's hardly surprising therefore that the Home Secretary has managed to alienate every single element which comprises our system of justice. Probation officers and magistrates are themselves currently challenging him within the courts and the Lord Chief Justice and Lord Donaldson seriously question his prison and sentencing policy both in terms of its effectiveness and the ramifications for the independence of the judiciary. Whilst attempting to fend off criticisms of despotism Michael Howard is at the same time within Europe blocking attempts to adopt a common policy against racism. This would have involved strengthening laws against public incitement to discrimination, violence or racial hatred; prohibiting participation in the activities of groups or organisations or associations concerned in such activities; and the prohibition of writings, pictures or other media containing racist or xenophobic manifestos. And again, whilst condemning the execution of Ken Saro-Wiwa as judicial murder, the government is unofficially notifying refugee groups in the United Kingdom that Nigeria is to be regarded as safe and therefore is part of an unofficial 'white' list of countries from which refugees are not acceptable.

W hat we have is the clearest form of moral bankruptcy, with no investment in principles concerned with human rights and justice. This explains why there has been no progress internally towards any reduction in the risks of miscarriages of justice. It is as if the iniquities suffered by the Guildford Four, the Birmingham Six, the Maguires, the Tottenham Three, the Cardiff Three and Judith Ward have never occurred. None of the lessons have been heeded and responsibility within the system has barely been recognised. Measures necessary for ensuring the protection of the vulnerable; full prosecutorial disclosure; the integrity of scientific evidence; the equality of access to financial resources and legal aid; and procedures for the thorough and efficient reinvestigation of wrongful convictions are not in place. These defects were all exposed in the cases cited, and the public, which voiced considerable disquiet at the time, may be forgiven for believing such remedies have been effected. Instead there has been disgraceful delay and inaction, in the hope that no one will notice and anxiety will be distracted by the 'law and order'-'prison works' debate.

The plethora of legislation railroaded through Parliament by the Home Secretary has either ignored the defects, exacerbated them or merely tinkered with them. The main statute, the Criminal Justice and Public Order Act 1994, most of which came into effect in 1995, substantially undermines any protection for the vulnerable and concentrates its attention on prison building, prison sentencing and limitations on the democratic freedom of assembly and protest. The Bill establishing the Criminal Cases Review Authority has merely produced a poor replication of the Police Complaints Authority; and despite being the one feature that most pundits agreed on, even before the Royal Commission required establishment, the review authority is still-born. In particular there is no authority established, as the Royal Commission indicated, for monitoring forensic science laboratories after poor, false or inadequate scientific and expert evidence. This was to have been a forensic science advisory council. The Crime Bill, as D.A. Thomas, this country's leading authority on sentencing, has argued, will simply add to a welter of ill thought out and inconsistent legislation. Additionally there are statutory proposals on disclosure - which have received support from Labour Party Spokesman Jack Straw - which will increase the burden on the defence and lessen it upon the prosecution.

'There is no real opposition to these moves other than within the legal fraternity itself'

Given what has been happening in the Courts while all this political machination has been occurring, there can be no cause for complacency; there should be considerable concern that there is no real opposition to these moves other than within the legal fraternity itself. Recent examples of miscarriages of justice demonstrate yet again how dire and urgent is the situation.

Let us examine the Rachel Nickell murder which occurred on Wimbledon Common on 15 July 1992. This is a case that is not subject to all the comments that were made about miscarriages arising in the 1960s; arrests in this case were made under provisions that are current, and in the wake of all those lessons supposedly learnt as a result of earlier miscarriages. However, this case suffered, yet again, from one of the fundamental and psychological difficulties that besets our system, as I tried to explain in my book *Presumed Guilty*: an investigative authority which imbues itself with an unmovable belief in the guilt of the suspect it decides to target. This view has been echoed recently by a member of the Crown

Prosecution Service who has resigned because of the pressure brought by police officers in charge of cases wanting 'their man' brought to court.

Colin Stagg was first arrested on 15 September 1992 and interrogated for three days. He answered every question put to him and gave a full account of his movements on the day in question.He offered an alibi for the material time and denied being responsible. His home was searched and nothing was found there or anywhere else which linked him or might have linked him with the crime. The police didn't even have enough evidence to warrant charging him and after three days he was released. However the police felt they had the right man and continued their pursuit of Colin Stagg by means of an undercover operation as a result of which he was rearrested. For the purposes of this operation they enlisted the services of a clinical psychologist, Paul Britton. He prepared a profile of the type of person he would expect the offender to be, bearing in mind the nature and general circumstances surrounding the killing. It was his opinion that the murderer would fall within a small subclass of male sexual deviants who would in his opinion betray a number of relatively peculiar characteristics or sexual idiosyncrasies. He thought that given the appropriate opportunity the murderer would be disposed to reveal extreme sexual fantasies and ultimately confess the murder. Thereafter a woman police officer set about seducing Colin Stagg over a period of some seven months. She introduced herself by letter and indicated an interest in sexual deviation and fantasy. There came a time when it appeared that no confession was forthcoming and the undercover officer then made it a condition of continuing her liaison with him that he should admit the murder. Despite initial denials he did begin to describe the nature of the killing as he understood it but there were serious discrepancies

'The investigative authority imbues itself with an unmovable belief in the guilt of the suspect'

with what had actually happened. Nevertheless, Mr Britton, who was described by the judge as pulling the strings of the operation throughout, was led to conclude a precise overlap between his profile killer and the man the accused revealed himself to be in the fantasies expressed to the officer. Colin Stagg was rearrested and interviewed but on the second occasion exercised his right to silence.

What is astonishing is not merely the nature of the investigation or the arrest, but the fact that the process of prosecution got under way and lasted as long as it did, right up to the doors of the Old Bailey - when it was only the intervention to the High Court Judge Mr Justice Ognall that prevented the risk of yet another miscarriage of justice occurring. He did so in strong and uncompromising terms: 'I would be the first to acknowledge the very great pressures on the police in their pursuit of this grave inquiry but I am afraid that this behaviour betrays not only an excess of zeal but a substantial attempt to incriminate a suspect by positive and deceptive conduct of the grossest kind.' This must have been plain from the outset to those in charge of the police inquiry, as well as to all those responsible for taking prosecutorial decisions; nevertheless this case survived the pre-committal stage of legal scrutiny, the committal stage in front of a magistrate, and the pre-trial stage through to 14 September 1994. It is one of the clearest examples of an attempt to circumvent both the letter and the spirit of the Police and Criminal Evidence Act 1984. It also invokes a highly questionable area of expert evidence. In the light of the abolition, effectively, of the right to silence - despite protestations to the contrary by the judiciary - one has to ask whether, were Colin Stagg to be arrested under the Howard regime, his silence on the second occasion on interview might not now be used as an extra limb of material to be held against a defendant at the trial stage.

The scope of scientific evidence gives rise to special concern. Firstly, there has been an increase in the use of experts for all sorts of purposes, sometimes without a proper consideration of whether there is a legitimate science underlying the expertise. Secondly this has occurred without provision of adequate facilities for the defence. This area demonstrates more clearly than any other the retrograde nature of our system of justice, dominated as it increasingly is by the exigencies of the market place. From now on police investigation is going to be encouraged through the Police and Public Order Act 1994 to concentrate on the interview room and to cut back on the expenditure involved in more reliable forms of investigation requiring careful and detailed analysis of the scene of a crime.

The most significant recent change to affect the application of forensic science to criminal investigation in England and Wales excluding London came with the introduction in 1991 of direct charging for scientific services to the Police. When this happened the police began to be charged for each item they submitted for examination and they became free to choose whether they stayed with the laboratories they usually utilised or chose something cheaper elsewhere. The knock-on effect is that officers in charge of investigation are extremely reluctant about sending more than they have to for forensic analysis; and as, on the whole, they are untrained in scientific analysis, they are unclear about what should be examined. This means they will not involve scientists at the scene of a crime, where the process of selection is most important and effective; where interpretation of aspects of the scene, blood stain patterns and trace elements are best discerned by a forensic scientist qualified to comment. Even with those items for analysis which the police choose to select, there is, it appears, an arbitrary limit on the amount of money that can be spent in relation to any particular exhibit. Some enquiries, for example fraud, will not involve any examination unless a certain value is triggered; that is, no fraud under £50,000 merits any kind of handwriting analysis should there be forgery in issue. The results of this approach are second-rate short-circuit solutions and it almost certainly means that evidence which might exculpate a suspect, or might provide innocent or alternative sources for incriminating evidence, will be

'Officers are extremely reluctant about sending more than they have to for forensic analysis'

overlooked or sidelined. The defence is equally trammelled by economic forces. The legal aid authorities are slow to authorise expenditure on forensic scientists; either they say none is required at all; or they say you have to choose someone geographically proximate to the scene; or they say you can only spend a specified sum of money; and in any event they delay final settlement of bills for an excessive period of time. The end result is a climate of fear within which lawyers and experts are reluctant to take any decisions lest at the end of the day there is no payment.

Beyond these complexities are some fundamental flaws. The main one concerns the complete absence of any system of accreditation and regulation within the forensic science profession. It is impossible for courts, let alone lay clients, to understand what scientific issues are involved and which experts are relevant to those issues. For example the study of DNA is not one cohesive science; DNA is not a finger print and it is not as reliable as it is made out to be. Yet there are major police enquiries proceeding on the basis that serious incursions into individual privacy can be made in order to obtain blood samples for comparison. And resistance to such invitations runs the risk of being interpreted as a sign of guilt. However, as the recent exposure by the Equinox television series showed, there are serious reservations about this area. It involves a multitude of disciplines including biology, chemistry, genetics and statistics. In all of these fields there is the readily understood propensity for human error. The DNA process involves at least eleven different stages. There is no one expert who can cover this adequately, and there is, as the Royal Commission reveals, a dearth of English experts in all these fields. What Michael Howard should be considering is a national forensic science service equally accessible to all, properly funded, with a research back-up, and an institute of forensic science attached to the major universities of this country. None of this is being currently contemplated. On the contrary, the forensic science services laboratory has shrunk dramatically, to a state in which, according to Angela Gallop of Forensic Access, 'it is barely recognisable'.

There is one startling instance which encapsulates many of the criticisms highlighted above. It is the case of Kevin Callan. In 1992 he was convicted of murdering his step-daughter Amanda aged 4 years. He was the only one at home at the time of her death, and the prosecution suggested that he had shaken her to death. He consistently denied this to the police and to the court. The principal evidence against him derived from two pathologists, Dr Freemand and Dr Garrett, both of whom deposed that the cerebral haemorrhage was

> 'The single judge originally refused leave to appeal, as well as legal aid, on the basis that this was a second bite of the same cherry'

caused by shaking and was not the result of a fall either downstairs or off a slide (which was the defence case). The defence contacted experts with similar experience and qualifications to those of the prosecution, who tended to concur with the prosecution experts.

What was required, however, were specialists with a different emphasis upon neurosurgery and neuropathology. After his conviction, the search for such experts was in fact undertaken by Kevin Callan himself, firing off a large quantity of letters to forensic science departments throughout the world. Fortunately a neurosurgeon in New Zealand, Mr Wrightson, began the road to recovery. Without the assistance of legal aid, further experts were obtained. Dr Whitwell, a distinguished and very experienced neuropathologist, concluded that the cause of death was direct trauma rather than shaking and that the condition of the brain prior to death had not been assessed with any degree of accuracy. In the end two further experts lent support to Dr Whitwell's conclusions and when the appeal was eventually heard the Crown conceded. Once again the system had failed to discern the injustice.

The injustice was the inability to identify the right issues and the right expertise. What is even more worrying is that after Kevin Callan was convicted, the single judge originally refused leave to appeal, as well as legal aid, on the basis that this was a second bite of the same cherry. This refrain is becoming increasingly common in fresh evidence appeals, and is resulting in an increasing number of refusals. No doubt the classic miscarriage appeals of the past, which relied upon further expert evidence, would now themselves not find favour in the Court of Appeal.

The Vilification of Gay Men and Lesbians:

Why Denying the Right to Serve Threatens Us All

Jonathan Cooper

In the recent 'MOD Four' case, it became clear that in Britain there is no legal basis for upholding the basic human rights of minorities.

The inability of the British constitution to promote and protect identified fundamental human rights was explicitly recognised at the end of 1995 by the courts' failure to guarantee lesbian and gay service men and women the right to serve in the armed forces.[1] That case has shown the folly of our present system. Four out of the five judges who examined the case expressed support for the applicants on the merits, but yet felt unable in law to interfere with the Ministry of Defence (MOD) policy - which is a blanket ban on any one of a homosexual orientation from serving in the armed forces. The applicants are presently seeking leave to petition the House of Lords. The consequence of the ban means that if a person of any rank acknowledges his or her attraction to the same sex, they face automatic discharge. Gulf War pilot heroes, costing millions of pounds to train, have been discharged under the policy; so have administrative staff with no combat

---

1. *R v MOD ex Parte Smith et al*, Court of Appeal, Unreported, 3/11/95.

role and nursing auxiliaries.

The case of the 'MOD Four', as it has come to be known, has obvious ramifications for the lesbian and gay community. However, there are also profound implications for British society as a whole. What the case has shown is that, in the absence of an incorporated Bill of Rights, fundamental human rights cannot be guaranteed to people within the jurisdiction. At least one of the judges, Lord Justice Simon Brown, was outspoken in his view that the appellants' human rights were being violated. Nevertheless, he felt unable to strike down the policy, as, in his opinion (in such an application for judicial review), he had to apply the following test: a policy, such as the one under review, is only unlawful if it is so unreasonable that no one in their right mind could have come to that same conclusion. As he believed that the policy had the implicit approval of Parliament, he considered that the test had not been satisfied. The consequences of that logic are self evident: identified human rights can be breached if there is sufficient will on the part of the Government to do so; and the judiciary, as the responsible guardians of our civil liberties, can only sit back and observe the situation.

President Clinton asserted during his speech last November to both Houses of Parliament, that on the whole we in Britain are a free people who love liberty, believe in reason, and struggle for truth, and that our legal system is built upon fairness and justice.[2] These proclamations may be true. However, as the 'MOD Four' case has shown, the British constitutional framework cannot protect the most vulnerable members of the community if Parliament, or those acting for Parliament, chooses not to protect them, or worse still decides to vilify them. Consequently, a Bill of Rights needs to be put in place, because without such an enshrined commitment to each individual, the majority, or those alleging to speak for them, are able to crush identifiable rights of minorities.

It is for this reason that Parliamentary sovereignty, in and of itself, does not necessarily act as a bulwark against arbitrary government. If the definition of democracy is to include the guarantee of the same rights as possessed by the majority to the social outcasts and marginalised people of our society, then those rights - which are universal, inherent and inalienable - have to be enshrined. By enshrining human rights, those who cannot protect their rights adequately through the

---

2. *Independent*, 30 November 1995.

democratic process are then placed beyond the reach of the majority and the vicissitudes of political controversy. The accessibility to fundamental rights, therefore, should not be submitted to the vote (which is the fundamental premise of parliamentary sovereignty) because that system is no guarantee that the most vulnerable amongst us will be protected.

That the MOD policy is in violation of fundamental human rights is not seriously in dispute. The blanket ban on serving in the armed forces if identified as having even the vaguest homosexual orientation (how gay do you actually have to be?) is a violation of the right to a sexual identity, and as such would constitute a breach of the appellant's right to respect for private life. This right is guaranteed by Article 8 of the European Convention of Human Rights (ECHR). The right to a sexual identity has been interpreted as forming a key aspect of each person's character. To this extent the right to respect for private life should be perceived as being akin to the right to respect for the dignity of a person, and their right to autonomy. The right to private life under Article 8 can be subject to state limitation. It may be lawful, for instance, for the state to impose certain limits on the expression of that identity, i.e. controlling aspects of sexual conduct. However, the nature of the MOD ban is such that it denies an individual their right to a sexual identity completely and, consequently, violates human rights. Additionally, the state is only able to interfere with the fundamental nature of the right under limited and prescribed circumstances. This interference must be according to law (which of itself cannot be arbitrary), proportionate to the legitimate aim pursued and necessary in a democratic society.

The MOD is of the view that to allow gay men and lesbians to serve in the armed forces would be disruptive and damage unit effectiveness. They have no evidence for their assertions. In reality, their argument boils down to whether or not it is reasonable for a straight man to have to shower with a man known to be gay. Why lesbians have also to be dismissed has never been made clear. Evidence was put before the court of other jurisdictions, alongside whom British soldiers fight, where the sexual orientation of the service men and women is considered irrelevant and strict codes of sexual conduct are in place. Despite this, the judges remained of the view that the policy was reasonable. Ironically, it is not deemed damaging to unit effectiveness to allow convicted murderers (Private Clegg) to remain part of the fighting force. However, if one of the nurses in a base hospital happens to be a lesbian (and lives off base with her girlfriend), she is considered to pose such a threat that she must be detained, interrogated, searched and, on the confirmation of her lesbianism, despite her excellent service record, be discharged.

The absurdity of the present constitutional framework is that the 'MOD Four' will eventually be able to assert their human rights violation before the European Commission and Court of Human Rights in Strasbourg. The frustration is that the judges, apparently willing to recognise the consequences of the policy, consider themselves trapped, and, like Pontius Pilate, only able to wash their hands of the matter. The folly of the current situation is that the European Court of Human Rights, instead of acting as the final arbiter of human rights questions, has in a UK context become the court of first instance. This is why there have been the many violations found against the UK government by the Strasbourg human rights mechanisms. The case of the 'MOD Four' will inevitably follow the same route.

Historically, however, it was not always possible to be as confident that the Human Rights Institutions in Strasbourg would uphold cases involving lesbian and gay issues. To this extent the ECHR, in its interpretation and in its form, has shown the potential limitations of articulated Bills of Rights. It is only within the last decade or so that Strasbourg was prepared to recognise that the denial of human rights to lesbians and gay men ultimately affects everyone's access to rights. The Convention should certainly not be considered as the global panacea to prevent discrimination and provide the cure for homophobia in Europe. The typical approach towards lesbian and gay issues has been characterised more by reticence than enthusiasm for the promotion of the right of an individual to express his or her sexual identity. Although that said, the Court has recognised that gay rights are a human right.

In the landmark decision, *Dudgeon v United Kingdom*, the Court found the United Kingdom in breach of Article 8 of the Convention in that the 1967 Sexual Offences Act (which decriminalised homosexual acts under certain circumstances) had not been applied to Northern Ireland.[3] The Court held that 'a person's sexual life is undoubtedly part of his private life, of which it constitutes an important aspect'.[4] As it happens, this was not a new development in Strasbourg case law. The significance of the Dudgeon judgment, and what was new, was that the Court was prepared to apply the same principles to a gay man as they would to a straight

3. *Dudgeon v UK*, Series A No 45, para 21.
4. Application No 5935/72, *X v FRG*, D&R 3/46.

man and accept that there was no pressing social need to criminalise same sex
sexual activity in private with a consenting adult over 21 years of age.

Prior to the decision in Dudgeon, the Strasbourg institutions were, however,
conspicuous in their failure to recognise lesbian and gay rights; and even now,
despite the progress made through decisions like Dudgeon, the Court and
Commission remain reluctant to acknowledge lesbian
and gay life styles. The overwhelming majority of the
previous relevant case-law of the European
Commission of Human Rights seems to indicate that
the Strasbourg institutions have approached lesbian
and gay issues with the same two misconceptions as
the UK judicial or legislative bodies. The first of these

'The European Court
of Human Rights
has, in the UK
context, become the
court of first
instance'

misconceptions is that the Convention should not be used to promote rights which
might, somehow, dilute their normal assumption of heterosexuality. The
Commission has, on no occasion, sought to examine, let alone uphold, lesbian
and gay rights in their own right. Their decisions have always been in relation to,
and compared with, a heterosexual view of normality. Secondly, the Commission
have approached gay issues, in particular, from what can only be interpreted as a
prejudiced and stereotypical perspective. In one case in the early 1970s the
Commission held that there was an objective and reasonable justification for
discriminating against gay men. The Commission was of the view that:

> studies have been made on several occasions... both on adult homosexual
> behaviour and on the effects of the personality of adolescents of homosexual
> relationships with adults. They have led to convincing conclusions as to the
> existence of a specific social danger in the case of masculine homosexuality.
> This danger results from the fact that masculine homosexuals often constitute a
> distinct socio-cultural group with a clear tendency to proselytise adolescents
> and that the social isolation in which it involves the latter is particularly
> marked.[5]

This view appears still to pertain. As recently as 1986, well over ten years after the
Commission had made the above comments, they had not developed their
argument. In a case concerning discrimination over the age of consent, where the

---

5.   X v FRG D&R 3/46.

police had raided a private gay party, the Commission stated:

> The Commission refers again to its previous case-law and would apply the same reasoning, namely that heterosexuality and lesbianism do not give rise to comparable social problems. Accordingly the Commission finds that any difference in treatment resulting from this legislation would have an objective and reasonable justification in the need to protect the individual, particularly the young and vulnerable.[6]

With the workings of the Strasbourg institutions as their model, and this pervasive attitude of the Commission, the lesbian and gay community could be forgiven for believing that the Convention was not in fact a Convention of Human Rights, but one of heterosexual rights. This is despite the fact that lesbians and gay men, on account of their sexuality, are, and have historically been, particularly vulnerable to a catalogue of abuses and violations of the Convention, and of human rights generally. It is reasonable to state that, by failing to uphold lesbian and gay rights in their own right, and by not attaching significant weight to the human consequences and misery of continuing the marginalisation of lesbians and gay men, the Commission has perpetuated lesbian and gay oppression.

Examples of the consequences of this approach by the Commission are numerous. They include the fact that all attempts to lower the age of consent and bring it in line with heterosexual sex have, to date, failed.[7] The Committee of Ministers has even felt unable to extend this protection from prosecution to all gay men who have reached their majority. That Committee decided that the conviction of a 26-year-old gay man for the offence of buggery with his 18-year-old boyfriend was not in violation of Article 8.[8] The applicant had been sentenced to two and a half years in prison. On his release he resumed his relationship with his apparent victim.

One Commission decision, and probably its most pernicious was the finding that lesbian and gay relationships do 'not fall within the scope of the right to respect for family life also guaranteed by Article 8'.[9] The Commission has given no reasoning to justify why lesbians and gay men are not entitled to respect for family life,

---

6. *Johnson v UK*, D&R 47/72.
7. See *Johnson v UK*, cited in note 6.
8. *X v UK*, Resolution DH (79) 5, D&R 19/66. This was decided before the Court's decision in *Dudgeon*, but after the Commission's admissibility decision.
9. *X & Y v UK*, D&R 32/220.

regardless of the stability and familial nature of their relationships.

As a result of this 'policy' decision a lesbian couple with a baby conceived through artificial insemination were denied family rights.[10] Other cases include a lesbian who was denied the right to adopt her girlfriend's son, as their 'domestic unit' was not considered sufficient to merit family right status.[11] A question which also remains unanswered, at least in any cogent, non-prejudiced manner, is why straight men and women are guaranteed the right to marry each other and found a family under Article 12 of the ECHR, while marriage - the mainstay of European society - is denied to those who may wish to marry someone of their own sex.

Perhaps the case which best sums up the Commission's prejudiced, albeit conventional, approach to lesbian and gay issues (outside of criminalisation) is that of *S v UK*.[12] This case involved the applicant's right to inherit her girlfriend's council tenancy following the latter's death. Heterosexual couples, though not married, but living as if they were, have that opportunity. The Commission were quite straightforward in their acknowledgement of the primacy of heterosexual relationships over gay and lesbian relationships. The Commission accepted that the treatment accorded to the applicant was different from the treatment she would have received if the partners had been of different sexes. They found that:

> the aim of the legislation in question was to protect the family, a goal similar to the protection of the right to respect for family life guaranteed by Article 8 of the Convention. The aim itself is clearly legitimate. The question remains, however, whether it was justified to protect families but not to give similar protection to other stable relationships. The Commission considers that the family (to which the relationship of heterosexual unmarried couples living together as husband and wife can be assimilated) merits special protection in society and it sees no reason why a High Contracting Party should not afford particular assistance to families. The Commission therefore accepts that the difference in treatment between the applicant and somebody in the same position whose partner had been of the opposite sex can be objectively and reasonably justified.

---

10. Application 14753/89, *X & Y v United Kingdom*, unpublished.
11. Application 15666/89, *Kerkhoven, Hincke, & Hincke v the Netherlands*.
12. D&R 47/274.

The case law of the Commission as it relates to sexual minority questions shows the conservative nature of the Strasbourg institutions, and how unwilling they are to interpret the Convention as a device to promote genuine equality of access.

Whilst the right to respect for private life is gratefully received, and is obviously crucial for a gay man or a lesbian be able to function as a sexual being, it is ironic that the one right guaranteed as a human right can also be interpreted as serving to compound the invisibility and repression which is the characteristic feature of the personal oppression of most gay men and lesbians. The right to private life resonates with the closet.

Without question the Commission and Court need to develop their approach to lesbian and gay issues. There seems to be evidence that a more universal approach to human rights is emerging which does include sexual minorities. In recent months tangible advances have taken place. For example, the Commission recently held that a transsexual has family rights.[13] In a slightly more mixed judgement, in a recent freedom of expression case concerning the showing of gay porn in a back room behind a shop, the Commission were particularly forceful in arguing that the case should still be heard by the Court, despite the fact that the applicant had since died.[14] In the event, however, the Court took the case out of the list. Their main argument was that no-one from the deceased's family had come forward to push for the case to be heard, despite the fact that the representative of the applicant's estate still wanted the case to go ahead - evidence, perhaps, of what happens when there is a failure to recognise chosen 'family' relationships instead of the more traditional models. The importance of the case remains, however, the Commission's support for a hearing for the deceased's violation.

The treatment of lesbian and gay issues under the Convention shows that a Bill of Rights, per se, is not necessarily a solution to minority issues, unless it explicitly recognises the rights of all minorities. Ideally this recognition needs be articulated within the text of the Bill: specific reference to sexual orientation should be included. Otherwise the provisions within a Bill of Rights must be broad enough to include an interpretation that embraces sexual orientation and sexual minorities. The International Covenant on Civil and Political Rights (ICCPR) has, for instance, not identified lesbians and gay men as being

13. Application 21830/93, *X & Y & Z v UK*, as yet unpublished.
14. *Scherer v Switzerland* 1994 EHRR.

explicitly protected by that instrument. However, the case law of the United
Nations Human Rights Committee (UNHRC) has since interpreted Article
26, which provides for an autonomous right of equality, and Article 2(1) (which
has its counterpart in Article 14 of the ECHR), as including sexual orientation
within the definition of 'sex'.[15] As such, full equality rights, where they relate
to discrimination on the grounds of 'sex', can now in theory be extended to
lesbians and gay men.

The approach of the UNHRC is clearly correct, that discrimination on
the grounds of sexual orientation is also discrimination on the grounds
of sex. The two battles for equality are, and should be seen, as the same
fight. Gay men and lesbians are dismissed because they do not conform to the
stereotype of what a 'man' or a 'woman' should be. Additionally, if a man (x) and a
woman (y) are both dating the same woman (z), only
y will be dismissed. If y had been x, a man, her job
would be secure. This is classic sex discrimination.
But there may also be a case to be made that, in order
to target the full range of human rights for lesbian and gay men, additional reference
should also be made to protecting sexual minorities.

'The right to private life resonates with the closet'

The Commission's history of dealing with such questions is an indication that
leaving everything up to the judges may bring with it more problems than solutions.
However this is partly a problem of the limitations within the ECHR itself. The
Convention is not the most comprehensive human rights document. Some of its
notable omissions, such as the lack of an autonomous right to equality, have meant
that it is unlikely that the Convention could ever systemically protect lesbians and
gay men. It is the denial of equality which lies at the heart of discrimination against
sexual minorities.

In effect the policy ban on homosexuals in the armed forces is 'a denial of
the right to have access on general terms of equality to public service'. As
such it constitutes a breach of Article 25(c) of the ICCPR. The ban also violates
Article 26 of the same Covenant which guarantees an autonomous right to equality
before the law and equal protection under it. (It should be pointed out that as a
result of the breadth and scope of the ICCPR it is a significantly more
comprehensive human rights instrument than its European counterpart.)

---

15. *Toonan v Australia*, Communication No 488/1992, UNHRC, 31 March 1994.

Since equality is an alien concept to the English common law, the British framework for the protection of human rights would develop significantly with the incorporation of the ICCPR.[16] This quantifiable lack of equality is emphasised by the 'MOD Four'. Their case has stressed how unequal gay men and lesbians are. In addition, one of the failings of British anti-discrimination law is its piecemeal approach. The MOD case has shown that the entire system for protection from discrimination needs to be overhauled and replaced with a single mechanism which promotes equality generally.

The 'MOD Four' case has brought to the boil what had previously been the simmering deficiencies of the British Constitution: violations of identified human rights cannot be remedied in English courts. The case has also highlighted the failure of the UK non-discrimination provisions. At the same time the case has proven the secondary status of lesbians and gay men in British society. But the overwhelming lesson to be learned from the situation of the 'MOD Four' is that the system upholding democracy in the UK is seriously flawed. Parliamentary sovereignty in and of itself is not sufficient to guarantee the civil liberties of people within the jurisdiction of the UK. Whilst the principle of parliamentary sovereignty may be theoretically laudable, if it doesn't function alongside an enshrined Bill of Rights, democracy will inevitably be diminished. However, as this brief examination of the treatment of lesbians and gay men under the European Convention has shown, such a Bill of Rights has to be carefully constructed to ensure that it can and will be used to protect the most vulnerable and disenfranchised of society. The simple incorporation of the limited provisions of the European Convention of Human Rights into UK law will not necessarily remedy the present circumstances of a number of minorities in Britain. Without the guarantee of inherent, universal and inalienable rights invested in each individual, allowing each individual to be equal with the state and other citizens, democracy may be nothing more than, at best, the despotism of the perceived majority and, at worst, mob rule.

---

16. *Applin v Race Relations Board* (1975) AC 259.

Politics, Race and US Penal Strategies

Ethan Raup

The Right in Britain would love to follow recent trends in the US, and to rely more and more heavily for public security on punitive coercion rather than measures to promote social cohesion.
Ethan Raup *here outlines the disastrous situation in the US, and warns against any imitation.*

In Seattle in 1995, a 29 year old man was convicted of robbing $337 from an espresso stand operator. In the past, the man would have faced a 3 to 4 year sentence. However, because the man had been convicted of both robbery and assault in the 1980s, he was sentenced to life in prison under Washington state's new 'three-strikes-and-you're-out' law. The victim, who had signed the petition to get the three-strikes proposal on the state ballot, expressed disbelief at the harsh sentence. 'I can't imagine him going to prison for the rest of his life for mugging me,' he said.

The tragic absurdity of this particular case aside, the combined impact of three-strikes laws, mandatory drug sentences and other retributive penal policies has had a sobering effect on the American prison system. By 1994, US prisons held over 1 million people, three times as many as in 1982, and far more than any other Western country. The rate of imprisonment per 100,000 in the US has grown from 100 in the late 1970s to 139 in 1980, and 210 in 1986. By 1994, America's incarceration rate reached 373, higher than South Africa's incarceration rate under Apartheid, three times that of Canada and England, and nearly nine times that of the Netherlands.

The fact that America has the most complex, most expensive, and most punitive criminal justice system in the world should be the topic of serious domestic political debate. Instead, this situation is routinely accepted in public discourse, which rarely rises above a shallow, sloganised discussion of crime enforcement and penal policies. For example, former Texas Governor Ann Richards ran a re-election campaign last year boasting that, under her watch, Texas had the highest incarceration rate in the country. Even that wasn't enough to satisfy voters; she was bested by an even tougher talking Republican opponent.

As Michael Howard exhibits portentous signs of American penal envy and prepares to take Britain down a similar path, complete with three-strikes type legislation and boot camps, it is worth examining not only current US penal strategies and their consequences, but also how and why Americans so readily accept such a punitive society. It is crucial to note that America's penal strategies cannot simply be blamed on widespread barbarism and/or racism. The circumstances that led to America's current prison crisis are much more complex, and are not unlike some circumstances in Britain. This inquiry should serve as a stern warning to Britain not only to avoid the outward manifestations of the prison crisis - three-strikes, mandatory drug sentences, boot camps, chain gangs - but also to be vigilant against the deeper causes of the American prison crisis.

American Penal Strategies: the politics of law and order
The law and order ideology

In America, as in Britain, there is a very close interrelationship between penal strategies, race, and politics. The political reliance on increasingly punitive crime enforcement strategies has been underpinned by conservative discourses on crime, which argue that the aspects of the welfare state which undermined free-market capitalism in the 1960s and 1970s were also responsible for the 'permissive' attitudes that led to increasing crime rates during the same period. The potential contradiction between *laissez-faire* economic and social welfare policy on the one hand, and increased criminal justice intervention on the other is thus resolved: if the welfare state was responsible both for America's economic decline, and for rising crime rates, then the government should be interventionist only in the area of law and order; indeed, the maintenance of law and order is necessary for the proper functioning of the market and society.

The doctrine of economic individualism found its echo in conservative explanations of crime, which held that the causes of crime must be located not in social conditions but in individual characteristics: like the consumer, the criminal is thought to engage in an overly simplistic process of rational decision-making, weighing the potential costs and benefits before acting. From this, it follows that, to deter crime, the government must toughen its criminal sanctions and tighten its mechanisms of carceral control.

As these conservative discourses on crime have gained credibility over the past three decades, there has been a corresponding loss of faith in social democracy. The sometimes ambivalent, and often hostile, view of social democracy stems in large part from a widespread belief that the welfare state has been unable to provide the glue with which to bind capitalist society together. If government cannot stabilise society through social welfare policies, then the obvious alternative is to accept the rapid transformations of the free-market, while relying on government to maintain social control through more coercive means; by shifting to a permanent carceral position, locking up, instead of helping, those who 'threaten' the social fabric.

Modern politics and crime

While these conservative discourses on crime have helped legitimise the law and order ideology, the realities of modern American politics have been the driving force behind an expansion of increasingly punitive crime enforcement strategies across the US. As the media have stepped into the vacuum left by traditional politics, arguably acting as a fourth branch of government, old affiliations and shared meaning regarding the nature and function of social democracy have been replaced by an image-based politics, where meaning and identities are built, broken down, and reconstructed at an unprecedented rate. This is not to suggest, as some post modern theorists claim, that social relations have become irrelevant, that they have been subsumed and dispersed within ever expanding cultural forms; rather that modern political forms have fundamentally altered relations between the electorate and public officials, the level of social and political discourse, and the character of political campaigns in a way that is consistent with law and order discourses and the rise of 'authoritarian populism'.

Whereas, previously, voter loyalties could be appealed to in a positive way, even in a 30 second television advertisement, it is now much more effective to give impressions, appeal to feelings, arouse emotions: wedged in the midst of advertisements for all types of products, the political spot must grab its audience. This practice tends to rule out even a substantive 30 second discussion of the issues. As political candidates steadfastly avoid engaging the public and each other in a meaningful discourse, choosing instead to exploit rising economic tensions with a divide and conquer strategy perpetrated through innuendo and accusation, America's political language and social discourse have been increasingly characterised by a rising tide of undirected anger, polarisation, and divisiveness, which is undermining America's already tenuous sense of common purpose.

The potential tyranny of this new form of politics found its single most disturbing manifestation to date in the Willie Horton ad campaign, aired during George Bush's 1988 presidential bid. The Bush campaign, facing the overwhelming popularity of Michael Dukakis several months before the election, decided they needed to transform Dukakis from a 'New Democrat' to a typical Northeastern establishment liberal. With the help of a focus group (an apparatus of the modern American electoral process designed to test the reaction of a particular demographic group to specific themes and attacks), the Bush team developed a series of devastating ads. Though each ad helped redefine Dukakis's image, one, featuring Willie Horton, a convicted murderer who raped a woman while on furlough from a Massachusetts prison, was of particular significance, for Horton was black, the woman white. Ostensibly questioning Dukakis's prison furlough plan, the advertisement's symbolism was powerful. As Susan Estrich, Dukakis's campaign manager, said after the election, 'you can't find a stronger metaphor, intended or not, for racial hatred in this country than a black man raping a white woman.'

Though the exact impact of this ad will never be known, many observers at the time and since have pointed to Willie Horton as the turning point in the election. Significantly, the ad also demonstrated the powerful dynamics between race, crime, and politics. While race will be explored in greater detail below, it is important to note here that the Horton ad further undermined a reasoned discussion of crime policies that were anything but tough. What Governor would be willing to even consider a furlough programme after Dukakis's public drubbing?

As the Willie Horton ad campaign is replayed and repackaged in varying degrees in local, state, and federal elections nationwide, any meaningful discourse on crime has been preempted by the compelling need for elected officials to maintain a hardened attitude toward criminals and law enforcement. With legislators at every level of government caught in a fierce competition to outdo each other's commitment to retribution and punishment, the 'law and order' ideology attained the level of social 'truth' in the late 1980s; the White House, Congress, the Supreme Court, state legislatures, academia, and the media all accepted its underlying assumptions as the reigning conventional wisdom.

The strength of the law and order ideology has continued unabated through the 1990s. In fact, the centre of the crime discourse has moved so far to the right that counter-discourses associated with 1960s liberalism have been relegated to the fringe of American politics. In his 1992 Presidential campaign, candidate Clinton confirmed that the traditional liberal pole on crime had finally collapsed. While Clinton paid lip service to a few 'smart on crime' programmes like Midnight Basketball, he employed a campaign strategy that emphasised he was as tough on crime as any Republican: he voiced strong support for the death penalty, focused repeatedly on his pledge to increase the number of police on America's streets by 100,000, and pointed with pride to his crime enforcement record as Governor of Arkansas.

Not surprisingly, in 1994, both Democratic controlled houses of Congress passed an anti-crime bill that expanded the death penalty by more than 50 additional offences, funded 100,000 new police, made 'three-strikes' applicable to federal courts, and allocated $8.8 billion towards new prison construction. Indeed, one of the few contentious issues was just how difficult to make death-row appeals. After winning control of both houses of Congress in the 1994 mid-term elections, one of the Republicans' first priorities was to repeal the 'Clinton Crime Bill' in order to gut the few token prevention programmes, enact new restrictions on death row-appeals, further weaken constitutional restraints on the police, and toughen sentencing stipulations.

Mandatory drug sentences

Though most resources allocated to fight the wars against drugs in the 1980s - which primarily targeted street drug-traffickers in disadvantaged urban minority communities - had little positive long-term impact, strict mandatory drug sentences enacted in the Reagan/Bush years have left a lasting legacy. The Anti Drug Abuse Act of 1986, which ushered in Reagan's second 'national crusade' against drugs, is the most comprehensive anti-drug legislation to ever pass Congress. In addition to tripling the budget for the war on drugs, this act stiffened penalties for manufacture, distribution and possession of illegal drugs. Persons convicted of major drug trafficking offences (those involving at least five kilograms of cocaine or one kilogram of heroin) were subject to a mandatory minimum sentence of ten years, considerably longer than the average federal sentence for homicide. This penalty doubled for a second conviction. Offences involving 100 grams of heroin, 500 grams of cocaine, or 5 grams of crack were subject to a five to forty year sentence, and a drug related death or serious injury was made punishable by a minimum twenty year sentence. Most states also toughened sentencing codes in some manner during the late 1980s: mandatory sentences and presumptive sentencing stipulations replaced indeterminate sentences; probation was terminated for an increasing number of crimes; sentence mandates were lengthened.

> 'It is no surprise that a baseball slogan has been transformed into a widely accepted penal policy'

Drug arrests resulting from Reagan's drug war of 1986 and Bush's drug war of 1988-1990, combined with these severe mandatory drug sentences, have been *the* major contributor to America's exploding incarceration rate. While incarceration rates for property and violent crime actually declined from 1977 to 1990, incarceration rates for drugs increased dramatically. From 1980 to 1992, adult drug arrests more than doubled from 471,200 to 980,700. At the same time, the likelihood of going to prison for that crime increased fivefold, from 19 sentences per 100,000 arrests to 104. As a result, the number of drug inmates soared from 7 per cent of new inmates in 1980 to 30 per cent in 1992. Moreover, while drug offenders accounted for 27 per cent of the total federal prison population in 1980, they accounted for 40 per cent following the 1986 Anti drug Abuse Act. By 1992, 58 per cent of federal inmates, and over 30 per cent of inmates instate prisons were drug offenders.

Three-strikes-and-you're-out

Considering the media's penchant for pithy phrases, it should be no surprise that a baseball slogan has been transformed into widely accepted penal policy. Passage of three-strikes legislation, which usually mandates life in prison for a third violent felony conviction, will ensure that the American prison population will grow even faster during the remainder of this decade. Variations of the three-strikes law are now operating in over thirty states, while, in Georgia, the Governor and Legislature felt three-strikes was too lenient, and passed a two-strikes bill.

California's experience with three-strikes legislation offers a fitting example of the convergence of the media, politics and crime in 1990s America. Though failing initially to gain much public support, the tragic kidnapping and murder of Polly Klaas transformed the three strikes proposal into a rallying point for an outraged public, with politicians, the media, and Hollywood celebrities stumbling over one another to voice support for the initiative.

The resulting legislation, embedded in the state's constitution, is the toughest, most sweeping three-strikes law in the country, requiring those convicted of a third felony to serve twenty-five years to life if their first two felonies were serious. Sentences of 'second-strike' felons are doubled, and 'first strike' violent felons must serve at least 85 per cent of their sentence.

Because California already had strict repeat-offender laws, any additional deterrent value is questionable, while the fiscal ramifications are staggering. A recent study by RAND, a California-based think-tank, concluded the cost would average at least $5.5 billion annually over the next 25 years. Already, there is a growing backlog of cases throughout the state due to defence lawyers' reluctance to plea bargain. Many fear a guilty plea to a felony may be a step toward a life sentence for a future crime. With potential three-strikers demanding a trial instead of pleading guilty, felony trials have increased 150 per cent since the law took effect. RAND estimates the state prison budget will have to increase from 9 per cent to 18 per cent by 2002 to accommodate the resulting expansion. Already, California spends more on its prison system than it does on higher education, once the best state system in the country.

In addition to being expensive, the law does not distinguish between minor and serious felony offences. As a result, nearly 500 crimes qualify as third strikes, including a wide range of petty felony offences such as shoplifting. One of California's first prosecutions under this law involved a 27 year old man subject to a life sentence for stealing a piece of pizza. He had twice previously pleaded guilty to two felonies: robbery and attempted robbery.

Such cases have prompted a revolt among California's judiciary, 85 per cent of whom were appointed by conservative Republican governors. Some have ruled the measure unconstitutional, arguing the harsh provisions violate the federal Constitution's ban on cruel and unusual punishment, while others have argued that its limit on judicial discretion violates the state constitution's separation of powers doctrine.

Chain gangs

After a sixty year hiatus, the return of chain gangs in Alabama, Florida, and Arizona in 1995 marked the most obvious return in America to punishment by public spectacle. While the criminal justice system has always relied on deeply symbolic images, the use of chain gangs marks a shift from strategies that emphasise efficient discipline toward those that emphasise more ritualistic forms of punishment.

Whereas the public humiliation of nineteenth century punishment took place in the town square or on Main Street, today's public humiliation, not surprisingly, relies largely on television and video images. In Alabama, for example, the debut of rock-breaking gangs at the Limestone Correctional Facility last summer was a staged and polished media event, with compelling video images of men shackled together struggling to crush rock beneath the weight of 10-pound sledgehammers.

Alabama Governor Fob James was elected last fall on a platform that promised tougher crime control measures. Tough talk is extremely popular with Alabama's electorate, and the spectacle of chain gangs will no doubt be worth at least one effective television commercial next time around. Ron Jones, commissioner of Alabama's corrections department, echoed the opinions of many in Alabama: 'It's time to change direction, and that's what we're doing in Alabama. The message is clear: we don't want you committing a crime in our state.'

In addition to crushing rock, the programme puts the unit's prisoners to work picking up trash along the state's public highways. During the one to three months prisoners spend on the gangs, they are deprived of the few basic amenities of prison life: television, radio, smoking, the right to purchase items at the prison store. Personal visits, even from family members, are strictly forbidden.

Governor James, ever mindful of the chain gang's racist past, ordered that each gang, which is comprised of five men, reflect the diversity of the prison population. Even so, because the majority of Limestone's prison population is black, each gang is comprised of at least three black men. This ratio, combined with the sight of white, shotgun-toting guards in mirrored sunglasses, makes comparisons with the days of slavery difficult to escape.

Nevertheless, proponents, echoing Speaker Gingrich's call for a return to 'Victorian values,' argue that parading chained prisoners before a scornful public will make them better citizens. Alabama prison officials also say chain gangs are cost effective, requiring fewer guards for prisoners joined at the ankle, and that unpleasant conditions encourage other prisoners to be less troublesome. Though most experts doubt that chain gangs will reduce Alabama's crime rate, or overcrowding in the state's prisons, it is too soon to tell if chain gangs will instil 'proper' morality or, alternatively, if they will create the deep-seated anger and despair that characterised chain gangs at the turn of the century, when desperate prisoners often turned to self mutilation — breaking legs, cutting tendons — to escape punishment.

Boot camps

The populist appeal of tough, old fashioned discipline has also boosted the popularity of military–style boot camps. Since they were introduced in Georgia and Oklahoma in 1983, various boot camp programmes have been set up by 30 states, 10 local jurisdictions, and the federal government. The Clinton Crime Bill of 1994 contained $150 million to fund alternatives to traditional incarceration, most particularly boot camps, and the Juvenile Justice and Delinquency Prevention Act of 1993 converted 10 former military bases into boot camps for youth offenders.

Common to each boot camp is the reproduction of military training and strict discipline. Penal boot camps include military-style drills and ceremonies, verbal assaults from correctional personnel masquerading as drill sergeants, and on-site punishments such as push-ups. Most boot camps target juveniles or young adult offenders, with sentences lasting from 90 to 120 days, followed by some form of supervised release back into the community.

While the most frequently stated goal of boot camps is to reduce recidivism by inculcating personal responsibility and discipline, some proponents also argue that boot camps cut costs by reducing massive prison overcrowding in existing correctional facilities. However, studies indicate that on both counts boot camps have been, at best, marginally successful: preliminary data suggest that recidivism rates have remained constant, while costs are saved only when boot camp selection procedures limit access to the prison bound.[1]

---

1. J. Simon, 'They Died with their Boots on; the boot camp and the limits of modern penality', *Social Justice*, Vol 22, No 2, 1995.

These questionable results have done little to erode the boot camp's popularity. As with most current penal strategies, facts and reason have little bearing on policy. Like chain gangs, images of boot camps resonate with the electorate and are consistent with the conservative argument that the collapse of personal discipline has caused the crime problem. With the 1996 Presidential race looming on the horizon, America can no doubt look forward to a fresh crop of 30 second commercials featuring a firm voice calling for personal discipline and a 'common sense' approach to crime, accompanied by images of young men dressed in stark clothing, marching in rank, and responding to a drill sergeant's orders.

Race and the US Criminal Justice System
Just as America's penal strategies cannot be divorced from its political culture, neither can they be separated from the impact of race. Indeed, a trend in the US prison system even more disturbing than the overall population explosion is the increasingly disproportionate black incarceration rate. Today, fully one-third of black men aged 20 to 29 are under some form of correctional supervision, while the incarceration rate for black Americans is four times worse than it was for black South Africans under Apartheid. Compared with an incarceration rate of 197 for white America, 1,534 of every 100,000 black Americans are in prison.

Profoundly repugnant as it is, the disproportionate black incarceration rate cannot simply be reduced to overt racism. As with the widespread acceptance of the law and order ideology, this phenomenon must be placed within the context of complex and antagonistic cultural forms and popular struggles; perceptions and realities of crime; political forms; and social discourses.

Race, ideology and the shift to carceral social control
Not only did conservative discourses on crime signify a general shift to the right and increased carceral control, they also created an ideological framework which targeted specific social enemies as more or less responsible for the moral breakdown and ensuing rise in crime. Indeed, as modern American politics have increasingly relied on divisiveness to build consensus, the capacity to build positive consensus has been lost, replaced by a need to scapegoat social enemies to construct a coercive moral unity.

As conservatives captured the 'family values' theme in the late 1980s they tied the apparent failures of social democracy to liberalism's connection with the civil rights movement. As a result, though the welfare state had initially been viewed as a family policy, by the mid-1980s it was associated with rising numbers of single mothers, particularly inner-city black women who were on welfare. Suddenly, the welfare state became the enemy of the family, promoting dependency, illegitimacy, 'permissiveness,' especially in the 'black underclass'.

Though black Americans have long struggled beneath the weight of dominant ideologies, the term 'black underclass' has done much more than past ideologies to dehumanise inner-city blacks. The development of this term has been highly political, representing a way of defining the problems of poor minorities in terms of a pathologically deviant sub-culture, rather than as the result of the flight of capital from inner-city areas, the effects of poor education, latent or overt racism, or lack of opportunity.[2]

'The incarceration rate for black Americans is four times worse than it was for black South Africans under Apartheid'

The concept of an 'underclass', a 'dangerous class', or a 'lumpenproletariat' has a long history in Western thought. However, from 1963 with Gunnar Myrdal's *Challenge to America*, the socially deviant 'underclass' began to describe a population of unemployed and eventually unemployable people at the bottom of society. The notion that this group was permanently unemployable, despite the best efforts of social democracy, was a significant step in the intellectual attack against the welfare state. The next step, linking this description with inner-city blacks, was made in the popular press towards the end of the 1960s. Moreover, through the late 1960s, American academics increasingly accepted the concept and existence of a permanent black underclass and began producing a significant amount of literature on the subject. These academic discourses overwhelmingly supported the view that poor black inner-city communities created and accentuated pathological traits which became a way of life that was passed from one generation to the next.

The proliferation of this discourse intensified in the 1970s as media commentators, politicians, and social scientists further legitimised and consolidated the belief that the black ghetto was mired in a 'tangle of pathology'. For example, in 1977 *Time* magazine published an article on blacks in New York, stating that 'The underclass has been left behind ... Its members are

2. L. Innis, J. Feagin, 'Race and Ideology in the 1980's: The Black 'Underclass' Ideology in Race Relations Analysis', *Social Justice*, Vol 16, No 4, 1988.

victims and victimisers in the culture of the street hustle, the quick fix, the rip-off, and, not least, violent crime'. Similarly, articles in such prominent magazines as *The New Yorker* and *The New York Times Magazine* began to appear, all of which reinforced the idea of a pathological inner-city black culture.

The power and widespread acceptance of this ideology in the media and popular culture continued through the 1980s and into the 1990s. Significantly, it also continues to be legitimised by American academics. For example, in 1987, William Julius Wilson published *The Truly Disadvantaged*, which quickly became the departure point for those concerned with inner-city blacks. There was little new or revolutionary about this work, however. Indeed, while Wilson sought to emphasise the role of joblessness, he also reinforced the most damning aspects of the black underclass ideology; namely, the socially–separate nature and internally–reproducing deviant values of this group.

'Before manufacturing industries abandoned the inner-city, there was no talk of a permanent black underclass'

It must be noted that before manufacturing industries abandoned the inner-city, there was no talk of a permanent black underclass. Indeed, in the 1950s, black out-of-wedlock birth rates were in the single digits, far lower than is true of non-urban whites today. By moving the public discussion away from decent paying jobs, capital flight, and racism, and toward the issues of crime, welfare dependency, illegitimacy, and self contained and automatically reproducing ghetto pathologies, the black underclass ideology not only helped legitimise existing racial inequalities, but it also dehumanised inner-city blacks and pointed to them as the cause of many social evils that were associated with liberalism, but that were, in reality, the product of a growing economic, political, and social crisis. Because this was both a permanent black underclass, and a social group that was entirely separate from the rest of society, there was little larger society or government could do to integrate inner-city blacks into the social system. Instead, the prudent response was to police deviant inner-city behaviour, ensuring that it had the least possible impact on the rest of society.

Anti-drug discourses: the inner-city and crack cocaine

If the black underclass ideology dehumanised inner-city blacks and pointed to them as the cause of many social evils, anti-drug discourses took the censure of inner-city blacks a step further, actively mobilising and legitimising political action against them. Though there were many drug discourses in the 1980s that targeted various types of behaviour, one particularly powerful and highly targeted anti-drug discourse linked 'crack' cocaine with 'underclass' pathologies, particularly violent crime. This link between crack and crime dovetailed with conservative discourses on crime, and was a necessary aspect of mobilising political forces against inner-city blacks, for if the real problem in the inner-city was drug related crime, then the answer was increased law enforcement, not social programmes.

In the mobilisation of political forces against inner-city blacks, the media not only played a vital catalytic role in defining inner-city drug abuse as a cause of crime and as a pandemic problem, but also in shaping the public's view of random drug violence. Though the cases of random violence are a real social tragedy and are not in any sense fabrications, the media have focused disproportionate attention on drug–related random violence, particularly black on white crime, such as car-jackings and drive-by shootings, which has helped perpetrate the image of a drug infested black inner-city that is a pervasive threat to white middle class suburbia.

This should not in any way suggest a conspiratorial construction of a moral panic between politicians and the media. Like any business, the media are motivated in large part by profit maximisation. And crime clearly sells. That is why crime, fire, war and similar such tragedy invariably lead on the local and national news, and why 'virtual reality' crime shows such as *COPS* and *Emergency 911* have proliferated so dramatically in the US. The media should not be excused from culpability, however. Through their irresponsible sensationalism, the shadowy figures of the Central Park jogger and the Long Island Commuter Train gunman, among other notable examples of random (generally black on white) violence, have been firmly embedded in America's collective social conscience.

This image of widespread random drug violence has helped mobilise an even more repressive response from middle class America towards the 'tangle of pathology' in the ghetto. In the *National Drug Control Strategy*, published in September 1989 as a blue print for Bush's drug war, William Bennett, the national 'Drug Czar', provided a suitable example of the way in which politicians have organised and targeted rising social concerns over crime and drugs in order to build a more coercive moral unity and legitimise increased carceral control.[3] According to Bennett, 'the intensifying drug-related chaos' may be predominantly attributed to crack: 'Our most intense and immediate problem is inner-city crack use'; this 'is spreading like a plague'(pp3-5). Moreover, 'anyone who sells drugs and anyone who uses them ... is involved in an international criminal enterprise that is killing thousands of Americans each year'(p4). The logical response, according to Bennett, is not to try a new approach, such as focusing on demand (education, treatment) rather than supply, but is to be 'tough on drugs - much tougher than we are now.' Toward this end, Bennett suggested that 'we should be extremely reluctant to restrict [drug enforcement officers] within formal and arbitrary lines.' In other words, since, as everyone can see in the press, the drug problem has become a crisis which is threatening to 'spiral out of control', the government must respond by redoubling its regulatory efforts, even if those efforts have to overlook certain inconvenient constitutional guarantees.

> 'Bennet characterises the effort to control drugs as essentially a struggle between good and evil'

Finally, in its discussion of drugs, particularly crack, Bennett's report characterises the effort to control drugs as essentially a struggle between good and evil: not only is drug use defined as a moral problem, but the populace is divided between the morally righteous majority of honest, hard-working Americans who abstain from drug use, and the drug users, who represent the forces of evil. However, the executive branch was not alone in offering a discourse which characterised drug consumers as tangible examples of moral depravity: the courts and Congress also reinforced this discourse and, more importantly, acted on Bennett's suggestion to get 'tougher', thus mobilising the full political force of the criminal justice system against that type of behaviour most associated with inner-city blacks.

The inner-city left to rot

The consequences of these dehumanising ideologies and corresponding strategies of carceral control have been profound. Through the 1970s and early 1980s, the rise in the black prison population mirrored the overall rise in the prison population. Thus, although black incarceration rates were already higher than those for other

3. W. Bennett, *National Drug Control Strategy*, Office of National Drug Control Policy, Washington 1989.

groups, the two-fold expansion in the prison population between 1973 and 1982 led to a parallel two-fold expansion in the black prison population. However, as the prison population exploded in the 1980s, the per centage of blacks incarcerated for drug-related offences made a dramatic 447 per cent increase between 1986 and 1991. By comparison, the per centage of whites incarcerated for similar offences increased by only 115 per cent during the same period.

Contrary to popular assumptions, most drug offenders sent to prison are minor offenders. In 1992, over two-thirds of the drug arrests were for possession, while less than one-third were for the sale or manufacture of drugs. Indeed, according to the Department of Justice, over 36 per cent of those sentenced for drug offences are low–level drug offenders with no current or prior violent offences and no previous prison time. Moreover, nearly all of those prosecuted for crack are black. The mandatory minimum sentence of five years for possession of 5 grams of crack or 500 grams of powdered cocaine has resulted in long sentences for black men from the inner-city, where crack is common, and correspondingly lenient treatment for white suburban residents who are more likely to use powdered cocaine. According to the US Sentencing Commission, 90 per cent of the 14,000 federal inmates serving time under the crack law are black, compared with about one third of those in prison for powdered cocaine.

Earlier this year the Sentencing Commission, which has never been accused of being 'soft' on crime, proposed removing the 100 to 1 disparity in sentencing for crack and cocaine possession. Congress responded quickly to this action, passing a bill that rejected the Sentencing Commission's proposal. After intense debate within the White House, Clinton signed the bill in late October, saying 'I am not going to let anyone who peddles drugs get the idea that the cost of doing business is going down.' Never one to exert courageous leadership in the face of strong public opinion, Clinton's capitulation on this issue provides even more evidence that inner-city blacks have been essentially 'left to rot' by a society that views them as so fundamentally deviant that there is little that can or should be done to integrate them within 'respectable' society.

Conclusion

A simple example can bring the racial resentment of crack sentences into sharp focus. Consider two men, one black, the other white, both aged 20, both with similar family backgrounds, and both with a single prior conviction resulting in a 15 month sentence. The white man faces sentencing for delivering 450 grams of powdered cocaine, while the black man stands convicted of selling 40 grams of crack. Under the federal sentencing law upheld by Clinton and Congress, the white man will receive a 57 to 71 month sentence, *while the black man will receive a sentence ranging from 108 to 135 months.*

Such disparities, by no means limited to crack sentences, help explain the wide gulf in perceptions of drugs, crime, and the criminal justice system between white and black America. Defined in terms of base morality, deviant pathological behaviour, and permissiveness, not explicitly in terms of race, most whites who support tough crime proposals also believe strongly that mandatory drug sentences and other penal strategies are race neutral. The new prisons being built across the country will be filled by whatever people the courts decide belong there, just as the drive to make single mothers work will apply to all those receiving welfare.

Inner-city blacks, on the other hand, who (inadvertently or not) feel the full force of law and order policies, have totally lost faith in the legal system and understandably view America's criminal justice apparatuses - law, prisons, courts, police - as overtly racist. One clear measure of the inner-city backlash against the criminal justice system has been the marked increase in jury nullification by minority-dominated juries. Increasingly, majority black urban juries have been returning acquittals in the face of strong evidence of guilt. With some black leaders, and many opportunistic defence lawyers, urging minority jurors to express their rage by voting not guilty, acquittal rates have reached 39 per cent in Washington DC, 42 per cent in Detroit, and 45 per cent in the Bronx, all of which are at least double the national average.

If the conservative impulse to entirely abandon social democracy and integrative social regulation in favour of increasingly repressive penal strategies continues, the quality of life, even for those whites who have remained aloof from the destructive effects of their social and economic policies, is likely to so degenerate that the drive for public order through increased carceral control will not only be counterproductive and immoral, but may well come to a violent conclusion. Britain would do well to heed this warning, and to not only approach repressive penal strategies with extreme caution, but also recognise and confront the tendencies that have underpinned America's prison crisis.

The case for a Constitutional Court

John Griffith

*In the last two decades the role of judges in Britain
has become more politicised. John Griffith argues
that this is a dangerous trend, and that
contemporary problems in the area of public law
can best be resolved through a constitutional court.*

My argument is that the influence of the senior judiciary has increased, is increasing,
and ought to be diminished. At this point in our long island history, this is an
unpopular view and might be thought more applicable to the early years of the
Stuarts or the late years of Queen Victoria. The present Government is unpopular
(which is usual) and ill-advised (which is not). But its shortcomings are providing
a springboard for judicial activism of a dangerous kind. This is not, however, a
situation that has suddenly arisen, nor is it one that will quickly disappear. Apart
from the present discontents, it emerges from the relationships between the three
principal institutions of our Constitution, and in particular from a newfound vitality
among the judges which, in a modest way, began to show itself in the early 1960s.
This activism has led the senior judiciary into areas of decision-making where their
particular expertise is limited, and where their judgment is open to criticism.

Causes for concern
Freedom of expression and of association
Over the years the judiciary have defined and re-defined the limits of these

freedoms. The presence or absence of a written constitution or of a Bill of Rights, while it shapes this process, does not otherwise greatly affect its outcome, which depends on a wide range of changing economic, political and social events. Two factors may have caused the large number of conflicts in the courts involving the media during the 1980s: the style of government and the growth of investigative journalism. In some cases Law Officers were clearly being driven by the insistence of Ministers, including the Prime Minister. In other cases, newspaper editors and television producers responded readily to information they received from unorthodox sources. But the decisions in the courts were those of the judges and often aroused resentment and, occasionally, ridicule.

In 1980 the Law Lords in *British Steel Corporation v Granada Television* upheld the Court of Appeal, and required the respondents to disclose the name of the BSC employee who had supplied them with confidential documents used in a televised interview with the chairman of the corporation. Lord Salmon, dissenting said: 'There are no circumstances in this case which have ever before deprived or ever should deprive the press of its immunity against revealing its sources of information.'

This decision was followed by *Secretary of State for Defence v Guardian Newspapers* (1984), where the copy of a 'secret' Ministerial document was delivered anonymously to the editor of *The Guardian* newspaper. The document concerned parliamentary and public statements to be made on 1 November 1983 about, and contemporaneously with, the delivery of Cruise Missiles from the USA to Greenham Common air base. A majority of Law Lords upheld the decision of the Court of Appeal requiring the newspaper to deliver the copy to the Department. This was despite the provisions of section 10 of the Contempt of Court Act 1981 which protected newspapers from disclosure unless this was shown to be necessary in the interests of national security (amongst other things).

In 1985 and 1986, articles appeared in *The Times* and the *Independent* written by a financial journalist, concerning two references to the Monopolies and Mergers Commission. Inspectors investigating insider dealings required the journalist to answer questions about the nature and sources of his information. His refusal to do so resulted in a fine of £20,000, a decision upheld by the Law Lords: *Re an Inquiry* (1988).

Section 10 of the Contempt of Court Act 1981 was further weakened by the Law Lords' decision in *X Ltd v Morgan Grampian* (Publishers) Ltd (1990) (an application is presently before the European Court of Human Rights, supported by a majority of the Commission). The journalist in this case was found guilty of contempt for refusing to disclose his source and threatened with imprisonment. In the event he was fined £5000 with costs believed to exceed £100,000. Disclosure in the 'interests of justice' under section 10 was held to extend to include 'interests in the administration of justice'.

A cognate case was *Home Office v Harman* (1981) by the Court of Appeal and a majority of Law Lords, where a solicitor was found to be in contempt of court for showing a journalist documents which had been made public in court. On the basis of these documents, the journalist wrote an article criticising the Home Office for what he called 'internal bureaucratic intrigue'. Subsequently the European Commission of Human Rights accepted a complaint against the Government and a settlement was reached.

Similarly, a majority in the Court of Appeal upheld the granting of an injunction restraining Thames Television from showing a film about the Primodos drug used in pregnancy testing. Lord Justice Shaw said, 'The law of England was indeed, as Blackstone declared, a law of liberty; but the freedoms it recognised did not include a licence for the mercenary betrayal of business confidences': *Schering Chemicals v Falkman Ltd* (1982). Lord Denning MR dissented on the ground that such prior restraints were not justified. The general attitude of the courts was further shown in the strong criticisms made by senior members of the judiciary, especially Lord Lane, of the BBC programmes *Rough Justice* and *Out of Court*.

But the overwhelming litigation was that surrounding Peter Wright's memoirs, *Spycatcher*. In September 1985, the Attorney General began proceedings in the Supreme Court of New South Wales, seeking to restrain publication of the book for breach of confidentiality. In July 1986, in the United Kingdom, the Attorney was granted injunctions, upheld by the Court of Appeal under Sir John Donaldson, preventing *The Guardian* and the *Observer* from publishing articles deriving directly or indirectly from Wright. In April 1987 they were joined by the *Independent* and in July 1987 by the *Sunday Times*.

By this time, the book was available in the United Kingdom, having been published in the USA. So *The Guardian* and the *Observer* in July 1987 sought the discharge of the injunctions against them. But, in crucial judgments, the Court of Appeal and, by a majority, the Law Lords continued the injunctions. In Lord Templeman's opinion, the continuance of the injunctions was fully consistent with the European Convention of Human Rights. This was when the reputation of the senior judiciary reached its lowest point, the absurdity of preventing newspaper publication in these circumstances being manifest.

Eventually the High Court, the Court of Appeal and, in October 1988, the Law Lords accepted that the injunctions must be discharged. But the damage had been done. As Sir Nicolas Browne-Wilkinson V-C had said on 22 July 1987 when supporting applications to discharge the injunctions (in which he was overruled):

> It is frequently said that the law is an ass. I, of course, do not agree. But there is a limit to what can be achieved by orders of the court. If the courts were to make orders manifestly incapable of achieving their avowed purpose, such as to prevent the dissemination of information which is already disseminated, the law would to my mind indeed be an ass.

A recent decision in this line of cases interfering with the freedom of expression was the upholding by the courts of the media ban on broadcasting any matter which included words spoken by a person representing or purporting to represent various organisations in Northern Ireland.

Seven journalists sought to have the ban set aside on the grounds that the ban was contrary to Article 10 of the European Convention of Human Rights; disproportionate to the mischief at which it was aimed; perverse in that no reasonable Secretary of State properly directing himself could have made it; and that the statute and licence did not empower him to give such directives, which prevented or hindered the broadcasting authorities from fulfilling their duties to preserve due impartiality: *ex parte Brind* (1991). The Law Lords rejected these arguments and held that the Secretary of State had not exceeded the limits of his discretion nor acted unreasonably.

A second fundamental freedom is that of association and membership of a trade union or other such body. Here the outstanding decision was that of the Law Lords upholding the Government's ban in December 1983 on trade union membership of civil servants at the Government Communications Headquarters (GCHQ): *Council of Civil Service Unions v Minister for the Civil Service* (1985). The Prime Minister's decision was taken without consultation with the union. The question before the courts was whether the failure to consult invalidated the decision to ban. Before the Court of Appeal, the Government claimed that consultation might have endangered national security, and supported this by an affidavit sworn by Sir Robert Armstrong as Secretary of the Cabinet and Head of the Home Civil Service. The crucial passage was in para 16:

> To have entered such consultations would have served to bring out the
> vulnerability of areas of operation to those who had shown themselves ready to
> organise disruption, and consultation with individual members of staff at
> GCHQ would have been impossible without involving the national unions.

The Law Lords accepted this claim without further investigation, although its substance was strongly denied by the trade unions. In this, as in other cases, the courts refused to question the validity of the Government's defence of 'national security'.

Miscarriages of justice

This group of cases requires little elaboration. Nothing contributed more to the decline in the reputation of the senior judiciary than their failures to respond to allegations of wrongful convictions.

The Guildford Four were convicted of murder in September 1975 and in 1977 were refused leave to appeal after the Balcombe Street arrests of IRA members who claimed responsibility. The new evidence gave rise 'to no lurking doubts whatever' in the minds of the Court of Appeal. The Maguire Seven were convicted of unlawfully handling nitroglycerine in 1976. They also were refused leave to appeal in 1977, no member of the Court seeing any reason for disturbing any of the convictions on the basis that they were unsafe or unsatisfactory.

Doubts about the rightness of the convictions of these eleven people persisted and in August 1987 the Avon and Somerset police were appointed to undertake an inquiry. Documents were found at Guildford which led to the conclusion of police fabrication and on 19 October 1989 the convictions of the Four were quashed. In June 1990 the Director of Public Prosecutions accepted that the convictions of the Maguire Seven were unsafe and unsatisfactory and could not be upheld.

On 21 November 1975 six men were convicted of the murder of twenty-one persons in a bomb attack at public houses in Birmingham. In March 1976 applications for leave to appeal were refused. When in 1980 the Court of Appeal accepted an application by the police to strike out civil proceedings brought by the Birmingham Six, Lord Denning MR said:

> Just consider the course of events if this action is allowed to proceed to trial. If the six men fail, it will mean that much time and money will have been expended by many people to no good purpose. If the six men win, it will mean that the police were guilty of perjury, that they were guilty of violence and threats, that the confessions were involuntary and were improperly admitted in evidence and that the convictions were erroneous. That would mean the Home Secretary would either have to recommend they be pardoned or he would have to remit the case to the Court of Appeal. This is such an appalling vista that every sensible person in the land would say: It cannot be right these actions should go any further.

In November 1981 the Law Lords upheld Lord Denning's judgment.

In 1987 the Devon and Cornwall police carried out an inquiry and subsequently the case was referred to the Court of Appeal. Lord Lane CJ, Lords Justices Stephen Brown and O'Connor reported in January 1988: 'The longer the hearing has gone on the more convinced this Court has become that the verdict of the jury was correct. We have no doubt that these convictions were both safe and satisfactory'. In August 1990, following the abandonment of the convictions of the Guildford Four and a further police investigation, the case was referred again to the Court of Appeal. On 14 March 1991 the Court set free the Birmingham Six.

Neither the conduct of the trial courts nor the evidence there adduced is here in issue. What matters are the misjudgments of the Court of Appeal, in refusing leave to appeal, and on referrals. On these the record was corrected only after continuous and persistent pressure from the Great and the Good, determined members of both Houses of Parliament, investigative journalists, and other campaigners.

The work and organisation of the legal profession

This was the title of the principal policy paper put forward by the Lord Chancellor in January 1989 (Cm 570). Two others concerned Contingency Fees (Cm 571) and Conveyancing by Authorised Practitioners (Cm 572). The response from the senior judiciary was extraordinary and verged on the hysterical.

Lord Lane CJ referred to the first paper as 'one of the most sinister documents ever to emanate from Government'. Lord Donaldson MR said he had 'absolutely no disagreement' with Lord Lane over the main issues. Lord Scarman criticised the papers as being 'ill-considered', 'superficial' in their reasoning, and 'flawed' in their logic. Lord Ackner spoke of the proposals as involving 'at the very least a substantial risk of the destruction of the Bar', of 'the myopic application of dogma'. The former Lord Chancellor, Lord Hailsham, was reported as saying that the Government was 'thinking with its bottom and sitting on its head'.

In a debate in the House of Lords on 7 April 1989, Lord Lane spoke of oppression not standing 'on the doorstep with a toothbrush moustache and a swastika armband' but creeping up step by step until all of a sudden the unfortunate citizen realised that freedom had gone. Lord Donaldson spoke of an 'unmitigated disaster', Lord Bridge of a 'deep sense of unease' felt by the great majority of the judiciary and of 'hasty and ill-considered legislation'. Lords Goff, Griffiths, Ackner and Oliver spoke in like terms. Much of this was repeated by Lords Ackner and Donaldson during the Lords' debate on the Courts and Legal Services Bill which implemented, in a modified form, Lord Mackay's proposals.

The extremity of the language and the vehemence in which it was couched seemed to suggest that the senior judiciary were not to be trusted with a calm consideration of where the public interest lay on matters affecting the legal profession and the administration of justice.

Future developments
The European Convention on Human Rights
The campaign for the incorporation of this Convention into UK domestic law has now attracted the support of many members of the senior judiciary. Whatever may be said of the substantive merits and demerits of this proposal there is no doubt that incorporation would greatly increase the political influence of the courts and lead to further judicialisation of the political process or, according to one's view, politicisation of the judicial process.

In recent debates in the House of Lords (the Third Reading was on 1 May 1995), Lord Lester's Human Rights Bill advocated incorporation and was supported by Lord Taylor CJ, Lord Woolf, Lord Browne-Wilkinson, Lord Lloyd and Lord Slynn. The Lord Chief Justice said he also spoke with the strong support of Sir Thomas Bingham MR. Other judges of lower rank have expressed their support for incorporation. The Labour and Liberal Democrat parties have both endorsed incorporation.

Incorporation can take several forms but may increase the political involvement of the judiciary in three ways. The first can be exemplified by Article 2 of the Convention. This provides: 'Everyone's life shall be protected by law'. Hitherto abortion and euthanasia have been matters for discussion and decision in Parliament. Under this Article, they will be transferred to the courts. In the USA, as is well-known, this has involved Presidential nominees for the Supreme Court in much controversy.

Secondly, if incorporation is to be properly entrenched it must empower the courts to declare Acts of Parliament invalid. This is the consequence favoured, as we shall see, by at least one Law Lord. Other forms of incorporation stop short of this. Nevertheless they are bound to give rise to much political argument in the courts.

Thirdly, the provisions of several Articles of the Convention empower the courts to rule whether or not a particular restriction on a conferred 'right' is legal, and to do so on political grounds. Thus Article 10 provides: 'Everyone has the right to freedom of expression'. It continues:

> The exercise of these freedoms, since it carries with it duties and responsibilities, may be subject to such formalities, conditions, restrictions or penalties as are prescribed by law and are necessary in a democratic society, in the interests of national security, territorial integrity or public safety, for the prevention of disorder or crime, for the protection of health or morals, for the protection of the reputation or rights of others, for preventing the disclosure of information received in confidence, or for maintaining the authority and impartiality of the judiciary.

This, in some respects, actually weakens the rights of the individual under the common law by the imprecision of categories such as 'protection of health or morals'. But, more importantly, it vests in the courts the power to decide what restrictions are 'necessary in a democratic society'. It is difficult to imagine any judgment more political and more comprehensive than that.

I am not here concerned with the arguments for or against incorporation, only to establish that incorporation seems likely to be enacted within the first session of a Parliament under a Labour or Liberal-Labour administration, and that this will result in a substantial transfer of political power to the senior judiciary.

The new jurisprudence

During the last few years, judges have actively extended their powers by the development of judicial review and other procedures. This has been spoken of largely as a reaction to the activities of over-zealous or careless Ministers, and no doubt this is part of the story. But the other part is the greater willingness of the courts to extend their jurisdiction. It is easy to applaud the decision in *M v Home Office* (1993) where the Law Lords held the Home Secretary to be guilty of contempt of court (albeit only in his official capacity, not personally), for disregarding an order of the court requiring an asylum seeker to be returned to the UK; and the requirement in *ex parte Hickey* (1994) that the Home Secretary disclose fresh information he receives following inquiries on a petition to refer a conviction to the Court of Appeal. But the critical lines that separate executive power from judicial power were shown dramatically in *ex parte Fire Brigades Union and others* (1995). By a majority of 3 to 2, the Law Lords held that the Home Secretary could not ignore a statutory provision enabling him to bring into force a statutory scheme for payment of compensation to victims of crime, while proposing a different non-statutory scheme of his own.

For the minority Lord Keith said: 'The fact that the decision is of a political and administrative character means that any interference by a court of law would be a most improper intrusion into a field which lies peculiarly within the province of Parliament'. He was joined by Lord Mustill who said that some of the argument addressed to their Lordships 'would have the court push to the very boundaries of the distinction between court and Parliament established in, and recognised ever since, the Bill of Rights 1689. 300 years have passed since then, and the political and social landscape has changed beyond recognition. But the boundaries remain; they are of crucial significance to our private and public lives; and the courts should, I believe, make sure that they are not overstepped'.

These recent cases may be seen as a continuation of the general trends of the 1980s. But there is another aspect. It seems there is a concerted drive by some members of the senior judiciary to extend their powers into new fields from which hitherto they have been excluded by the conventional laws of the constitution.

In 1995 in an article in *Public Law* entitled 'Law and Democracy', Mr Justice Laws, a judge of the High Court, spoke of the principles which lie behind judicial decisions. It is obvious that judges must often have regard to the public interest and that this will be shaped by their own personalities and experiences. But Sir John Laws went much further when he spoke of

> the deeper question, whether good judicial decisions are themselves fuelled by ideals which are not normally neutral, but which represent ethical principles about how the state should be run, and in that sense may be said to be political principles ... The substantive principles of judicial review are judge-made, owing neither their content nor their authority as law to the legislature ... They constitute ethical ideals as to the virtuous conduct of the state's affairs.

It is far from obvious that judges should apply their own political philosophy - 'how the state should be run' - in the determination of cases that come before them.

Sir John then hugely magnifies his claim of judicial supremacy by calling into existence a 'higher-order law' which could not be abrogated by Parliament. In his formulation it is the Constitution that is sovereign, not Parliament, and judges are the Constitution's custodians. We should recognise, says Sir John 'the moral force of the basis on which control of public power is effected by the unelected judges'. This is reminiscent of the old story of Labouchere who said that he did not object to Gladstone's always having the ace of trumps up his sleeve, but only to his pretence that God put it there.

Sir John makes clear how far his doctrine of judicial supremacy may go. First he considers Article 9 of the Bill of Rights, protecting the freedom of speech and debates or proceedings in Parliament from being impeached or questioned in any court or place out of Parliament. This he calls 'a statute like any other' and so subject to judicial interpretation. To be specific, he says he is 'not convinced' that an MP who, motivated by actual personal malice, defames, in the course of debate, an individual outside Parliament, 'should not' be subject to 'the ordinary law of defamation', presumably in the ordinary courts 'out of Parliament'. He adds: 'Article 9 could *readily* be construed conformably with such a state of affairs" (my emphasis).

In the same issue of *Public Law*, Lord Woolf writes on 'Droit Public - English Style', and he is prepared to take the final step: 'I myself would consider there were advantages in making it clear that ultimately there are even limits on the supremacy of Parliament which it is the courts' inalienable responsibility to identify and uphold.' He concludes that this is necessary 'to enable the rule of law to be preserved'.

Over the years, judges have from time to time claimed this pre-eminence which today seems to be couched in the strongest terms. Those who take this view see themselves as occupying a position above Parliament as guardians of some ultimate political principles which they enshrine. In these days of 'sleaze' and Lord Nolan's committee such a claim may be popular. But it is dangerous in the extreme and the record of the courts in recent times does not begin to justify acceptance of such a position. In Britain's democracy, 'how the state should be run' must be determined by the Queen in Parliament, not by judges, however eminent.

The present situation is not remediable by merely procedural changes to the method of appointing judges. I suggest that it requires structural and institutional reform and the appointment of new non-legal members to the highest court.

A Constitutional Court

Whatever procedural changes may be suggested in the appointment of judges - such as a Judicial Commission, a Minister of Justice responsible to the House of Commons, or a wider recruitment to all levels of the bench from amongst legal practitioners - in my view something extra is needed to deal properly with the mix of legal, political and social problems presented by public law cases. A new structure is needed that will address the complex issues in this area, issues which are at present too often decided by the judiciary. For this purpose I propose the creation of a Constitutional Court composed in part of judges and in part of persons from outside the legal profession.

Such a Court could take many forms. What follows is one model, in the barest outline.

Jurisdiction: This would include: (1) all judicial review cases; (2) all referrals in cases of alleged miscarriages of justice (to investigate which the Court would need special powers); (3) all cases involving contempt of court or breaches of confidentiality where the public interest was involved; (4) all cases brought under the European Convention on Human Rights if incorporated in UK domestic law.

Membership: This would consist of panels of: (1) 10 judges appointed by the same person or body entrusted with the appointment of judges generally; (2) 10 councillors (or some other such title) appointed by the Queen, on the nomination of the Prime Minister. Appointments to the Court of judges and councillors would be for five years, not renewable. One judge and one councillor would be designated Joint President. The panel of judges would be drawn from senior judges already in office who would continue to be available to hear cases in their own courts. The panel of councillors would be drawn from those having experience in the conduct of public affairs or in business, trade unions, the media, the voluntary sector, or the professions. Excluded from nomination would be practising members of the legal profession, MPs and peers, those holding offices of profit under the Crown, and the employees of local authorities. The appointments would be part-time.

Sittings: Cases would, ordinarily, be heard by 3 judges and 3 councillors. Exceptionally, plenary sessions would consist of 5 judges and 5 councillors. Sitting members would be chosen by their respective Joint-Presidents (who might also sit as one of the members).

Access: Leave to appeal to the Constitutional Court from either the court of first instance or the Court of Appeal would be granted only by the Constitutional Court who would need to be satisfied that a matter of sufficient public interest was involved. Leapfrogging over the Court of Appeal from the court of first instance to the Constitutional Court would be common.

Presentation: Written submission of argument would be the practice, followed by a short hearing. *Amicus* and Brandeis briefs, bringing before the Court advice and argument from individuals and groups having special knowledge relevant to the issues, would be encouraged. If the Court split 3-3 or 5-5, the appeal would be lost.

This is only one possible model, and obviously it is only a sketch. However, it is my view that such a court could play a crucial role both in giving serious attention to difficult and complex areas of public law, and in restraining the judiciary from their increasing intervention into areas that more properly belong in the political sphere.

The Law and Social Rights

Keith Ewing

*Keith Ewing argues that social and economic rights,
especially for trade unions, need to be protected by
statute. In addition, it should be Parliament, not the
law courts, that is the guardian of these rights.*

David Wilson is a journalist who was employed by the *Daily Mail*. In 1989 the
employer decided to terminate the collective bargaining arrangements then in force
and invited all those employed under the collectively agreed terms to sign what
are sometimes referred to as 'personal contracts'. Those who agreed to the personal
contracts were given a 4.5 per cent backdated pay increase while those who did
not remained employed on the terms and conditions in force when the collective
bargaining arrangements were terminated. As a senior trade union representative
at the *Daily Mail*, Mr Wilson refused to accept the new terms and so did not
qualify for the increase. The simple question which these simple facts presented
was whether the employer had done anything unlawful in discriminating against
Mr Wilson?

An industrial tribunal held that the employer had acted unlawfully, but this
was reversed by the Employment Appeal Tribunal which in turn was reversed by
the Court of Appeal, the original decision thereby being restored. But before the
appeal could be heard by the House of Lords the government intervened, in May
1993, with a late amendment to the Trade Union Reform and Employment Rights
Bill authorising employers to discriminate against trade unionists in the way of the
Daily Mail. The House of Lords was later to reveal that the government's indecent
haste was uncalled for; reversing the Court of Appeal it was unanimously held
that the current statutory protection against discrimination on the grounds of trade

union membership does not apply to the conduct of the employer in this case. The employer was concerned not by membership of the union but only by a desire to get rid of collective bargaining.

There are many who would see this distinction as mere sophistry, based on an impossibly narrow perception of the statutory protection of trade union membership. Essentially, the House of Lords was saying that people are protected in being in association with others but not if they seek to enjoy the benefits or services of the association. Other distinctions drawn by the House of Lords would be treated with equal disdain, including in particular the holding that the discrimination against Mr Wilson was an omission which did not constitute 'action' against him as the statute required, an aspect of the decision which was all the more puzzling for the fact that the Act expressly states that 'action' includes 'omission' (unless the context otherwise requires). It was of no comfort to Mr Wilson that the unanimous decision of the Lords was taken 'with regret' by at least one of them.

The erosion of trade union rights

The *Wilson* case raises many awkward questions. The most obvious relates to the performance of the judges. This was a court which included two past presidents of the Employment Appeal Tribunal, people with some experience of labour law. It was a decision taken with at least one of its members knowing that it would leave 'an undesirable lacuna in the legislation protecting employees against victimisation'. And it was a decision reached only by reversing the Court of Appeal below. The other question raised by the case relates to the statutory framework of workers' rights. Not only does it raise the issue of the narrow drafting of the protection against discrimination. Even more importantly, it highlights the absence of any provision preventing employers from derecognising a trade union, the decision which set in motion the events which led to the House of Lords decision. Perhaps more that anything else the importance of the *Wilson* case lies in this highlighting of the consequences of the lack of a legally underwritten guarantee of the employees' right to a collective voice at work.

In this respect the case reveals a more general concern about the erosion of social and economic rights in this country since 1979, as successive Tory governments have moved gradually to dismantle the structure built up carefully in the 1970s. Although gradual the change has been relentless. An average of one major piece of legislation has been introduced every two years, and further restrictions have been introduced by secondary legislation, or, as in the case of the trade union ban at GCHQ, under the royal prerogative. These measures have attacked along two broad fronts, with the first serving to deregulate the basic employment protection standards, and the second to withdraw the rights of trade unions. So far as the former is concerned we have seen the abolition of the wages councils which set minimum conditions for the most vulnerable workers, and we have seen also the extension of the qualifying period for the bringing of an unfair dismissal action, from 6 months to two years, arguably the most cruel of a number of measures which invite that sobriquet.

In the area of trade union rights, we have seen the removal of a number of measures introduced to underpin by legislation the process of collective bargaining. We have seen also the introduction of a number of wide ranging restrictions on the operation of the right to strike; the combined effect of these is to make it very difficult for trade unions to organise industrial action within the law. The purposes for which industrial action may be taken have been significantly narrowed; the tactics which might be employed in the course of a dispute have been reduced by restoring liability for secondary and sympathy action; and a complex framework of highly prescriptive procedural obligations has been imposed requiring both mandatory postal ballots (at the unions' expense), and the giving of various forms to notice to the employer. Even where these formalities are met strikers may still be dismissed by the employer, though non strikers may not be expelled from the union.

These great legal changes have accompanied equally momentous social and economic changes in Britain since 1979. Indeed it may well be that the legal changes contributed to these other developments. For example, we can point to a significant decline in the levels of trade union membership and collective bargaining density, with only 1 in 3 workers now thought to be unionised, and with less than half of the labour force now covered by collective bargaining. These figures compare with a level of trade union density of about 62 per cent in 1980, and a level of collective bargaining (and wages council order) coverage in excess of 80 per cent at about the same time. Although other countries have also seen a decline in the level of trade union influence there are few countries where this has been as marked as in Britain. Subject to the terms of employment protection legislation it means that most workers must now depend on their own personal bargaining power as a guarantee against unfairness at work.

Alongside the decline in the levels of trade union and collective bargaining density, we can point also to an unprecedented increase in levels of income inequality and job insecurity. Indeed it was estimated by the Rowntree Inquiry into Income and Wealth earlier this year that the increase in income inequality since 1977 grew faster in Britain that in any other OECD country with the exception of New Zealand. As the Institute of Employment Rights points out in *Just the Job?*, a consultation paper on the future of employment law issued earlier this year, this rise in inequality of incomes, together with cuts in social security, has contributed to an increase in household poverty. Job insecurity is clearly much more difficult to measure, but it has been estimated by Cambridge economists that there are now some 9 million disadvantaged workers in this country, that is to say people without secure or well paid employment, living as a result in either insecurity or comparative poverty. Indeed this is thought to account for as many as 30 per cent of British workers.

Possible codes of social and economic rights

A good starting point for any progressive policies for the future is to look at the international treaties to which this and other countries are parties - legacies of a bygone era. Perhaps the most significant of these are not the treaties of the EC or EU, but those of the International Labour Organisation, a UN agency of which this country is a member, and which by its constitution is committed to the realisation of a number of social goals.

These include full employment and the raising of standards of living; the ILO is also committed to 'policies in regard to wages and earnings, hours and other conditions of work calculated to ensure a just share of the fruits of progress to all, and a minimum living wage to all employed and in need of such protection'; and to the 'effective recognition of the right to collective bargaining', and to the 'co-operation of management and labour in the continuous improvement of productive efficiency'.

The constitutional objectives of the ILO have been translated into 176 Conventions and 183 Recommendations. Many of these have been ratified or adopted by United Kingdom governments, including the two most fundamental treaties of the ILO, namely Conventions 87 and 98 which deal respectively with Freedom of Association and the Right to Organise, and the Right to Organise and Collective Bargaining. It is the breach of these measures in particular which has brought Britain to the edge of international shame: it is the recommendation of the supervisory agencies based in Geneva that much (though not all) of the legislation of Tory governments passed since 1980 violates the guarantees of these fundamental texts. This is true, for example, of the trade union ban at GCHQ, many of the restrictions which have been imposed on the right to strike, and much of the legislation interfering with the autonomy of trade union government. Remarkably the Government has done nothing to fall into line behind the judgment of its international peers and continues to defy the rule of international law.

At a time of vibrant debate about constitutional reform it behoves us to consider the extent to which social and economic rights, of which the ILO Constitution and Conventions are singular examples, can be brought within the framework of any new constitutional settlement. Although there is quite rightly concern about the need for the better protection of civil and political liberties, social and economic rights have in practice been shown to be more vulnerable to erosion and more in need of protection. Indeed one of the great unfulfilled promises of the twentieth century has been to secure the implementation of the type of programme crystalised in the ILO Constitution. So while there may be a case for protecting important liberal values such as freedom of speech and assembly, it is also important that the state recognises its obligations to all of its citizens in terms of their social and economic welfare.

The question which then arises, however, is whether there is a role for formal legal measures to entrench or recognise these rights. Or does social and economic progress depend on the development of social forces which constitutions and legislation are powerless to mould? There are few who would defend such a position, and fewer still who would argue that progress can happen only when changes have taken place in the economic structure of society. There is no alternative - and there never has been - here or elsewhere in western Europe, to seeking to embrace, adopt and employ the constitutional machinery of the state for the purpose of promoting social and economic progress. Indeed to deny that change can be directed by the juridical and political superstructure would be to deny the legitimacy of the ILO, and to undermine the work of those campaigning to expand the social constitution of the European Union.

So where do we go from here? The answer depends on how far constitutional reform is to be taken. If, however, it is proposed to incorporate the European Convention on Human Rights into domestic law as a restraint on the power of Parliament, there is no justification for doing so in isolation, and without also incorporating parallel texts, such as the Council of Europe's Social Charter of 1961. Similarly, if it is proposed to have a distinctively British Bill of Rights there is no reason why it should be confined to civil and political liberties, and should not also include social and economic rights including for example the right to a minimum wage, to a safe and healthy working environment, and to protection from unfair treatment at work. There is also no reason why it would not include the right to form and join trade unions, the right of a trade union to be recognised by an employer in accordance with procedures laid down by law, and the right to strike in accordance with restrictions or limitations laid down by law.

Problems of enforcement

It is one thing to contemplate the possibility of the entrenchment of certain documents, or of certain rights, as part of a tailor made document; it is another matter altogether to contemplate the possibility of the enforcement of such measures. Civil and political rights are relatively easy to deal with in the sense that, if you have the money it is usually pretty straightforward to be able to challenge a government decision, for example on the ground that it violates the right to freedom of expression. But social and economic rights are different. The party violating the rights is not usually the government, but an employer in the private sector. There is, however, no reason why this should be an impediment, for the constitution need not be confined to the relationship between the citizen and the state, but may also address certain relations between individuals and groups within the community. However, there do exist two main problems for the enforcement of social and economic rights through the judiciary.

The first problem is the nature of the judiciary: the courts have been a major problem with regard to the delivery of social justice. An indication of why we should continue to be cautious was provided in the landmark GCHQ case, when the civil service unions challenged the decision of the responsible minister in the courts, after having convinced the ILO's Freedom of Association Committee (the appropriate supervisory body) that the ban by the Government violated ILO Convention 87. This provides that workers, 'without distinction whatsoever', have the right to establish and join trade unions of their own choosing without prior authorisation. In the proceedings before the domestic courts one of the issues which arose for consideration was whether the government's conduct could be said to be irrational because of its failure to comply with international labour standards. The Court of Appeal not only answered in the negative, but in an extraordinary example of forensic arrogance also held that there was no breach of Convention 87, notwithstanding the view expressed by the Freedom of Association Committee to the contrary.

This case is relevant because this is the type of document that we would be asking the courts to protect were we to constitutionalise social and economic rights. The courts, predictably, got it wrong, even though the correct answer had already been provided for them. They consciously chose to ignore the correct answer, by indulging themselves in a very literal interpretation of the treaty, in a manner appropriate for the interpretation of a tax statute. This is not to say that the courts are always on the side of the Government. We can now point to some great and creative decisions of the senior courts, especially in the area of equal opportunities law. For example, moulding the language of the Treaty of Rome and Directives made thereunder, the House of Lords swept away the exclusion of part-time workers from unfair dismissal and redundancy payments, and the Court of Appeal has also ruled against the qualifying periods for both. The fate of David Wilson is, however, a timely reminder that the leopard has not changed its spots, the House of Lords in that case being willing to reverse the decision of the Court of Appeal, despite the acknowledgement that it could thereby leave union activists exposed to the risk of victimisation.

The second problem with judicial review as a method of entrenchment is the question of constitutional principle. Although it is increasingly heretical to say so in the new liberal age, the principle of parliamentary sovereignty is an important principle of constitutional law which should not be lightly surrendered. It is also a principle which provides important opportunities for the implementation of practical measures of social and economic progress. Although it is true that the principle of parliamentary sovereignty was established in the pre-democratic time, it was nevertheless the first essential step on the road to democracy, and continues to perform a democratic function, indeed a function which might be said to be peculiarly sensitive to the constitutional principles of democratic socialism. For the essence of a democratic socialist constitution is the principle of popular sovereignty, and whatever Dicey and other writers may have thought when writing in a different age, the principle of parliamentary sovereignty can be defended now as the constitutional or legal principle which best reflects and gives effect to the political principle of popular sovereignty.

So we are impaled on the horns of a dilemma. There is a demand for constitutional reform. And there is an argument that social and economic rights have as great a claim to constitutional recognition as do civil and political rights and freedoms. (Indeed the claim is all the greater in the sense that people in this country still have the right to vote and the right of freedom of expression, if they can afford to exercise it. But there is no right to be represented by a trade union, to have one's union recognised by an employer for the purposes of collective bargaining, or to be protected from dismissal for taking part in a strike or other industrial action.) Yet there is concern about leaving the enforcement of social and economic rights to the courts, partly because of the record of the courts in this area, but partly also because of the need not to usurp the proper role of Parliament. All of this suggests that the way forward may depend on a system of entrenchment which relies on Parliament rather than the courts, and is for the protection not only of social and economic rights but also civil and political rights.

The solution to this problem is in fact provided by institutional structures currently in place in Sweden. Although these were mainly designed for the safeguarding of constitutionally protected civil and political rights, they are capable of adaptation to serve a much wider need. The principal method for the safeguarding of constitutionally entrenched rights is the Constitutional Committee of the Riksdag. If it were to find that a Bill violates the Constitution, the Bill could be delayed for a year unless it has the support of 5/6 of the members of the House. It is not suggested that this type of constitutional scrutiny should be adopted in Britain in precisely this form, but it does provide some food for thought. One possibility would be to establish such a Committee in Parliament (questions will arise as to appointment and composition) and to entrust it to scrutinise legislation and secondary legislation to ensure compliance with treaties such as the European Convention on Human Rights and ILO Conventions 87 and 98. Questions would then arise as to the powers of such a Committee and whether there should be parallel structures in the second chamber (or indeed whether there should be a joint committee of the two Houses).

Although there are many drawbacks with a regime such as this, it also has many attractions, not the least of which is that it leaves responsibility for the enforcement of rights with Parliament. Moreover, by providing that civil and political rights would be protected in the same way, it thereby reduces the risk of important measures of social progress being undermined by judicial review at the suit of companies with their well filled money bags. In effect it restores the role of Parliament as the defender of the rights of individuals within the community; it does not authorise the sacrifice of social and economic rights on the alter of civil and political liberty; and it does not make the vindication of rights dependent on people's ability to litigate. It does mean, however, that the rights in question would not be self-executing and that implementing legislation would be necessary to give them content and substance. The scheme proposed here would be designed to operate as a restraint on any erosion, by government sponsored legislation, of the constitutionally entrenched provisions. The constitutional entrenchment of social and economic rights would thus have to be accompanied by measures for their statutory implementation.

A code for trade union rights

The task then is to draw up a statutory code appropriate for the domestic legal agenda, a code to replace that which we currently have, now extending to over 400 pages in what will be three consolidation Acts. This is not to suggest that we can or should contemplate a statutory code which would regulate every worker for every moment of the working life. But it is to suggest the need for a comprehensive code to replace the deregulatory and deconstructionist structures which we currently have in place. Unless we are to return to the common law, whatever replaces the current framework will inevitably and unavoidably provide a comprehensive platform of minimum rights covering a wide range of issues (drawing on ILO and EC standards), and will also seek to restore power to trade unions to act on behalf of workers and to build upon the platform of statutory guarantees.

There is a need for a strong framework of legislation which guarantees rights in respect of trade union membership, trade union organisation, and trade union representation and recognition. It is true that we already have rights in respect of trade union membership, in the sense that workers may not be dismissed or have action short of dismissal taken against them because of their trade union membership, or their participation in trade union activities at an appropriate time. The *Wilson* case, however, exposed the limitations of the current protection, which in any event was further weakened by the legislation passed in the wake of the Court of Appeal's decision that the employer acted unlawfully. There is thus a need, as an early priority, for the current protection to be extended by providing that people are entitled to protection from discrimination not only on account of their trade union membership or activities, but also on account of enjoying the benefits or services of membership.

On the question of trade union organisation rights, the aim here is to enable unions to build up their strength in the workplace in order adequately to represent members employed there. But as matters currently stand, the only effective organisational right which British unions enjoy is the right of their lay officials to have time off work with pay in order to carry out their industrial relations duties or to undergo training in these duties. Based on ILO Convention 135, this clearly contemplates the possibility of lay officials being entitled to paid time off work to seek to recruit newly hired employees, to hold meetings of the membership at the workplace, and to represent members in grievance or disciplinary proceedings or before outside bodies such as industrial tribunals. But all this applies only where the union is already recognised by the employer, and moreover it fails to address adequately the problems which unions face in trying to recruit and represent members in a hostile environment.

There are in fact three organisational needs for unions. The first is the right of full time or branch officials to enter a workplace in order to meet workers employed there; the second is the right of the union in the workplace to hold meetings and elections at the workplace; and the third is the right to distribute material about the union to members and other workers employed there. There is a case for saying that organisational rights, which are designed principally to build up strength and a presence in the workplace, are in fact a necessary prerequisite to recognition and should be acknowledged as such. There is thus a strong case for arguing then that these rights should depend not on the union being recognised by the employer but on its being represented in the workplace - though clearly it is open to consideration whether a single member should be enough to unlock the door for the union, or whether a more substantial level of representation should be required.

Apart from trade union membership rights and trade union organisation rights, the third factor in the equation is trade union representation and recognition rights. Here there are two offerings on the menu, both of which look appetising, though neither of them may on its own satisfy the real hunger for legislation. One option is that developed by the campaign group Press for Union Rights under the NUJ General Secretary John Foster. This proposed that workers should have the right to individual and collective representation by a trade union on all matters relating to their working conditions.

Developed in a document entitled *Workers' Rights: The Next Step*, the proposal for collective representation has proved to be the most controversial. It would give workers the right to nominate a trade union to act on their behalf collectively with other workers, the employer being under a duty to meet the union officials representing the workers in question, a duty which would apply regardless of the number of workers who had elected in favour of collective representation of their interests.

The other option is that which was recently proposed by the TUC in their document *Your Voice at Work*, in which trade unions would be entitled to recognition for the purposes of collective bargaining where they could demonstrate either majority membership or majority support in the appropriate bargaining unit. Where a union fails to secure majority support but has the support of at least 10 per cent of the workers in the unit in question it would be entitled to general consultation rights which would include the right to be consulted about matters prescribed by EC law. In workplaces where there is no trade union support of this level, the employer would be required to establish an elected body to represent the workforce as a whole, with which the employer would be required to consult on the matters prescribed by EC law, currently business transfers and collective redundancies. Unions would have the right to nominate candidates for what would in effect be a works council.

The implementation of either or both of these proposals would go a long way towards helping trade unions to expand their role in the workplace, and would at the same time help people like David Wilson in the future. But whether they will be enough on their own to restore collective bargaining to the levels to which we were accustomed before 1980 is an open question. As already pointed out, it is now estimated that collective agreements reach only 47 per cent of the labour force, compared with a remarkable 82 per cent in the mid 1970s (if wages council orders are also taken into account). In other words, less that half of British workers are now covered by collective bargaining, a shocking statistic when compared with the levels of coverage in other major OECD countries where (with the exception of Canada, the United States and Japan) the levels are typically much higher. OECD figures suggest that the level of coverage in Austria is 98 per cent, Belgium 90 per cent, Germany 90 per cent, Netherlands 71 percent and Sweden 83 per cent.

It is difficult to avoid the conclusion that if we are to have a new constitutional settlement under a new left of centre government, it must necessarily give prominent scope to social and economic rights, if only because they have proved to be the most vulnerable to erosion. But any new settlement must also be mindful of the difficulties in relying on the courts for the effective implementation of social and economic rights, and must acknowledge also the constitutional role and function of Parliament. This has implications not only for social and economic rights, but also for the civil and political liberties, which should enjoy no elevated constitution status, but which should be enforced in the same way as social and economic rights. A new commitment to social and economic rights would not then rely solely on a commitment to their constitutional recognition, but above all on a comprehensive statutory code for their effective implementation.

Historically we might have hoped that collective bargaining would have been the primary vehicle for the delivery of social and economic justice. But the erosion of collective bargaining density is such that is open to question whether this is a realistic option unless a determined effort is made to re-establish effective and comprehensive bargaining machinery. The current proposals of bodies like the TUC and the Press for Union Rights group would clearly go a long way towards closing the representation gap in British workplaces. But it remains to be seen whether they will be enough, without the accompaniment of some kind of joint or tripartite sectoral employment regulation. Unless a commitment of this kind is undertaken we are facing the unavoidable prospect of workers relying on the state for the direct regulation of their working conditions in numbers much larger than would have been considered acceptable or desirable in the past.

One step nearer to genuine citizenship:

Reflections on the Commission of Social Justice Report

Ruth Lister

Citizenship should still be based on rights and duties, argues Ruth Lister. But the nature of these rights and duties should reflect the massive changes that have taken place since the postwar settlement, especially the changes in women's lives and the pervasive lack of security in employment.

A culture of citizenship

One step nearer to genuine citizenship...a remarkable document, for throughout there is the point/counterpoint between the economic, social and political that must be at the heart of any reform programme. And if a still intellectually timid Labour Party could be persuaded to sign up wholeheartedly there would be a transformation of British political life - and a genuine threat to sleaze and social injustice at the same time.

Will Hutton's positive interpretation of the *Commission on Social Justice Report* highlights its potential for the development of a culture of citizenship in the UK.

The Commission's conceptualisation of social justice was grounded in the belief that 'the foundation of a free society is the equal worth of all citizens, expressed most basically in political and civil liberties, equal rights before the law, and so on,' and that 'everyone is entitled, as a right of citizenship, to be able to meet their basic needs for income, shelter and other necessities'. Moreover, 'self-respect and equal citizenship demand more than the meeting of basic needs: they demand opportunities and life chances', thereby underlining the importance of 'the primary distribution of opportunity, as well as its redistribution'.

This emphasis on the primary distribution of opportunity over the secondary redistribution of income and wealth - symbolised in the notion of an 'investors" as opposed to a 'Levellers" Britain (and we were justly criticised for the historical illiteracy of the latter label) - has inevitably attracted considerable criticism from the left. Even a *Guardian* editorial argued that 'not nearly enough is done to reverse Britain's inequalities. Just because Labour wants to drop its tax and spend image is no reason for Borrie to ignore justice'.

While I do not accept that we 'ignored justice', I do have considerable sympathy with those who have criticised the Report's lack of redistributive force in the face of the massive increase in inequality engineered by the Tories. That said, these critics do tend to over look those recommendations for a fairer tax system which would tax back at least some of the gains made by the better off. It is also worth repeating our restatement of an old principle: 'Taxes are the contribution that we all make towards building a better society. Taxation in a democratic society is based upon consent; it is a desirable good, not a necessary evil...fair taxes, wisely and efficiently used, are a responsibility we should share and accept'. Unfortunately, in trying to compete with the Tories as the party of low taxation, Labour is in danger of losing sight of this principle and of reinforcing the increasingly dominant view of taxation as inherently undesirable.

Taxation represents one of the fundamental responsibilities of citizenship. It is not, however, taxation that politicians - Labour as well as conservative - have had in mind as the language of obligations rather than that of rights increasingly dominates political discourse. The Labour Party's new statement of aims and values offers the ideal of 'a community...where the rights we enjoy reflect the duties we owe'. The implication of this is that duties stand morally and logically prior to rights; and the danger in this position is that rights can be fundamentally compromised if they become subservient to specific obligations. The Commission on Social Justice's (hereafter CSJ) position was rather different: 'The reality is that rights and responsibilities go together. To strengthen social rights (which is essential), responsibilities must be clarified'. Thus, rights and responsibilities are understood as standing in a relationship of broad reciprocity, a position which still leaves many difficult questions to be resolved but does provide one element of a framework for thinking about modern citizenship.

An often overlooked chapter of the Report outlines various aspects of community responsibility, drawing on Robert D. Putnam's notion of 'social capital', that is 'the networks, norms and trust that facilitate co-ordination and co-operation for mutual benefit'. The Commission took inspiration from its 'outreach visits', from the strength and vibrancy of many community-based organisations, often driven by women, which make up what Putnam has dubbed 'the capillaries of community life'.

In order to enhance this culture of 'active citizenship' (a far cry from paternalistic Tories' use of the term), various proposals were put forward to promote bottom-up community regeneration, including the establishment of community development trusts. Support for such trusts has also come from the independent Opsahl Commission into the future of Northern Ireland. They were defined by a Northern Ireland community group as 'an independent, not for profit organisation which takes action to renew an area physically, socially and in spirit. It brings together the public, private and voluntary sectors, and obtains financial and other resources from a wide range of organisations and individuals. It encourages substantial involvement by local people and aims to sustain their operations at least in part by generating revenue'.

There is, of course, a danger that the language of community and citizenship can obscure difference and divisions. The Commission acknowledged this, noting that '"community" may bring about the best of local loyalties; or it may be racist, discriminatory and exclusionary'. Elsewhere in the Report it made the case for the strengthening of existing anti-discrimination laws and their extension to minority groups not currently covered by them. It also floated the idea, promoted by some at an earlier major Liberty conference on rights, of a comprehensive anti-discrimination law to be enforced and promoted by a single powerful Human Rights Commission.

Central to the CSJ's aim of 'building strong communities' is the notion of *investment* in the social capital which is essential to the reconstruction of what have been described as 'landscapes of despair'. If there is one theme that can be said to run through the Report as a whole it is that effective citizenship rights and responsibilities need to be underpinned by investment - economic, educational and social. The importance of such investment is heightened by the insecurities which increasingly characterise both 'public' and 'private' life, another theme which recurs through the pages of the Report.

Social and economic citizenship rights

It was partly these insecurities which encouraged the Commission to reject the siren 'modernising' voice - on the left as well as the right - which had been calling for it to abandon Labour's traditional commitment to universalism as opposed to means-testing as the basis for social rights. Instead, it demonstrated that it is means-testing and not universalism which is anachronistic, for the former is ill-suited to modern conditions of rapid change, fluctuating incomes and insecurity and, because it is based on the joint incomes of couples, it threatens to undermine women's financial independence.

The Report contained a clear, principled statement against means-testing which can be used by universalists inside and outside the Labour Party in support of their cause. However, the Commission was also conscious that its Report was likely to be dismissed as 'old Labour', if it simply reiterated the policy of across-the-board increases in child benefit and the basic pension on which Labour fought the last election. Although research has cast doubt on the thesis that such commitments, and the higher taxes needed to fund them, were responsible for the loss of that election, it nevertheless retains a powerful grip on Labour Party thinking.

The Commission attempted to square the circle by suggesting a number of ways in which social rights could be better 'targeted' without recourse to conventional means-testing. Thus, for instance, it proposed a significant increase in child benefit, to be funded by the virtual abolition of the married couple's tax allowance (with the alternative option that some of these savings might be channelled into nursery education) and the taxation of the child benefit paid to higher rate taxpayers. In the Commission's view, without some element of selectivity the chances of the Labour Party committing itself again to a significant increase in child benefit were virtually nil. Of course, there are both logical and practical arguments against any form of taxation of child benefit but that it would represent an extension of means-testing is not one of them. Means-testing and taxation are very different animals, as anyone who has been subjected to the former could testify; the point of proposing an element of taxation was to head off the growing calls for the benefit's means-testing.

A second example of 'targeting' is the proposal for a 'minimum pension guarantee', under which total pension income would be guaranteed at a level above both the current basic pension and income support rates. This does come closer to means-testing although under one of the two options suggested it eschews traditional means-testing of income and assets by taking account only of pensions and significant earnings. Moreover, although this was not made explicit, it was the Commission's intention that eventually the guarantee should be met on an individual basis, thereby safeguarding the financial independence of older women.

> 'Paid work remains the best pathway out of poverty, as well as the only way in which most people can hope to achieve a decent standard of living'

Although the CSJ did not go as far as many would have liked towards eliminating means-testing, it did propose a two-fold alternative strategy for the promotion of the social and economic security and rights of the population as a whole and not just those in poverty. This strategy was based on the one hand on the recasting of social insurance and on the other on 'welfare-to-work' mechanisms and an attack on low pay, in the belief that 'paid work remains the best pathway out of poverty, as well as the only way in which most people can hope to achieve a decent standard of living'.

The recasting of social insurance so as to cover those groups currently excluded by a scheme predicated on male employment patterns is central to the Commission's attempt to create a social security scheme in tune with contemporary employment and family patterns. Part-time workers, in particular, would enjoy new rights.

By now the kind of 'welfare-to-work' measures proposed by the Commission have already become part of a consensus which, according to Nicholas Timmins, the *Independent*'s public policy editor, stretches across the political spectrum to the left of Michael Portillo. However, the CSJ's strategy is a far cry from the Government's, which aims to price the unemployed into low paid work, free of any minimum wages protection and with minimum employment rights, subsidised by an increasingly extensive patchwork of means-tested benefits. In contrast, the CSJ predicated its welfare-to-work strategy on a minimum wage (without specifying a level), a Jobs, Education and Training Programme to raise the skills of the long term unemployed and lone parents, the strengthening of employment rights and a decent social infrastructure, including adequate child care facilities.

In nailing its flag to the mast of the objective of full employment (covering women as well as men, part-time as well as full-time work) and of the centrality of paid work at a decent wage as the best route out of poverty, the Commission was effectively positioning itself to reject the main alternative non means-tested strategy to that of social insurance, i.e. a citizen's income. However, in doing so, and having considered the main arguments for and against a benefit of this kind, paid totally unconditionally to every individual citizen, the CSJ advised against ruling out any move to citizen's income in the longer term: 'if it turns out to be the case that earnings simply cannot provide a stable income for a growing proportion of people, then the notion of some guaranteed income, outside the labour market, could become increasingly attractive. Work incentives might matter less and those who happened to be in employment, knowing that they probably would not remain so throughout their "working" lives, might be more willing to finance an unconditional payment'.

Citizenship obligations

Another reason for not adopting citizen's income was that whilst it might appear the epitome of a citizenship benefit, it 'does not require any *act* of citizenship; it would be paid regardless of whether someone was in a job or looking for one, caring for children or other dependants, engaged in voluntary work or not'. Thus, it would upset the reciprocity-based balance of rights and obligations espoused by the Commission.

Critical here is the question of the nature of any obligation to undertake paid work for those of working-age able to do so. Increasingly influential is a strand of US new right thinking which advocates the enforcement of work obligations through the welfare system, as representing as much a badge of citizenship as do rights. The ultimate solution, under this creed, is workfare under which social security claimants are required to undertake paid work or training as a condition of receiving benefits. Although the British government has backed off workfare as such, the increasingly restrictive conditions imposed on eligibility for benefits for the unemployed have been widely interpreted as steps in that direction and there have been hints that it may be contemplating experimenting with local pilot schemes.

The CSJ came out firmly against workfare but endorsed the long-standing principle in the British social security system that unemployed claimants should be available for work and be expected to accept a reasonable offer of work or training. This endorsement does not extend, however, to the increasingly punitive interpretation and application of these principles under the Tories. There is a distinction to be made between measures which accept that unemployed people have a responsibility to be available for work which it is reasonable to expect them to do, and at a reasonable wage, and measures designed to force the unemployed into inappropriate and unacceptably low-paid jobs.

One of the more controversial of the Report's recommendations was that the parents (lone and married) of older children should be required to register for part-time work, provided adequate child care facilities were available and subject to various safeguards. The proposal would only be activated in the context of the successful introduction of the proposed Jobs, Education and Training package. This has been interpreted in some quarters as an attack on the rights of lone mothers. However, the UK is very unusual in allowing lone parents to remain on social assistance until their youngest child is aged 16 and it is debatable whether such a liberal rule is actually in lone parents' own interests. The evidence of the long-term damage done to the economic interests of women absent from the labour market for long stretches led us to conclude that we are doing mothers no favours by assuming that they can continue to remain outside the labour market for so long.

The proposal highlights a tension at the heart of the Report: how to reconcile the commission's identification of paid work as the best antidote to poverty and economic insecurity with its recognition of the value to society and citizenship of the unpaid caring work still primarily undertaken by women. This tension also runs through the politics and theorisation of women's social citizenship rights. In an attempt to transcend the long-standing 'equality' *v* 'difference' dilemma, in which women's demands are constructed either on the basis of their equality with or difference from men, many feminists today are attempting to accommodate the two. The difficulties at a policy level are encapsulated in the question of how best to validate and support, through some form of independent income maintenance entitlement, the caring work for which women still take the main responsibility in the 'private' sphere, whilst not locking them into this responsibility and out of the 'public' sphere and potential economic and political autonomy.

Part of the answer, as the CSJ recognised, has to lie in tackling men's absenteeism from the caring responsibilities undertaken in the 'private' sphere. Here the Commission looked to countries such as Sweden for inspiration. As well as recommending improvements to maternity leave and a new right to paternity leave, it supported the longer term introduction of paid parental leave. The experience of other countries suggests that this would need to be earnings-related, and part of the leave reserved for fathers, if men are to make use of it. More effective anti-discrimination and equal pay laws would also help by closing the pay gap.

In addition, we attempted to resolve the dilemma of valuing caring work whilst promoting paid work, within the framework of also improving women's access to an independent income, in two main ways. First, were our proposals, mentioned above, for a modernised social insurance scheme that would reflect the realities of women's employment patterns and provide better support for those with caring responsibilities. A stronger, more inclusive social insurance scheme is, we believed, the best route available at present to promote women's independent social security income.

Second, we supported the idea of a participation income which would provide a modest income (financed initially by the conversion of personal tax allowances) on an individual basis. A participation income could be seen as a step down the road to a fully fledged citizen's income, but it is subject to a condition of active citizenship for those of working age able to work. This would include caring work and, in some versions, voluntary work.

For some feminists, the central attention given by the Report to women's position and concerns is one of its great strengths. As Anne Showstack Sassoon observed recently, 'it puts women at the very centre of its analysis and their life chances at the core of its proposals'. For once, a report of this kind has not been conceived through a uni-focal male lens.

However, there is also a strand of feminism which is very critical of what it sees as an endorsement of 'flexible' working practices which have disadvantaged women. In fact, our proposals would do much to protect the rights of these female workers through, for instance, the extension of part-time workers' rights; the outlawing of zero-hours contracts and the introduction of a minimum wage. The fact is that for many women part-time work is their favoured way of reconciling the conflicting demands of paid work and family. Acknowledgement of this does not have to mean acceptance of the *status quo* under which such women are all too often exploited, provided it is combined with the kind of measures recommended and with serious attempts to shift the domestic sexual division of labour so that it is no longer only women who are faced with such choices.

Conclusion

The CSJ's Report clearly raises a wide range of issues. It was not intended to provide a blueprint for a single parliament but a longer term strategy which we offered for public debate. It is therefore disappointing that, within the Labour Party itself, this debate appears to have disappeared behind closed doors. Discussion of the Report throughout the Party was effectively sidelined by the Clause IV consultation. I fear that the New Labour leadership is unlikely 'to sign up wholeheartedly' to the kind of strategy proposed but instead will cherry pick those elements of the Report which chime most closely with the New Labour agenda.

At the same time, there is a danger that the immediate needs of those unable to cross the bridge from welfare to work will be forgotten in the rush to sign up to this agenda - which, according to Tony Blair, is not about 'better benefits', which a number of Labour spokespeople now seem to associate with a 'dependency culture' which research has yet to show exists. Clearly, the success of any 'welfare-to-work' strategy is dependent on the creation of suitable jobs, which is not guaranteed and which will, in any case, take time. The CSJ Report acknowledged the need to tackle the poverty experienced by those still reliant on benefit through, for instance, its support for a benchmark minimum income standard and recommendations for the overhaul of the social fund. A new Labour government, committed to social justice and the extension of citizenship, will need to combine the kind of long-term structural strategy proposed by the Commission with some immediate help for those who have been the main victims of over a decade of redistribution from the poor to the rich.

Soundings

Soundings is a journal of politics and culture. It is a forum for ideas which aims to explore the problems of the present and the possibilities for a future politics and society. Its intent is to encourage innovation and dialogue in progressive thought. Half of each future issue will be devoted to debating a particular theme: topics in the pipeline include: Heroes and Heroines, The Public Good, and the Media.

Why not subscribe?
Make sure of your copy

Subscription rates, 1996 (3 issues)

INDIVIDUAL SUBSCRIPTIONS
UK   £35.00
Rest of the World   £45.00

INSTITUTIONAL SUBSCRIPTIONS
UK   £70.00
Rest of the World   £80.00

Please send me one year's subscription starting with Issue Number _____

I enclose payment of £ _____

I wish to become a supporting subscriber and enclose a donation of £ _____

I enclose total payment of £ _____

Name _____

Address _____

_____

_____ Postcode _____

Please return this form with cheque or money order payable to Lawrence & Wishart Account No. 3 and send to:
Soundings, c/o Lawrence & Wishart, 99A Wallis Road, London E9 5LN

Social rights and responsibilities

Anna Coote

Anna Coote looks at the politics of social rights.

It has become fashionable, right across the political spectrum, to talk about 'rights' in relation to health and welfare services. The language of rights is deployed by politicians and analysts of various persuasions - with different but overlapping meanings. For some, the concept of social rights can seen as part of a broader effort to diminish the role of the state. Promoting individual rights, with corresponding responsibilities, helps to set limits upon collective activity.

The Patient's Charter is a case in point. It talks about individuals having rights to health care. But it circumscribes provision - by what it leaves out. For example, it proclaims a right to treatment within two years of being placed on a waiting list, but there is no right to be put on the waiting list in the first place. It gives patients the right to complain when things go wrong, but no right to appeal against unwelcome decisions.

Others see entitlement to social goods as a way of strengthening and deepening democracy. Rights to education, health care and a basic income, for example, are regarded as essential components of citizenship, because these things make it possible for individuals to exercise their civil and political rights, and more generally to participate in society. For example, your right to vote is impaired if you can't read; you can't enjoy freedom of speech and rights of movement and assembly if you are too poor or sick to go out of doors. So democratic society depends upon the just distribution of social goods - and these should be a matter of right, not privilege.

Linked to this is the idea that social rights help to shift power from planners and providers of social goods, to citizens and service users. This suggests a model of welfare built not on paternalism or philanthropy but on the principle of equal citizenship and self-determination. Instead of being at the mercy of politicians and professionals who decide who needs what, individuals should be able to claim what has been designated, by prior agreement through the democratic process, as theirs by right.

Rights may also be a means of guaranteeing some forms of welfare provision against the vagaries of short-term political interests. If something is a right there may be an appeal to law which can override political decisions: this depends, of course, on how the right is formulated and how easily it can be revoked by new legislation or undermined in practice. But it must surely be easier for a politician to call for a new right than to call for the abolition of a right that already exists in law.

More generally, the language of rights is used as a way of expressing ideas about social justice. People will say 'we have a right to proper health care' or 'we have a right to a decent education', not because they know the courts would enforce their claims to health care and education, but because there is a widely held view that this is what ought to be available to everyone in a civilised society. In this sense, rights are about intentions or desires rather than enforceable entitlements. This use of the language of rights is increasingly common, even while (or perhaps because) social conditions are deteriorating. It implies a demand for more, rather than less, collective provision. On the whole people who can afford to buy health care or education do not bother to assert these as a 'right'.

'Rights are about intentions or desires rather than enforceable entitlements'

I do not intend to go into the philosophical arguments about what is a real right and what is not. But I do want to address two more practical arguments which are deployed against social rights, as opposed to civil and political rights. The first is that enforcing social rights is far more expensive than enforcing civil and political rights. While it costs money to uphold civil liberties (by means of police, courts, lawyers, judges, prisons), these costs are more modest, more controllable and more predictable than the costs of enforcing substantive social and economic rights. If all citizens had equal and enforceable rights to health care, education and housing, for example, then the state would have a duty to provide extensive - and expensive - services. It would be hard to control the costs of providing such services, or to predict the volume of demand.

The second is that, if the aim is to empower individuals, there are better ways of achieving this - namely *choice/exit* and *voice*. Or, put another way, the market, or democratic accountability.

The main problem with choice as a means of empowerment is that some citizens have more power to choose than others - because of where they live, how much they earn, how much they know, or how deftly they can manipulate the system to their advantage. The powers of choice can accumulate with those who are already powerful and drain away from the powerless. Some people seem to accept that cumulative inequalities are a reasonable price to pay for protecting 'freedom' of choice. But for anyone who wants to reconcile this freedom with the principle of equal citizenship, it will be necessary to orchestrate and regulate the conditions in which choices are made.

The second strategy, voice, involves members of the public having a say, through lobbying, campaigning, consultation, negotiation, voting - or a combination of these - in things like planning services, setting priorities and allocating resources. These are important elements of the democratic process but, like choice, they are limited in their capacity to empower the citizen. The distance between the elector and the decision, and the decision and its implementation, is considerable, and the bigger and more complex the society, the greater this distance can be. I shall argue that social rights are not an alternative to choice or voice, but essential as a way of making them fair and equitable.

Putting rights into practice

If we are to try to make social rights work in practice, how do we proceed? We can't escape the fact that rights to health care, education and social services are likely to be *much more* expensive to enforce than traditional liberties. In addition, there is the problem of political viability. The idea that citizens should have civil and political rights is well-established in judicial and political circles, even though many of these rights are in practice fragile or illusory. But the idea that they should also have social and economic rights remains controversial in political terms, and unrealised in practice. The case for introducing such rights would need, at the very least, to be built upon some positive experience of codified human rights. In some countries, notably the UK, there is little experience of that kind.

Rights can be expressed in different ways. For example, as duties imposed on authorities or as entitlements held by individuals. Individual entitlements are unenforceable without corresponding duties, but duties do not always imply specific entitlements. Most national legislation under which health care and education are provided do not allow for individual enforcement. There are also diverse ways in which new rights may be established and enforced. They can be introduced by statute, with or without entrenchment, or by means of ministerial regulation; they can be set out in statutory or non-statutory codes; they can be issued unilaterally by the authority, or negotiated with groups of citizens or service users. Rights may be enforced through the courts by means of judicial review, through courts or tribunals by individual claims, or through designated complaints and appeals procedures, which may or may not involve a final appeal to the courts.

Where there are no means of enforcement, rights can be expressed as a declaration of purpose: in this case, they may be implemented by administrative procedures, such as the setting of goals and timetables, with designated strategies for achieving targets. Where there are no means of implementation, the language of rights is purely aspirational: a right is not what *is*, but what *ought to be*.

In practice, the elasticity of the idea of rights is probably its greatest strength. I don't think we should assume a scale of worthiness, stretching from 'good/real' enforceable individual entitlements at the top to 'bad/unreal' aspirational rights at the bottom. At best, enforceable entitlements can bring tangible benefits to individuals and help to promote the fair distribution of power and autonomy. At worst, they can clog up the courts, make hay for the lawyers, favour better-off litigants and play havoc with public finances. At worst, aspirational rights can act as a cynical camouflage for government inaction, and deceive and alienate the public. At best, they can play a useful role in raising public expectations, creating a climate of opinion favourable to equal citizenship and providing a focus for campaigns. What is probably needed is a strategic mix of different kinds of rights, addressing the different places where power is located and the different ways in which power is exercised.

'In practice, the elasticity of the idea of rights is probably its greatest strength'

There are pragmatic, if not principled, grounds for treating social and economic rights differently from civil and political ones. Political and civil rights can be a route to social and economic rights, but not *vice versa*. If all individuals in a society were comfortably housed and enjoyed reasonable standards of health care, education and social insurance, but had no civil or political rights, they would have no constitutional means of winning the rights they lacked. By contrast, a society in which individuals enjoyed the right to vote, freedom of speech, assembly, movement and so forth, would hold out the possibility of winning social rights through the democratic process. Social rights may be necessary for the just enforcement of existing civil rights, but on their own they cannot be a means of achieving them. And indeed, without civil rights, social rights are almost certainly unenforceable and therefore meaningless.

Another reason for treating social and economic rights differently is that civil and political rights are already part of the picture. They are widely accepted, even if they are not widely enforced. But we are not yet accustomed to the judges interfering in the allocation of public resources for social goods.

There is a useful distinction to be made between substantive and procedural social rights, and these two kinds of rights can be tackled in different ways. Substantive rights are rights to actual benefits and services: to a hospital bed, a secure income, a school place, a home care attendant. Procedural rights are rights to the fair treatment of individuals as they come into contact (or try to come into contact) with service providers.

How can the idea of social rights be transformed into a tangible asset for citizens? On one side, there could be a new 'Social Charter' for the UK, based on international treaties, such as the European Social Charter, to which Britain is already committed. This charter could embody substantive rights, such as rights to medical care, social security and housing. It could be introduced by an ordinary Act of Parliament. It need not be directly enforceable by individuals. It could impose duties on public bodies and lay down procedures for setting targets and monitoring progress towards them. It would act as a important guide for interpreting and formulating laws - and a set of criteria for measuring the performance of public bodies.

Procedural rights

Such a Charter, for all its limitations, would provide a framework of aims and values within which procedural rights could be introduced - and here it is possible to envisage individuals having some enforceable entitlements. Although procedures do cost money, they do not have the same implications for resource allocation as do substantive rights. It is almost certainly easier to predict and control the costs of enforcing fair procedures, whereas the introduction of enforceable rights to services and benefits would imply unpredictable and open-ended demands on public funds. Procedural rights would be based on principles of fairness which are already well established in law. In effect, it would mean extending civil liberties to the realm of social provision.

The basic principles of fair treatment recognise a citizen's rights to:

a fair hearing

equal and consistent treatment

unbiased decisions

structured discretion (where a decision involves an element of discretion, for example, an expert's assessment of an individual's predicament, it should follow explicit guidelines)

reasons for decisions (when a decision is reached, reasons should be given)

appeal and complaint (the person concerned should have a right to appeal against a decision, or to complain about any action that is taken as a result of a decision)

There is no single formula for putting these principles into practice. Each area of provision would have to be examined separately to find out the most appropriate ways of applying procedural fairness. A package of rights (and mechanisms for implementing them) could be custom-made for each one, following the same principles and set within a common framework of aims and values.

Enforcing rights

There are clearly tensions between the desire to confer genuine and empowering rights on individuals, and the desire to avoid rigidity and proliferation of rules and regulations, to keep open the channels of democratic debate and to keep lawyers at bay. But there are ways of enforcing rights which do not inevitably fall into these traps. For example, we can make more of non-statutory codes and procedures. We can further develop the role of the Local Ombudsman, the Health Service Commissioners and the Audit Commission. We can resolve not to use courts where tribunals will do and to strengthen advice and advocacy systems so that lawyers are brought in only as a last resort. Any attempt to increase rights - political, civil or social - should in any case be part of a broader campaign to modernise the British legal system and reform the judiciary.

Deciding about rights

A strategic mix of rights, of the kind outlined above, would require a considerable amount of devolved decision-making, particularly in developing procedural social rights. The matter of how decisions are made and by whom, as well as how decisions are reviewed and their impact assessed, therefore becomes crucial. If decisions about rights are to check and redirect the flow of power and opportunity, they cannot be left to those who already have more than their fair share of both. In this sense, rights and 'voice' are like a horse and carriage. You can't have one without the other. They are interdependent and can reinforce each other. However, it is neither possible nor desirable for everyone to participate in all decisions: so the ideal of maximal participation is tempered by the practical requirements of modern government.

> 'The 'public interest' is multi-dimensional and often inharmonious'

Working out how the public should participate in decisions about rights is not just a technical matter: it is highly political. The 'public interest' is multi-dimensional and often inharmonious. It is not just that different communities and groups have different and conflicting interests; individuals can have more than one set of interests, reflecting different relations with state and society. We are 'customers' when we use public services, and as such we are concerned with how we ourselves and our immediate family are affected by various forms of provision at the point of use. We are 'citizens' not by virtue of our use of services but because we are part of a community. As citizens, we have wider concerns - not just about ourselves, but about our neighbours and other members of the community, both now and in the future. The interests of customers and citizens may conflict, within and between individuals and groups. Citizens' rights and customers' rights are different, but related, instruments. Customers and citizens exert power, and experience powerlessness, in different ways and with different consequences.

So what are the means of public participation in political decision-making? Representative democracy with universal suffrage and regular elections is of course the best known form of collective decision-making. In theory, at least, it addresses the diverse and shared interests of the population as a whole. But in a large and complex society, the distances between the decision and the elector are so great that the amount of power actually exercised by the individual citizen is negligible. How else may the public participate?

One option is for members of the public to vote on a specific question or series of questions, in local or national referenda. There are examples (in the US) of 'people's referenda' where an issue is raised in the community and, if sufficient support is demonstrated, must then be put to the vote. A referendum may prompt an extensive and well-informed public debate, or railroad public opinion into over-simplified decisions about complex questions. A great deal depends on how much the public knows and understands about the issue in question, on how the question is worded, and on how power is distributed between those who campaign for and against.

Another possibility is to apply the jury principle to some local decisions. Individuals would be selected at random from the electoral register to form a citizen's jury for a finite period, to deliberate upon matters of local concern. There are various ways in which the juries might be used - for example, to monitor performance following decisions taken by elected representatives or government agencies, to assess and review decisions before they are implemented, to advise on decisions yet to be taken, or to take decisions on behalf of the community, which would then be implemented by the elected authority. A selected jury could perform a local function similar to that of either a select or a standing parliamentary committee. How well this worked would depend on how the juries received evidence, on what resources they had at their disposal, and on procedures for deliberation.

The idea of public consultation overlaps with that of citizens' juries, but offers further possibilities. Its effectiveness, from the public's point of view, depends on what questions are asked, by whom, of whom, by what means and on the basis of what information; on whether any dialogue takes place and, if so, with whom; on how the answers are processed and conclusions drawn, and on what action is taken as a result. All these decisions remain in the hands of those who consult - as is the decision whether or not to consult in the first place. At worst, public consultation can be a highly manipulative process, benefiting no-one but the consulting body. At best, it can be a route towards more open and appropriate decisions, more enlightened decision-makers and a better-informed public.

There is a critical difference between consultation and negotiation, in that the latter culminates in some form of shared decision-making. One model is provided by the local service agreements pioneered by a handful of local authorities in the UK. Well-publicised open meetings are called at which members of the public are invited to discuss in detail the planning of a local service. These neighbourhood forums are asked to suggest improvements. Officers respond and a dialogue takes place, leading to a negotiated agreement which embodies changes to the service. This is published and distributed in each neighbourhood as a form of guarantee, with a procedure for complaining if the terms are breached.

Negotiated agreements call for clear and thorough communication of relevant information. They can set high standards of participative democracy and can be expected to raise the expectations of the public about the quality of service. The success of this approach depends upon a supportive political culture, not just on the part of the local authority, but within the local community. This can be nurtured but cannot be sustained unless the formula is applied sparingly. Negotiation takes time and energy, which are scarce and precious resources - especially among women. If every service were subjected to local negotiation, the likely result would be increasing apathy and disbelief, leading to anger and resentment.

There is no perfect way of deciding about rights. But the process of making such decisions is a vital one which must be seen to be fair and which could itself be subject to a rights-based approach. If the principles of judicial fairness were applied, decision-making would have to be open and to follow explicit guidelines, to be unbiased and to treat individuals equally and consistently. Reasons for decisions would have to be given, with rights of appeal. Procedures for decision-making could be established nationally or locally, and could be set out in statutory or voluntary codes. The rights of appropriate associations to be consulted in policy formation, to participate in decisions and to pursue complaints and appeals could be promoted through similar means.

Rights have an intrinsic and an instrumental value. They express the just claims of the individual upon the community, and enforceable rights provide a means for ensuring those claims are met. Neither choice nor voice does this. As a declaration of aims and aspirations, such as might be found in a Social Charter, rights have a unique part to play in creating a climate of opinion favourable to the goals of social justice. Furthermore, rights can protect the interests of individuals against the volatility of political and administrative decisions, as well as against the arbitrary and random effects of professional discretion. Voters don't like the idea of rights being taken away from them.

Rights can help to reconcile choice with the principle of equal citizenship. They can create a framework of shared aims and values in the form of a Charter of Rights which places duties on government bodies. Procedural rights, meanwhile, can help to equalise the power of choice. Suppose Citizen A and Citizen B have vouchers to buy education for their children: both choose to send their children to the same school; the school has only one place, but Citizen A knows the head teacher and Citizen B does not and consequently the A child gets the place. A right of appeal could help Citizen B to fight through the web of privilege which divides her from Citizen A. If choices are made within a framework of judicial fairness, they are less likely to compound existing inequalities.

It is a matter of opinion whether rights weaken democracy: that depends how much faith one has in the effectiveness of voice, and in the capacity of representative democracy to protect and empower individuals - especially vulnerable minorities. In my view, social rights can help to ensure that all citizens are able to exercise their civil and political rights (e.g. through a Charter which expresses rights to education and health care, even if only in aspirational terms). They can enhance the effectiveness of voice as a means of empowerment through a statement of rights which makes shared aims and values explicit rather than implicit. Voice may also be strengthened by means of group rights and by applying the principles of judicial fairness to decision-making procedures.

Talking about rights in abstract terms can be an important consciousness-raising exercise. Putting rights into practice, so that people can feel the difference, is a daunting and complicated task. The strength of the rights-based approach lies in its flexibility, if we can work out ways of applying it in different ways to different power relationships. The approach must be gradual and experimental, so that lessons can be learned along the way, and public support encouraged and sustained. But if the goal of a democratic state is to create the conditions for all citizens to enjoy autonomy in equal measure, then citizens need rights. They must have a fair say in how they are developed, and they must know what to expect from whatever rights are produced by that process.

Law and injustice:

Is there an exit from the post-modern maze?

Bill Bowring

Bill Bowring *looks at ways of theorising the relationship between law and justice, and between law and society. He argues that a fruitful approach to critical legal theory is to be found in the 'critical realism' associated with Roy Bhaskar.*

This article seeks to situate the preceding sections within a paradoxical contemporary phenomenon: the infiltration of so many areas of contemporary life, riddled as they are with uncertainty and risk, by the law (which is not the same thing, in most cases, as justice). This is what the theoretician of public law Martin Loughlin has described in the context of local government as 'juridification': the replacement of convention and informality by increasing legal formality, and recourse to and intervention by the courts. In effect, in the absence of any other means of collectively deciding on right or wrong, law becomes the only framework for human judgement. I aim to explore four of the ways in which this process has been theorised, and to ask whether postmodernism and the ethics of 'alterity', currently fashionable in critical legal circles, hold any answers. The issue at stake, I argue, is human emancipation, for which realism, in a special sense which I explain, is a necessary precondition.

The dominance of law

What is to hold contemporary Western society together? People no longer define and constitute themselves through tradition: traditions now for many people in the world are commodities, part of the virtual worlds of advertising and tourism. Moreover, even religion is no longer the pervasive and inescapable matrix of the lived world. It is a matter of choice. Even religious fundamentalism is not a return to roots, more a chosen, if perhaps subjectively inescapable, act of rebellion. In every society religion has, since time out of mind, shared with law, with which it is so intimately connected, its pre-eminence as a supremely complex and characteristically human construct. But today it is law rather than religion which is increasingly called upon to provide the remedies and safeguards which society craves in an ever more unpredictable human environment.

'Law rather than religion is increasingly called on to provide the remedies and safeguards which society craves'

Many of the other pieces collected together in this section of *Soundings* concern the failings and disasters of the law, its inadequacy in the face of deprivation and oppression. Yet without exception the remedies put forward by the various authors, even John Griffith with his well-founded distrust of the judges, or Mike Mansfield with his unrivalled experience of law at the coal-face, invoke the law. That is, law is either challenged to become more just, more congruent with social needs; or is asked to act as a shield against oppression, or an instrument for social change.

There was a time when socialists thought that the law and lawyers, like the state, would wither away. Law would cease to be necessary when the production relations became transparent and just. In the years which followed May-June 1968, the ideas of the early Soviet theorist Yevgeny Pashukanis, who asserted that bourgeois law reflected the capitalist system of exchange, were widely read. But E.P. Thompson, in *Whigs and Hunters*, signalled a sea-change within Marxist thought.[1] Responding to the lack of democracy, and history of human rights abuses in the USSR, he undertook his rehabilitation of the rule of law. He insisted that even in a socialist society the rule of law would continue to be an essential component of democracy, and must provide protection against the arbitrary exercise of authority.

1. E. P. Thompson, *Whigs and Hunters: The Origin of the Black Act*, Penguin, Harmondsworth 1975.

The hegemony of human rights, at home and abroad

This is the context in which so many on the British left now seek legal and constitutional answers to society's ills. Charter 88 is no longer quite so prominent, but perhaps this is because there is a growing political consensus, most of all among the senior judges, that a Bill of Rights must be enacted; or that at any rate the European Convention on Human Rights must be incorporated into English law. Constitutional reform is at the centre of Labour's agenda. As militant organised labour and mass left politics have shown signs, at least in Britain for the moment, of becoming exhibits in the museum of working-class history, every pressure group tends to make use of the rhetoric of legal rights, flawed as this language is by its origin in liberal theory. Patricia Williams, the black American legal academic, speaks of the 'alchemy of race and rights' - the base metal of the language of power transmuted by its capture for the struggles of the oppressed into the gold of an authentic weapon for emancipation.[2] At the same time, Tory rule since 1979 has been marked by a ceaseless flood of new legislation and regulation, whether seeking to eviscerate local government, or to inhibit public protest. Even that cornerstone of the 'rule of law', the right to silence, has been undermined by the Criminal Justice and Public Order Act 1994, which also defines and restricts 'rave' parties, and criminalises hunt saboteurs.

Much the same processes can be seen at work in the international arena. Every state in the world now uses and abuses the rhetoric of human rights. The most recent universal human rights instrument, the United Nation's Convention on the Rights of the Child, opened for signature as recently as 1989, yet came into force in 1990 and has now been ratified by the great majority of states. It may be the first such treaty to achieve universal ratification. The United States of America, always slow to fall in line with the international human rights consensus, felt in 1992 obliged to ratify the International Covenant on Civil and Political Rights of 1966. Not surprisingly, the US ratification is so hedged about with reservations as almost to negate itself. But it remains the case that no state in today's world, even those most criticised by Amnesty International, will now openly boast of the regular application of torture or other gross violations of human rights. The British government was acutely embarrassed by the recent decision of the European Commission on Human Rights in the case of the Gibraltar shootings -

2. Patricia Williams, *The Alchemy of Race and Rights: Diary of a Law Professor*, Harvard, Cambridge Mass.1991.

the Death on the Rock case.

But perhaps the most significant victory for the new 'dominant discourse' of politics was the abrupt abandonment by the Soviet leadership, led by Mikhail Gorbachev and Aleksandr Yakovlev from 1985 onwards, of Marxism-Leninism - otherwise known as scientific communism - and its replacement by the ideology of 'common human values', to be brought to life in a 'rule of law state'. This has meant, above all, that pride of place is now given in the constitutions and laws of the states now 'in transition to democracy' to the civil and political rights which were once the ideological weapon of the West. At the same time, these states witness the abandonment of the social and economic rights to work, to free education and health care, and to housing, which were the more or less redeemed pledges of the former regime. All the states on the eastern side of the Iron Curtain have rushed to join the Council of Europe, and to subscribe to its European Convention on Human Rights. Ukraine and Moldova are at the time of writing the most recent recruits, and Russia will surely follow. These states join for the privilege of letting all those within their jurisdiction, whether citizens or not, apply to the Commission and Court of Human Rights at Strasbourg to complain about violations of their rights.

This is not to deny that there is more than a degree of cynicism involved here. Russia is the state whose government in 1993 trashed its Constitution and shelled its own Parliament into submission, and in 1994-1995 perpetrated a number of egregious massacres in Chechnya - Shamashki is a name stained with blood. Russia's first Human Rights Ombudsman, Sergei Kovalyov, lasted only one year before his dismissal both by the State Duma, and by his immediate boss, President Yeltsin, because of his outspokenness not only on prison conditions and racist housing registration policies, but also for his stand on Chechnya. Turkey, a long-standing member of the Council of Europe, has oppressed its Kurdish minority through the mass destruction of villages, murder, torture, and gross violations of the right to freedom of expression, and now finds itself arraigned before the European Commission on Human Rights in respect of hundreds of applications.

In spite of these limitations, as acute a critic of modern capitalism as Marshall Berman has recently applauded the inexorable spread of human rights language as an important step towards human emancipation.[3] In his view, despite the fact that

3. Marshall Berman, 'Modernism and Human Rights Near the Millennium', *Dissent*, Summer 1995.

many people, movements and governments are still trying to smash the rights of man, 'this will be harder than it was two centuries ago, because the idea of human rights today is far more historically grounded and concrete, attuned to experiences that so many people around the world really go through and desires they really feel.' And the visionary Portuguese scholar Boaventura de Sousa Santos sees the discourse as a terrain which can and must be captured by the forces of emancipation.[4] It is surely the case that the language of rights, dressed as it is in the natural law doctrines peculiar to the West, has already achieved global currency, and will last well into the next millennium.

How has this process been theorised?

The liberal quandary

Most British judges, if they have thought about the question of the relationship between law and society, and the increasing process of juridification - and many have - probably subscribe to one of the contemporary versions of liberal theory on offer. The pre-eminent authors of contemporary liberalism are John Rawls and Ronald Dworkin. They both subscribe to theories of justice - justice as fairness. For Rawls, at least in an earlier incarnation when he wrote *A Theory of Justice*, the norms of justice can be reliably identified by a kind of thought experiment, in which the reader is encouraged to place herself in an 'initial position', behind a 'veil of ignorance', in which nothing is known of inherited life chances or inequalities.[5] It is then a question of what the rational subject would desire for everyone. Under pressure from communitarian critics, Rawls has more recently taken the view that liberal values are historically and contingently located in western capitalist societies (or 'well-ordered democratic societies', as he defines them), and can be defended only from that position, with all its contradictions.

For Dworkin, who sympathises with Rawls, the law can and should appeal to strong principles of justice, what he describes as 'rights as trumps'. This position appeals to many at the sharp edge of constitution-building: Kader Asmal, who played a leading role in negotiating South Africa's interim constitution, has placed particular emphasis on Dworkin's work. Moreover, Dworkin has taken a public stand castigating the decay of civil liberties in Britain, and calling for the

---

4. See a report of a keynote address by Santos, in Bill Bowring, 'Human Rights in the New World Order', *Socialist Lawyer*, No19, 1993.
5. John Rawls, *A Theory of Justice*, University Press, Oxford, 1971.

incorporation of a Bill of Rights.[6] But unfortunately for the legitimacy of Dworkin's system, his principles of justice are to be derived ultimately from the values held by the community at large, not the best recipe for the defence of unpopular minorities, even if rights are to be trumps. Furthermore, both Rawls and Dworkin are heavily influenced by American philosophical pragmatism and legal proceduralism, and are its contemporary exponents. Their project is hegemonic in character. It is universalist, in the sense that 'justice as fairness' is to be applied to everyone, everywhere. It seeks to establish foundations for right conduct in government and society. It is no accident that Dworkin's best known book is entitled *Law's Empire*.[7]

> 'Rights were seen not only as problematic, but as an integral part of the machinery of oppression'

These are attractive doctrines. They admit of a certain egalitarianism, based as they are on distributive justice. For example, there is Rawls' 'difference principle', that social and economic inequalities are only justified if to the greatest benefit of the least advantaged members of society. But in the end they are hardly subversive of the machinery of law which has been responsible for so many miscarriages of justice.

Critical legal theory and postmodernism

Beginning in the 1970s, first the US and then Britain saw the rapid growth of a movement of 'critical lawyers', largely from academic backgrounds. This was quite different from the generations of lawyers, going back in Britain to Ernest Jones the Chartist, barrister, editor and convicted state criminal, and Fred Engels's friend and translator Sam Moore, who had sided with the oppressed. At first, these new critical lawyers drew from Marxist critiques of law and rights, and sought to place law in its social and economic context, as an instrument of state power and policy, or as an obfuscation, legitimising exploitation and oppression. In the US, rights were 'trashed' - made to display their indeterminacy and incoherence, and their ultimate subservience to the interests of the oppressors. Rights in particular, or 'rights discourse' talk about or rhetoric of rights were seen not only as ambiguous and problematic, but as an integral part of the machinery of oppression. In more recent years in Britain, critical legal theory has moved away from Marxism, and drawn on a wider range of theoretical inspirations; but it has continued to see

6. Ronald Dworkin, *A Bill of Rights for Britain*, Chatto Counterblasts, London 1990
7. Ronald Dworkin, *Law's Empire*, Fontana, London 1986.

itself as the *enfant terrible* of contemporary legal studies. It delights in shocking what it takes to be the legal establishment.'[8] Each year, at a different university, there is a gathering of several hundred academics under the banner 'Critical Legal Conference'. There is even a more radical student offshoot, the 'Critical Legal Groups', with their own annual conference. These meetings are characterised by an extraordinary pluralism, even eclecticism.

Recently, however, this pluralism has tended to be skewed by something of a new hegemony. In Britain especially, critical lawyers have increasingly been influenced by the theories of French thinkers such as Jean-François Lyotard and Jacques Derrida, loosely described as post-modernism; they have become highly critical both of rights discourse and of Marxist economic determinism. (Of course, Derrida has somewhat disgraced himself in the last couple of years for some admirers, in his book *Spectres of Marx*, by revealing himself as - perhaps - a closet Marxist and supporter of human rights doctrine.[9])

'Critical lawyers have increasingly been influenced by the theories of French thinkers such as Jean-François Lyotard and Jacques Derrida'

The post-modernists condemn what they describe as foundationalism - the idea that there is a 'foundational' real reality, which can be distinguished from unreality or falsehood. For example, they dismiss the Marxist contention that theory is the ideological superstructure of economic processes. They disparage the 'grand narratives' of Marxism and other theories drawing from the rationalist traditions of the enlightenment. They insist that since Auschwitz and the holocaust it is no longer possible to place events and ideas in a single narrative of progress, or within a theory capable, at least in principle, of explaining human and natural phenomena. They deny the possibility of progress. Indeed, they claim that since German-speaking Europe was the home of the thinkers who epitomised the enlightenment - Kant, Goethe, Hegel, Marx and Freud - yet still gave birth to fascism, it is a delusion to believe that the problems of humanity can be solved through the exercise of rational thought. They argue that, in the name of enlightenment, difference, in particular the voices of women and minorities, has been suppressed; and that the white male voices which have been heard have

---

8. Alan Hunt, *The Critique of Law: What is 'Critical' about Critical Legal Theory?*, in Fitzpatrick and Hunt (eds), Critical Legal Studies, Blackwell, Oxford 1987.
9. Jacques Derrida, *Spectres of Marx*, Routledge, London 1995.

been characterised by 'binary oppositions' - good/bad, true/false, working-class/ruling class; furthermore, there can no longer be a belief in the existence of a grounded subject of theory, able to discriminate between truth and falsity, or to judge between competing viewpoints or ethical considerations.

But most of all, following the 'linguistic turn' in philosophy, in which the object of intellectual engagement is not the world and its living people, but language, discourse and text - theory has nothing more to do with a 'real' world capable of generating criteria of truth. Each voice or story has equal validity with all others. The thinker is to discriminate between rival accounts not by way of reasoned judgment, but instead, at best, through a process akin to aesthetic appreciation. This is, of course, a recipe for relativism, or even nihilism. And an approach to the law based on such theories can hardly be described as critical, much less subversive; it fails to ground a response to the evident failings of the British legal system, and the chasm between law and justice, since it has no evaluative criteria, and no theory of the relationship between law and justice.

A number of critical legal scholars who subscribe to the theories described above have theorised an ethical dimension to post-modern legal theory, albeit recently elaborated. It is argued that law and justice occupy radically different universes, the synchronic and diachronic. Law falls within the realm of reason, thought and analysis, occupying lived time and space. Justice, on the other hand, is instantaneous, outside time. Following the French Jewish philosopher Emmanuel Levinas, justice is said to come before all thought and judgment, in the inescapable appeal of the Other, whose suffering face confronts each of us and demands a response. This school of thought has found recent expression in the book *Justice Miscarried: Ethics, Aesthetics and the Law* by Costas Douzinas and Ronnie Warrington.[10] In this work they describe a number of miscarriages of justice, and, focusing on the notorious case of the Tamil refugees, argue for a radical shift in the ethical perceptions of judges, a new concern and compassion for the other. But the approach is in the end ahistorical and ungrounded in any social context. By way of prescription, the judges are called upon to do what they almost certainly consider they are doing anyway - that is, hearing both sides, and giving more concern to the suffering other.

---

10. Costas Douzinas and Ronnie Warrington, *Justice Miscarried: Ethics, Aesthetics and the Law*, Harvester Wheatsheaf, 1994. See also Zygmunt Bauman, *Postmodern Ethics*, Blackwell, Oxford 1993.

Habermas and discourse ethics

Is there any other project capable, in the realm of theory and critique, of reconnecting law and justice? The most intelligent analysis of the liberal thought of Rawls and Dworkin, and the most uncompromising opposition to the post-modern fashion, comes from a contemporary German, Jürgen Habermas - whom Berman describes as 'the most serious theorist of human rights today'. Habermas is already known for his lucid account of the legitimation crisis of contemporary capitalism; and for his analysis of the struggle between the ever-encroaching systems (whether of money or of welfare) of modern society and the intimate lifeworld inhabited by the human person. Habermas has developed his own account of the ethical perceptions of women and men in a world in which there is no uncontested conception of what constitutes the good life, and in which people find themselves cut adrift from traditional beliefs and values. He calls his theory 'discourse ethics'. He argues that what goes on in relations between human beings is 'communicative action', in which communication is only possible on condition that speakers adhere to certain principles, in particular the sincerity of what they say, and its susceptibility in principle to external verification and modification through argument.

Thus, his theory of ethics does not pretend to tell us what the good life is, or how we should decide important moral issues. Instead, it explains the ethical conditions for arriving at such decisions in a rapidly changing society in which there are no moral certainties. But this is not Kant's system, in which the individual, through a process of ratiocination arrives at universalisable maxims - the categorical imperative. Habermas takes on board Hegel's critique of Kant. Habermas' discourse ethics is intersubjective; it can only be worked out in and through society, between persons who have attained the capacity to recognise the dignity and autonomy of others as a precondition for their own human realisation.

It can be no surprise, therefore, that Habermas has increasingly turned his attention to questions of law and justice. His latest massive text is entitled *Facticity and Validity* (*Faktizität und Geltung*, 1992, as yet untranslated), two words which closely parallel law and justice. It sets out to show how a constitutional state, based on rational principles of proceduralism and human rights, is possible. It contains powerful critiques both of the liberalism of Rawls and Dworkin, and of the postmodern response, and seeks to show how a comprehensive theory of rights can be built on the foundation of discourse ethics. But despite its impressive architecture, Habermas's theory has little to say about the economic and social injustice inherent in modern capitalism, and can, indeed, be read as an apologetics or justification of the modern German state.

Realism, and a (qualified) return to Marx

Is there any other theoretical framework for genuinely critical legal theory? The British left has long had an uneasy affinity with Marx. On the one hand his critique of capitalist exploitation continues to resonate. But on the other, as is well known, Marx was a fierce critic of bourgeois rights, the civil and political rights of the American and French revolutions, as much in the *Critique of the Gotha Programme* as in the much earlier *On the Jewish Question*.

It has been doubted whether Marx had other than a contradictory and inadequate approach to ethics. For Steven Lukes, Marx's was a narrow and impoverished view of the meaning of the rights of man... it treated them *only* as symptomatic of the individualism and contradictions of bourgeois life.[11] According to Christine Sypnowich, Marxists argue that the institutions of justice are historically specific to societies based on private property. Furthermore, rights find their fullest expression in the society of private property *par excellence*, as the superstructural effect of capitalist relations of property and exchange.[12] Tom Campbell also comments that 'it is unlikely that there can be any Marxist indulgence for the pretensions of those theories of justice which present themselves as the embodiment of universal truths which have application to any and every stage of historical development'.[13] Nevertheless, among a number of recent commentators, Philip Kain suggests that Marx was, on the contrary, seeking to transcend equal rights and justice; the justice of the communist society being an ideal which we seek to realise.[14]

But there is another level at which, arguably, Marx can still provide a vital emancipatory resource. As Etienne Balibar has recently pointed out language was for Marx as well as Habermas a 'communicative action'.[15] Marx put it this way: 'language *is* practical consciousness that exists also for other men, and for that reason alone it really exists for me personally as well; language,

---

11. Steven Lukes, *Marxism and Morality*, Oxford University Press, Oxford 1988.
12. Philip Kain, *Marx and Ethics,* Oxford 1988.
13. Christine Sypnowich, *The Concept of Socialist Law*, Oxford University Press, Oxford 1990.
14. Tom Campbell, *Justice*, Macmillan, London 1990.
15. Etienne Balibar, *The Philosophy of Marx*, Verso, London 1995.

like consciousness, only arises from the need, the necessity, of intercourse with other men'.[16] But Marx does not subject such action *a priori* to any logical or ethical norm, instead tying it firmly to labour, production and history. Law, as a discursive practice, inseparable from language, is no less historically and materially grounded. On another level, the symbolic structure common to both economic and juridical 'fetishism' is *generalised equivalence*, which subjects individuals, abstractly and equally, to a kind of circulation, whether of values or of obligations. Marx's critique of human rights enables such rights to be seen both as rhetoric which serves to disguise exploitation, and as a means by which class struggle by the oppressed can find expression - for example, in his time, 'the modest Magna Carta of the legally limited working day', by which the workers have compelled 'the passing of a law, an all-powerful social barrier by which they can be prevented from selling themselves'. That is, rights and the law can be understood as *objects of struggle*.

Of course, Marx is no longer fashionable, in academe or for New Labour. But in recent years there has emerged in Britain an attempt to complete Marx's philosophical project, and at the same time to provide not only a theory of society, but also a practical ethics, capable of guiding human emancipation. This school is known as 'critical realism', and has seen itself as a socialist philosophy, a resource for the socialist movement.[17] It is counterposed to positivism as much as to liberalism. Roy Bhaskar, its progenitor, started as a philosopher of science, arguing for realism - the intransitive and deep nature of the world, independent of human observation - as against the fashionable 'social constructivists' who see all human knowledge, including scientific research, as essentially limited by and to language - that is, as human constructs, incapable of justification by reference to any world outside.

In the social sciences, Bhaskar has worked to undermine the traditionally impenetrable barrier between 'fact' and 'value': the doctrine that it is logically impermissible to argue from what is, from knowledge of a state of affairs, to what ought to be, or what one ought to do. Instead, Bhaskar argues that from research into the deep and structured workings of modern society, based as it is on exploitation and oppression, the necessity of action may be derived. Bhaskar has a transformational conception of social activity: social structures exist only by virtue

16. Karl Marx, *German Ideology*, Lawrence & Wishart, London 1970.
17. Bhaskar, Arthur, Benton *et al*, *A Meeting of Minds*, Socialist Society, 1991.

of the human activities which reproduce or transform them, activities for which such structures are in turn a necessary condition. Furthermore, emancipation means the transformation of such structures, the transition from unwanted, unneeded and oppressive sources of determination to wanted, needed and empowering ones. In his most recent work, particularly in *Dialectic, the Pulse of Freedom*, Bhaskar argues for moral realism and ethical naturalism.[18] This leads him to a greatly expanded understanding of rights in the context of human emancipation. But can such theoretical underlabouring serve the interests of critical lawyers?

More recently, a number of critical legal scholars, notably Alan Norrie, have begun the application of Bhaskar's methodology to law - particularly in the field of criminal law.[19] There are two requirements for such an approach. First, it must constantly be borne in mind that society and its structures, including law, are not reducible to individuals and their activities, but rather to the 'persistent relations' between individuals and groups - of which law is an essential example - and the relations between these relations. By virtue of its subject-matter, this requires a dialectical approach. Second, law must be re-linked to a realist ethical foundation, capable of drawing conclusions for action from research carried out in accordance with the principles described above.

Conclusion

British lawyers - or at least a small group of them - have an honourable record of placing themselves at the service of the oppressed, and in particular the organised working class. But such engagement has either been informed by Stalinist Marxism, as with D. N. Pritt QC, one of the founders of the Haldane Society, or by one of the varieties of neo-Marxism. There has been little theory-guided practice. But the present crisis of British constitutionalism, and the widespread public dissatisfaction with the machinery and content of justice, calls for serious analysis guided by methodology capable of judgment and of prescription. It may well be that critical or dialectical realism, in one of its materialist, non-relativist variants, can provide such essential tools.

---

18. Roy Bhaskar, *Dialectic, the Pulse of Freedom*, Verso, London 1994. For a recent application of critical realism in the field of sociology, see Margaret Archer, *Realist Social Theory: the Morphogenetic Approach*, Cambridge University Press, Cambridge 1995.
19. Alan Norrie, *Crime, Reason and History: A Critical Introduction to Criminal Law*, Weidenfeld & Nicolson, London 1993.